Add your opinion to our next book

Fill out a survey

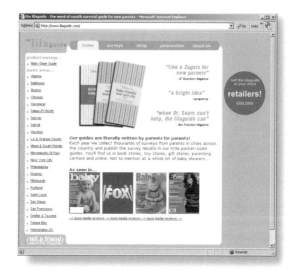

visit www.lilaguide.com

the lilaguide

by PARENTS *for* PARENTS

baby-friendly seattle area

NEW PARENT SURVIVAL GUIDE TO SHOPPING,
ACTIVITIES, RESTAURANTS AND MORE...

2ND EDITION

LOCAL EDITOR: KRISTEN RAGAIN

PUBLISHED BY THE LILAGUIDE/OAM SOLUTIONS, INC.
SAN FRANCISCO, CA   WWW.LILAGUIDE.COM

Published by:
OAM Solutions, Inc.
139 Saturn Street
San Francisco, CA 94114, USA
415.252.1300
orders@lilaguide.com
www.lilaguide.com

ISBN. 1-932847-31-6
First Printing: 2005
Printed in the USA
Copyright © 2005 by OAM Solutions, Inc.

07   about the lilaguide
09   thank yous
10   disclaimer
11   how to use this book

Shopping
13   baby basics & accessories
63   maternity clothing

Fun & Entertainment
77   activities & outings
101   parks & playgrounds
119   restaurants

Health & Support
147   doulas & lactation consultants
149   exercise
157   parent education & support
165   pediatricians

Other Necessities
171   breast pump sales & rentals
177   diaper delivery services
179   haircuts
185   nanny & babysitter referrals
191   photographers

indexes
200   alphabetical
205   by city/neighborhood

No, for the last time, the baby does not come with a handbook. And even if there were a handbook, you wouldn't read it. You'd fill out the warranty card, throw out the box, and start playing right away. Until a few hours passed and you were hit with the epiphany of, "Gee whiz honey, what in the wide, wide world of childcare are we doing here?"

Relax. We had that panicked thought when we had our daughter Delilah. And so did **all the parents** we talked to when they had their children. And while we all knew there was no handbook, there was, we found, a whole lot of **word-of-mouth information**. Everyone we talked to had some bit of child rearing advice about what baby gear store is the most helpful. Some **nugget of parenting wisdom** about which restaurant tolerates strained carrots on the floor. It all really seemed to help. Someone, we thought, should write this down.

And that's when, please pardon the pun, the lilaguide was born. The book you're now holding is a guide **written by local parents for local parents**. It's what happens when someone actually does write it down (and organizes it, calculates it, and presents it in an easy-to-use format).

Nearly 7,000 surveys have produced this first edition of **the lilaguide: Baby-Friendly Seattle**. It provides a truly unique insider's view of over 1,100 "parent-friendly" stores, activities, restaurants, and service providers that are about to become a very big part of your life. And while this guide won't tell you how to change a diaper or how to get by on little or no sleep (that's what grandparents are for), it will tell you what other **local parents have learned** about the amazing things your city and neighborhood have to offer.

As you peruse these reviews, please remember that this guide is **not intended to be a comprehensive directory** since it does not contain every baby store or activity in the area. Rather, it is intended to provide a short-list of places that your neighbors and friends **deemed exciting and noteworthy**. If a place or business is not listed, it simply means that nobody (or not enough people) rated or submitted information about it to us. **Please let us know** about your favorite parent and baby-friendly businesses and service providers by participating in our online survey at **www.lilaguide.com**. We always want your opinions!

So there you have it. Now go make some phone calls, clean up the house, take a nap, or do something on your list before the baby arrives.

Enjoy!

Oli & Elysa

Oli Mittermaier & Elysa Marco, MD

PS

We love getting feedback (good and bad) so don't be bashful. Email us at **lila@lilaguide.com** with your thoughts, comments and suggestions. We'll be sure to try to include them in next year's edition!

We'd like to take a moment to offer a heart-felt thank you to all the **parents who participated in our survey** and took the time to share their thoughts and opinions. Without your participation, we would never have been able to create this unique guide.

Thanks also to **Lisa Barnes**, **Nora Borowsky**, **Todd Cooper**, **Amy Iannone**, **Katy Jacobson**, **Felicity John Odell**, **Shira Johnson**, **Kasia Kappes**, **Jen Krug**, **Dana Kulvin**, **Deborah Schneider**, **Kevin Schwall**, **April Stewart**, and **Nina Thompson** for their tireless editorial eyes, **Satoko Furuta** and **Paul D. Smith** for their beautiful sense of design, and **Lane Foard** for making the words yell.

Special thanks to **Paul D. Smith**, **Ken Miles**, and **Ali Wing** for their consistent support and overall encouragement in all things lilaguide, and of course **our parents** for their unconditional support in this and all our other endeavors.

And last, but certainly not least, thanks to **little Delilah** for inspiring us to embark on this challenging, yet incredibly fulfilling project.

participate in our survey at

ratings

Most listings have stars and numbers as part of their write-up. These symbols mean the following:

❺ / ★★★★★ extraordinary
❹ / ★★★★☆ very good
❸ / ★★★☆☆ good
❷ / ★★☆☆☆ fair
❶ / ★☆☆☆☆ poor
✓ available
✗ not available/relevant

If a ★ is listed instead of ★, it means that the rating is less reliable because a small number of parents surveyed the listing. Furthermore, if a listing has **no stars** or **criteria ratings**, it means that although the listing was rated, the number of surveys submitted was so low that we did not feel it justified an actual rating.

quotes & reviews

The quotes/reviews are taken directly from surveys submitted to us via our website (**www.lilaguide.com**). Other than spelling and minor grammatical changes, they come to you as they came to us. Quotes were selected based on how well they appeared to represent the collective opinions of the surveys submitted.

fact checking

We have contacted all of the businesses listed to verify their address and phone number, as well as to inquire about their hours, class schedules and web site information. Since some of this information may change after this guide has been printed, we appreciate you letting us know of any errors by notifying us via email at **lila@lilaguide.com**.

baby basics & accessories

Seattle

★★★★★
"lila picks"

- ★ Babies R Us
- ★ Barneys New York
- ★ Clover
- ★ Curious Kidstuff
- ★ Izilla Toys

- ★ Kid's On 45th
- ★ Land of Nod
- ★ Merry Go Round
- ★ Top Ten Toys

Again & A Gain ★★★☆☆

❝...a great place for gently used baby stuff, especially toys and books... a bit messy, but you can find most things you are looking for... owner and staff very helpful... a bit overpriced for consignment... small play area makes shopping with kids easy... a lot for small sizes and maternity... give yourself time to dig through their goods, there are some gems... ❞

Furniture, Bedding & Decor	✓	$$	Prices
Gear & Equipment	✓	❸	Product availability
Nursing & Feeding	✓	❸	Staff knowledge
Safety & Babycare	✓	❹	Customer service
Clothing, Shoes & Accessories	✓	❸	Decor
Books, Toys & Entertainment	✓		

WEST SEATTLE—4832 CALIFORNIA AVE SW (AT SW EDMUNDS ST); 206.933.2060; M-SA 10-7, SU 10-5

All For Kids Books & Music ★★★★⯪

❝...the best store in the city for children's books and music... test drive the music before you buy... great play area for the kids... knowledgeable staff and great selection... huge selection of books for and about kids... just a wonderful, wonderful book shop... helpful staff... one of Seattle's best... you can find just about anything here... ❞

Furniture, Bedding & Decor	✗	$$	Prices
Gear & Equipment	✗	❹	Product availability
Nursing & Feeding	✗	❺	Staff knowledge
Safety & Babycare	✗	❹	Customer service
Clothing, Shoes & Accessories	✗	❹	Decor
Books, Toys & Entertainment	✓		

WWW.ALLFORKIDSBOOKS.COM

UNIVERSITY DISTRICT/UNIVERSITY VILLAGE—2900 NE BLAKELEY ST (AT UNIVERSITY VLG MALL); 206.526.2768; M-SA 10-6, SU 12-5

Alphabet Soup Books ★★★★☆

❝...the woman who runs this store is very helpful and enthusiastic about kid's books... newly-opened bookshop offers new, used, and

participate in our survey at

'vintage' children's books... the perfect place for books you haven't seen since kindergarten, and the best place to buy your childhood favorites for your child, even if they are out of print... very friendly staff... **99**

Furniture, Bedding & Decor	✗	$$$ .... Prices
Gear & Equipment	✗	❹ .... Product availability
Nursing & Feeding	✗	❹ .... Staff knowledge
Safety & Babycare	✗	❺ .... Customer service
Clothing, Shoes & Accessories	✗	❺ .... Decor
Books, Toys & Entertainment	✓	

WALLINGFORD/FREMONT—1406 N 45TH ST (AT INTERLAKE AVE N); 206.547.4555; DAILY 10-9

Anthropologie

66 *...beautiful store with cute knits, ornate T-shirts and dresses... fun retro toys and unique books... high-end, nicely designed duds for girls (no boys clothing)... the stores are nicely designed and enjoyable to shop in... great for clothes to be used for somewhat special occasions...* **99**

Furniture, Bedding & Decor	✗	$$$ .... Prices
Gear & Equipment	✗	❸ .... Product availability
Nursing & Feeding	✗	❸ .... Staff knowledge
Safety & Babycare	✗	❸ .... Customer service
Clothing, Shoes & Accessories	✓	❸ .... Decor
Books, Toys & Entertainment	✗	

WWW.ANTHROPOLOGIE.COM

DOWNTOWN—1509 FIFTH AVE (AT PIKE ST); 206.381.5900; M-SA 10-8, SU 11-6

UNIVERSITY DISTRICT/UNIVERSITY VILLAGE—2520 NE UNIVERSITY VLG ST (AT UNIVERSITY VLG MALL); 206.985.2101; M-SA 9:30-9, SU 11-6

April Cornell

66 *...beautiful, classic dresses and accessories for special occasions... I love the matching 'mommy and me' outfits... lots of fun knickknacks for sale... great selection of baby wear on their web site... rest assured your baby won't look like every other child in these adorable outfits... very frilly and girlie—beautiful...* **99**

Furniture, Bedding & Decor	✗	$$$ .... Prices
Gear & Equipment	✗	❸ .... Product availability
Nursing & Feeding	✗	❹ .... Staff knowledge
Safety & Babycare	✗	❹ .... Customer service
Clothing, Shoes & Accessories	✓	❹ .... Decor
Books, Toys & Entertainment	✗	

WWW.APRILCORNELL.COM

BELLEVUE—215 BELLEVUE WY SE (AT MAIN ST); 425.455.9818; M-SA 9:30-9:30, SU 11-7

DOWNTOWN—400 PINE ST (AT WEST LAKE CENTER); 206.749.9658; M-SA 9:30-9, SU 11-6

Ashleigh's Attic

66 *...great place to check out if you are looking for a baby product, but are hesitant to pay full price... you can get great deals on a wide variety of used items... all of the baby and toddler gear you might need... the store is crammed, so not the easiest place to shop with a little one in tow... prices are a bit high... items not always in the best condition so be sure to look closely... disinterested staff...* **99**

Furniture, Bedding & Decor	✓	$$ .... Prices
Gear & Equipment	✓	❸ .... Product availability
Nursing & Feeding	✓	❸ .... Staff knowledge
Safety & Babycare	✓	❸ .... Customer service

Clothing, Shoes & Accessories ...... ✓   ❷ .... Decor
Books, Toys & Entertainment .... ✓

REDMOND—16360 REDMOND WY (AT GILMAN ST); 425.867.1007; T-SA 10-6

Babies R Us ★★★★★

"...everything baby under one roof... they have a wide selection and carry most 'mainstream' items such as Graco, Fisher-Price, Avent and Britax... great customer service—given how big the stores are, I was pleasantly surprised at how attentive the staff was... easy return policy... super busy on weekends so try to visit on a weekday for the best service... keep an eye out for great coupons, deals and frequent sales... easy and comprehensive registry... shopping here is so easy— you've got to check it out... **"**

Furniture, Bedding & Decor .... ✓	$$$ .... Prices	
Gear & Equipment .... ✓	❹ .... Product availability	
Nursing & Feeding ...... ✓	❹ .... Staff knowledge	
Safety & Babycare .... ✓	❹ ....Customer service	
Clothing, Shoes & Accessories ...... ✓	❹ .... Decor	
Books, Toys & Entertainment .... ✓		

WWW.BABIESRUS.COM

LYNNWOOD—19500 ALDERWOOD MALL PKWY (AT 196TH ST NW);
425.672.3220; M-SA 9:30-9:30, SU 11-7; PARKING IN FRONT OF BLDG

TUKWILA—17500 SOUTHCENTER PKWY (AT SOUTHCENTER MALL);
206.575.1819; M-SA 9:30-9:30, SU 11-7; MALL PARKING

Baby Depot At Burlington Coat Factory ★★★⯪☆

"...a large, 'super store' layout with a ton of baby gear... wide aisles, packed shelves, barely existent customer service and awesome prices... everything from bottles, car seats and strollers to gliders, cribs and clothes... I always find something worth getting... a little disorganized and hard to locate items you're looking for... the staff is not always knowledgeable about their merchandise... return policy is store credit only... **"**

Furniture, Bedding & Decor .... ✓	$$ .... Prices	
Gear & Equipment .... ✓	❸ .... Product availability	
Nursing & Feeding .... ✓	❸ .... Staff knowledge	
Safety & Babycare .... ✓	❸ ....Customer service	
Clothing, Shoes & Accessories ...... ✓	❸ .... Decor	
Books, Toys & Entertainment .... ✓		

WWW.BABYDEPOT.COM

AUBURN—1101 SUPERMALL WAY S1126 (AT THE SUPERMALL OF THE
GREAT NORTHWEST); 253.735.9964; M-SA 10-9, SU 11-6; FREE PARKING

EDMONDS—24111 HWY 99 (AT 240TH ST SW); 425.776.2221; M-SA 10-9, SU
11-6

BabyGap/GapKids ★★★★☆

"...colorful baby and toddler clothing in clean, well-lit stores... great return policy... it's the Gap, so you know what you're getting—colorful, cute and well-made clothing... best place for baby hats... prices are reasonable especially since there's always a sale of some sort going on... sales, sales, sales—frequent and fantastic... everything I'm looking for in infant clothing—snap crotches, snaps up the front, all natural fabrics and great styling... fun seasonal selections—a great place to shop for gifts as well as for your own kids... although it can get busy, staff generally seem accommodating and helpful... **"**

Furniture, Bedding & Decor .... ✗	$$$ .... Prices	
Gear & Equipment .... ✗	❹ .... Product availability	
Nursing & Feeding .... ✗	❹ .... Staff knowledge	
Safety & Babycare .... ✗	❹ ....Customer service	

participate in our survey at

Clothing, Shoes & Accessories	✓	
Books, Toys & Entertainment	✗	

 .... Decor

WWW.GAP.COM

BELLEVUE—108 BELLEVUE SQ MALL (AT BELLEVUE WY NE); 425.454.9132

DOWNTOWN—1530 5TH AVE (AT PIKE ST); 206.254.8000; T-SA 9:30-9, SU 10-8

LYNNWOOD—3000 184TH ST SW (AT ALDERWOOD MALL); 425.776.8214; M-SA 10-9:30, SU 11-7

NORTH BEND—521 S FORK AVE SW (AT BENDIGO BLVD S); 425.831.2470; M-SA 10-8, SU 10-6

REDMOND—16428 NE 74TH ST (REDMOND TOWN CTR); 425.869.9772

TUKWILA—1048 SOUTHCENTER MALL (AT TUKWILA PKWY); 206.242.8087

UNIVERSITY DISTRICT/UNIVERSITY VILLAGE—2730 NE UNIVERSITY VLG (AT NE PACIFIC ST); 206.525.2146; M-SA 9:30-9, SU 11-6; PARKING IN FRONT OF BLDG

Barneys New York ★★★★★

"...pretty much what you would expect from Barneys—totally decadent, sensationally cool, big price tags... adorable designer clothes for tots... you can find wonderful little gifts at reasonable prices... a great place for gifts—my friends get so excited when they see the Barneys box... when you're in the mood to impress, Barneys is a sure bet... yes it's pricey, but the experience is so wonderful... **"**

Furniture, Bedding & Decor	✓	$$$$		Prices
Gear & Equipment	✗	❹		Product availability
Nursing & Feeding	✓	❹		Staff knowledge
Safety & Babycare	✗	❹		Customer service
Clothing, Shoes & Accessories	✓	❹		Decor
Books, Toys & Entertainment	✓			

WWW.BARNEYS.COM

SEATTLE—1420 5TH AVE; 206.622.6300; M-F 10-7, SA 10-6, SU 12-5

Bella Rose ★★★★☆

"...lovely shop, but not a great place to take kids—access for strollers difficult and many fragile and tempting objects for small fingers!.. good place to find special gifts... limited selection, but very good quality, stylish products... **"**

Furniture, Bedding & Decor	✗	$$$		Prices
Gear & Equipment	✓	❹		Product availability
Nursing & Feeding	✗	❹		Staff knowledge
Safety & Babycare	✗	❹		Customer service
Clothing, Shoes & Accessories	✗	❹		Decor
Books, Toys & Entertainment	✗			

WWW.BELLAROSEFINEGIFTS.COM

CAPITOL HILL—2811A E MADISON ST (AT MLK JR WAY); 206.322.1977; M-SA 10-6, SU 11-4

Bellini ★★★★☆

"...high-end furniture for a gorgeous nursery... if you're looking for the kind of furniture you see in magazines then this is the place to go... excellent quality... yes, it's pricey, but the quality is impeccable... free delivery and setup... their furniture is built to withstand the abuse my tots dish out... they sell very unique merchandise, ranging from cribs to bedding and even some clothes... our nursery design was inspired by their store decor... I wish they had more frequent sales... **"**

Furniture, Bedding & Decor	✓	$$$$		Prices
Gear & Equipment	✗	❹		Product availability
Nursing & Feeding	✗	❹		Staff knowledge
Safety & Babycare	✗	❹		Customer service

Clothing, Shoes & Accessories ....✗	❹ .... Decor	
Books, Toys & Entertainment ....✓		

WWW.BELLINI.COM

BELLEVUE—10635 NE 8TH ST (AT 106TH AVE NE); 425.644.8288; M-SA 10-6,
SU 12-5

Birth & Beyond ★★★★⯪

"...almost everything you need to support the more 'natural' approach to mothering... beautiful accessories and gifts... small shop, but packed with great finds... excellent selection of nursing supplies and bras... friendly informed staff... lots of alternative, healthier choices here... the dreamiest baby blankets... special services like shopping by appointment, after hours and travel packages (note their shortened hours in Issaquah)..."

Furniture, Bedding & Decor...........✗	$$$..Prices	
Gear & Equipment ....✓	❹ ....Product availability	
Nursing & Feeding ....✓	❺ .... Staff knowledge	
Safety & Babycare ....✓	❹ ....Customer service	
Clothing, Shoes & Accessories ......✓	❹ .... Decor	
Books, Toys & Entertainment ....✓		

WWW.BIRTHANDBEYOND.COM

ISSAQUAH—317 NW GILMAN BLVD (AT 224TH AVE SE); 425.392.6665; M-F
10-11:30AM; PARKING LOT BY BLDG

MADISON VALLEY/MADISON PARK—2610 E MADISON ST (AT 26TH AVE E);
206.324.4831; M-F 10-6, SA-SU 11-5; STREET PARKING

Bootyland ★★★★☆

"...fun, friendly, funky, laid back... where else can you find red leather cowboy boots and a t-shirt with Buddha on it for a four year old girl... some new, some old, all of it supercool... punk logos on onesies, organic clothes, handmade clothing and slings—super cool... a small shop with great prices and fun people—the place to go if you're a hipster mom... great selection of vintage clothing... great for one-time outfits like Halloween costumes or Christmas dresses..."

Furniture, Bedding & Decor...........✓	$$..Prices	
Gear & Equipment ....✓	❹ ....Product availability	
Nursing & Feeding ....✓	❹ .... Staff knowledge	
Safety & Babycare ....✓	❹ ....Customer service	
Clothing, Shoes & Accessories ......✓	❹ .... Decor	
Books, Toys & Entertainment ....✓		

WWW.BOOTYLANDKIDS.COM

CAPITOL HILL—1321 E PINE ST (AT 13TH AVE); 206.328.0636; M-SA 11-5:30,
SU 12-5; STREET PARKING

Boston Street Baby Store ★★★★☆

"...something for everyone's budget... you are sure to find the right gift here... I love the unisex basics... great quality... bright, colorful, handmade fabric items... inexpensive cotton knits... amazing sales (Cotton Caboodles clothing for $5)... stores are full of excellent ideas... the kind of stuff that makes you a favorite at parties... not a ton of space so you might have to leave your stroller outside..."

Furniture, Bedding & Decor...........✗	$$$..Prices	
Gear & Equipment ....✗	❹ ....Product availability	
Nursing & Feeding ....✗	❹ .... Staff knowledge	
Safety & Babycare ....✗	❹ ....Customer service	
Clothing, Shoes & Accessories ......✓	❹ .... Decor	
Books, Toys & Entertainment ....✓		

PIKE MARKET—1902 POST ALLEY (AT STEWART ST); 206.634.0580; DAILY
10-6

participate in our survey at

Capers

"...lots of interesting and unique baby items... beautiful home decor with a small amount of clothes... beautiful one of a kind items that come with a price tag, but nice quality... not a huge selection... wonderful books and other finds, great for gifts... I found it pricey..."

Furniture, Bedding & Decor	✗	$$$$ .... Prices
Gear & Equipment	✓	❸ .... Product availability
Nursing & Feeding	✗	❸ .... Staff knowledge
Safety & Babycare	✗	❸ .... Customer service
Clothing, Shoes & Accessories	✓	❹ .... Decor
Books, Toys & Entertainment	✓	

WALLINGFORD/FREMONT—716 N 34TH ST (AT FREMONT AVE); 206.545.7876

WEST SEATTLE—4521 CALIFORNIA AVE SW (AT SW OREGON ST); 206.932.0371; M-F 7:30-8, SA 8-6, SU 8-5

Carter's

"...always a great selection of inexpensive baby basics—everything from clothing to linens... I always find something at 'giveaway prices' during one of their frequent sales... busy and crowded—it can be a chaotic shopping experience... 30 to 50 percent less than what you would pay at other boutiques... I bought five pieces of baby clothing for less than $40... durable, adorable and affordable... most stores have a small play area for kids in center of store so you can get your shopping done..."

Furniture, Bedding & Decor	✓	$$ .... Prices
Gear & Equipment	✗	❹ .... Product availability
Nursing & Feeding	✗	❹ .... Staff knowledge
Safety & Babycare	✗	❹ .... Customer service
Clothing, Shoes & Accessories	✓	❹ .... Decor
Books, Toys & Entertainment	✓	

WWW.CARTERS.COM

AUBURN—1101 SUPERMALL WY (AT SUPERMALL OF THE GREAT NORTHWEST); 253.804.3155; M-SA 10-9:30, SU 11-6; PARKING COMPLEX

NORTH BEND—461 S FORK AVE (AT FACTORY STORES AT NORTH BEND); 425.888.6370; M-SA 10-8, SU 10-6

Children's Closet

"...great resale shop with good prices... helpful, friendly staff... always new merchandise... clothes from size zero to size 12... furniture, toys, books, dvds, shoes, and more..."

Furniture, Bedding & Decor	✗	$ .... Prices
Gear & Equipment	✗	❸ .... Product availability
Nursing & Feeding	✗	❹ .... Staff knowledge
Safety & Babycare	✗	❺ .... Customer service
Clothing, Shoes & Accessories	✓	❺ .... Decor
Books, Toys & Entertainment	✗	

WWW.CHILDRENS-CLOSET.NET

KENT—230 WASHINGTON AVE S (AT W MEEKER ST); 253.813.3090; M-F 10-6, SA 12-6

Children's Place, The

"...great bargains on cute clothing... shoes, socks, swimsuits, sunglasses and everything in between... lots of '3 for $20' type deals on sleepers, pants and mix-and-match separates... so much more affordable than the other 'big chains'... don't expect the most unique stuff here, but it wears and washes well... cheap clothing for cheap prices... you can leave the store with bags full of clothes without putting a huge dent in your wallet..."

Furniture, Bedding & Decor	✗	$$ .... Prices

Gear & Equipment	✗	❹	Product availability
Nursing & Feeding	✗	❹	Staff knowledge
Safety & Babycare	✗	❹	Customer service
Clothing, Shoes & Accessories	✓	❹	Decor
Books, Toys & Entertainment	✓		

WWW.CHILDRENSPLACE.COM

ALGONA—1101 SUPERMALL WY (AT SUPERMALL OF THE GREAT NORTHWEST); 253.333.1109; M-SA 10-9, SU 11-6

BELLEVUE—250 BELLEVUE SQ (AT NE 4TH ST); 425.455.0823; M-SA 9:30-9:30, SU 11-7

DOWNTOWN—400 PINE ST (AT 4TH AVE); 206.264.0389; M-SA 9:30-9, SU 11-6

TUKWILA—1062 SOUTHCENTER MALL (AT SOUTHCENTER MALL); 206.444.6497; M-SA 10-9, SU 11-7; MALL PARKING

Children's Shop, The ★★★⯪☆

"...beautiful clothes and the nicest owner!.. well worth the price and the sidewalk sales are amazing... cute shop in the heart of Madison Park—really nice owner is helpful... good selection of Petite Bateau... high price, high-quality... **"**

Furniture, Bedding & Decor	✗	$$$$	Prices
Gear & Equipment	✗	❹	Product availability
Nursing & Feeding	✗	❹	Staff knowledge
Safety & Babycare	✗	❹	Customer service
Clothing, Shoes & Accessories	✓	❹	Decor
Books, Toys & Entertainment	✗		

CAPITOL HILL—4114 E MADISON ST (AT 41ST AVE E); 206.328.7121; M-F 10-6, SA 10-5

Childrens Warehouse, A ★★★⯪☆

"...high-quality, name brand clothes in excellent condition at this consignment store... tons of new and used stuff!..a bit pricier than some other consignment shops, but more availability... carries some new items too... maternity and older kid's clothing also... **"**

Furniture, Bedding & Decor	✗	$$	Prices
Gear & Equipment	✗	❹	Product availability
Nursing & Feeding	✗	❹	Staff knowledge
Safety & Babycare	✗	❹	Customer service
Clothing, Shoes & Accessories	✓	❹	Decor
Books, Toys & Entertainment	✗		

MUKILTEO—10809 MUKILTEO SPEEDWAY (AT 106TH ST SW); 425.349.1919; T-TH 10-5:30, F 10-4, SA 11-5; PARKING LOT

Childs Closet, A ★★★★☆

"...an amazing find for gently used high-quality clothing... we haven't shopped for 'new' clothes since we found this shop... a Hanna Anderson jacket for $4.99, you can't top that... secondhand clothes typically in good condition... great place for high-end kids clothes on the cheap... well organized and clean for consignment... selection sometimes so-so... **"**

Furniture, Bedding & Decor	✓	$$	Prices
Gear & Equipment	✓	❹	Product availability
Nursing & Feeding	✓	❹	Staff knowledge
Safety & Babycare	✗	❹	Customer service
Clothing, Shoes & Accessories	✓	❸	Decor
Books, Toys & Entertainment	✓		

WWW.ACHILDSCLOSET.COM

UNIVERSITY DISTRICT/UNIVERSITY VILLAGE—5025 25TH AVE NE (ACROSS FROM UNIVERSITY VLG MALL); 206.985.4402; M-SA 10-6, SU 12-4; PARKING IN FRONT OF BLDG

City Kids ★★★☆☆

"...a great consignment shop with clean and good quality items... pricing is just right... if you don't mind sorting through a mess of items definitely go for it... great customer service—they'll call when something comes in... cramped store with odd hours... lots of variety... good for baby gear, nursery and maternity..."

Furniture, Bedding & Decor	✗	$$ .... Prices
Gear & Equipment	✓	❸ .... Product availability
Nursing & Feeding	✓	❹ .... Staff knowledge
Safety & Babycare	✗	❸ .... Customer service
Clothing, Shoes & Accessories	✓	❸ .... Decor
Books, Toys & Entertainment	✓	

EDMONDS—C-9726 EDMONDS WY (AT 100TH AVE W); 425.775.7627

City Peoples Mercantile ★★★☆☆

"...a nice neighborhood spot where you can always find a gift for all ages... not a large selection... eclectic inventory for the home and garden... little shopping carts my daughter loves to push..."

Furniture, Bedding & Decor	✓	$$$ .... Prices
Gear & Equipment	✗	❸ .... Product availability
Nursing & Feeding	✗	❸ .... Staff knowledge
Safety & Babycare	✗	❸ .... Customer service
Clothing, Shoes & Accessories	✗	❹ .... Decor
Books, Toys & Entertainment	✓	

LAURELHURST/SANDPOINT—5440 SAND POINT WY NE (AT PRINCETON AVE NE); 206.524.1200; M-F 9-7, SA 9-6, SU 10-6

Clover ★★★★★

"...a sweet little store—a much needed addition to the baby scene... a little spendy... huge selection of inspired European, educational and wooden toys... my favorite shop... the toys are old world and wonderful, makes me want to be a kid again... neat, thoughtful and unusual toys and baby items, but pretty pricey... darling linens and nice selection of sturdy dress up clothes... for gifts you won't find in the chains... no Barbies to be found here..."

Furniture, Bedding & Decor	✗	$$$ .... Prices
Gear & Equipment	✓	❹ .... Product availability
Nursing & Feeding	✗	❹ .... Staff knowledge
Safety & Babycare	✗	❹ .... Customer service
Clothing, Shoes & Accessories	✓	❺ .... Decor
Books, Toys & Entertainment	✓	

WWW.CLOVERTOYS.COM

BALLARD—5335 BALLARD AVE NW (AT 22ND AVE NW); 206.782.0715; M-SA 10-6, SU 10-5

Costco ★★★☆☆

"...dependable place for bulk diapers, wipes and formula at discount prices... clothing selection is very hit-or-miss... avoid shopping there during nights and weekends if possible, because parking and checkout lines are brutal... they don't have a huge selection of brands, but the brands they do have are almost always in stock and at a great price... lowest prices around for diapers and formula... kid's clothing tends to be picked through, but it's worth looking for great deals on name-brand items like Carter's..."

Furniture, Bedding & Decor	✓	$$ .... Prices
Gear & Equipment	✓	❸ .... Product availability
Nursing & Feeding	✓	❸ .... Staff knowledge
Safety & Babycare	✓	❸ .... Customer service
Clothing, Shoes & Accessories	✓	❷ .... Decor
Books, Toys & Entertainment	✓	

WWW.COSTCO.COM

EVERETT—10200 19TH AVE SE; 425.379.7451; M-F 11-8:30, SA 9:30-6, SU 10-6

FEDERAL WAY—35100 ENCHANTED PKWY S; 253.874.3652; M-F 11-8:30, SA 9:30-6, SU 10-6

ISSAQUAH—1801 10TH AVE NW; 425.313.0965; M-F 11-8:30, SA 9:30-6, SU 10-6

KIRKLAND—11831 120TH AVE NE (AT NE 118TH ST); 425.825.4500; M-F 10-8:30, SA 9:30-6, SU 10-6

KIRKLAND—8629 120TH AVE NE (AT NE 85TH ST); 425.827.1693; M-F 10-8:30, SA 9:30-6, SU 10-6

MONTLAKE—1175 N 205TH ST (AT AURORA VLG); 206.546.0480; M-F 11-8:30, SA 9:30-6, SU 10-6

SODO—4401 4TH AVE S (AT SPOKANE ST); 206.622.3136; M-F 11-8:30, SA 9:30-6, SU 10-6

TUKWILA—400 COSTCO DR; 206.575.9191; M-F 11-8:30, SA 9:30-6, SU 10-6

Cotton Caboodle ★★★★☆

"...I hesitate to give a great review for fear my favorite outlet spot for good deals will become mobbed... a fun spot to pick out made in the USA duds at a fair price... Cotton Caboodles is pretty pricey at the noutiques, but here everything is priced from $5 to $10... look for coupons in the circular for even better deals... especially great for girl's clothes... a bit of a hit or miss, but the hits are great... **"**

Furniture, Bedding & Decor	✗	$$ .... Prices
Gear & Equipment	✗	❸ ...... Product availability
Nursing & Feeding	✗	❸ ...... Staff knowledge
Safety & Babycare	✗	❹ ...... Customer service
Clothing, Shoes & Accessories	✓	❸ .... Decor
Books, Toys & Entertainment	✗	

QUEEN ANNE—203 W THOMAS ST (AT 2ND AVE W); 206.352.3763; M-F 10-5

Curious Kidstuff ★★★★★

"...an 'alternative' toy store that focuses on creative wooden toys rather than plastic junk... no 'violent' toys here... one of those shops that everyone talks about... everything in this store seems to be chosen with love by an enthusiastic and knowledgeable buyer... many of the nicest presents my kids have received came from here... gift wrapping is always free—perfect for gift shopping... **"**

Furniture, Bedding & Decor	✗	$$$ .... Prices
Gear & Equipment	✗	❹ ...... Product availability
Nursing & Feeding	✗	❹ ...... Staff knowledge
Safety & Babycare	✗	❹ ...... Customer service
Clothing, Shoes & Accessories	✗	❹ .... Decor
Books, Toys & Entertainment	✓	

WWW.CURIOUSKIDSTUFF.COM

WEST SEATTLE—4740 CALIFORNIA AVE SW (AT SW ALASKA ST); 206.937.8788; M 9-5, T-F 9-8, SA 9-5, SU 11-5; PARKING LOT AT 42ND AVE

Essenza ★★★★☆

"...funky store with neat one of a kind type baby gifts... soft blankets in fun patterns and colors... not your everyday baby mall type store... terrible stroller access... nice products and something different... sometimes great finds are left over when they have sales... very high-end... **"**

Furniture, Bedding & Decor	✗	$$$$ .... Prices
Gear & Equipment	✓	❹ ...... Product availability
Nursing & Feeding	✗	❹ ...... Staff knowledge
Safety & Babycare	✗	❹ ...... Customer service

| Clothing, Shoes & Accessories | ✓ | ❺ | Decor |
| Books, Toys & Entertainment | ✗ | | |

WALLINGFORD/FREMONT—615 N 35TH ST (AT EVANSTON AVE N);
206.545.9121

Finders ★★★★☆

"...lots of great gifts... very cute and frilly, but also some more standard styles as well... very cute picture frames and embroidered items... if you needed a baby gift, I'm sure you'd find it here... very helpful and friendly service..."

Furniture, Bedding & Decor	✗	$$$	Prices
Gear & Equipment	✗	❹	Product availability
Nursing & Feeding	✗	❹	Staff knowledge
Safety & Babycare	✗	❺	Customer service
Clothing, Shoes & Accessories	✓	❺	Decor
Books, Toys & Entertainment	✓		

WWW.FINDERSGIFTS.COM

MERCER ISLAND—7607 SE 27TH ST (AT 76TH AVE SE); 206.236.1110; M-SA
10-9, SU 1-5

Fireworks Galleries ★★★☆☆

"...interesting gifts and room decor that I haven't seen elsewhere... cool stuff, not cool prices... unique funky gifts—many made by local artisans... spendy, but interesting gifts and room decor that I haven't seen elsewhere... cool stuff, not cool prices... unique funky gifts-many made by local artisans... spendy, but high-quality... not a huge selection, but interesting... too many breakables and aisles too narrow to bring the little ones... super colorful and fun place where you never know what whimsical and unique items for baby's room you can find... this store is worth an outing—what fun..."

Furniture, Bedding & Decor	✗	$$$$	Prices
Gear & Equipment	✓	❹	Product availability
Nursing & Feeding	✗	❹	Staff knowledge
Safety & Babycare	✗	❹	Customer service
Clothing, Shoes & Accessories	✓	❺	Decor
Books, Toys & Entertainment	✓		

WWW.FIREWORKSGALLERY.NET

BELLEVUE—196 BELLEVUE SQ (AT BELLEVUE WY NE); 425.688.0933; M-SA
9:30-5:30, SU 11-7

DOWNTOWN—400 PINE ST (AT WESTLAKE CENTER); 206.527.2858; M-SA
9:30-9, SU 11-6

PIONEER SQUARE—210 1ST AVE S (AT S WASHINGTON ST); 206.682.8707;
M-SA 10-5:30, SU 11-5:30

UNIVERSITY DISTRICT/UNIVERSITY VILLAGE—2617 NE VILLAGE LN (AT
UNIVERSITY VILLAGE); 206.527.2858; M-SA 9:30-9, SU 11-6

Flora and Henri ★★★★☆

"...an emporium of high-end, stylish, well-made kids clothes with prices to match... quality is great, but range of items is limited... gorgeous and ridiculously impractical clothes at mind boggling prices... beautiful looking store... great quality beautiful clothes for when you want to splurge... good for gift shopping..."

Furniture, Bedding & Decor	✗	$$$$	Prices
Gear & Equipment	✗	❸	Product availability
Nursing & Feeding	✗	❹	Staff knowledge
Safety & Babycare	✗	❹	Customer service
Clothing, Shoes & Accessories	✓	❹	Decor
Books, Toys & Entertainment	✗		

WWW.FLORAHENRI.COM

CAPITOL HILL—705 BROADWAY E (AT E ROY ST); 206.323.2942; M-F 9-5

DOWNTOWN—717 PINE ST (AT 7TH AVE); 206.749.9698; M-SA 10-6, SU 12-5

Fred Meyer

❝...a good selection of inexpensive clothes, toys, gear, food and more... suitable for my infant as well as my thirteen year old, so I can get a bunch of shopping done at once... play land for older kids lets me shop while they have fun... not much customer service to speak of, but the prices are right... one-stop shopping—food, clothing and home supplies all in one place... ❞

Furniture, Bedding & Decor	✗	$$	Prices
Gear & Equipment	✓	❹	Product availability
Nursing & Feeding	✓	❸	Staff knowledge
Safety & Babycare	✓	❸	Customer service
Clothing, Shoes & Accessories	✓	❸	Decor
Books, Toys & Entertainment	✓		

WWW.FREDMEYER.COM

BELLEVUE—2041 148TH AVE NE (AT NE 29TH ST); 425.865.8560; DAILY 7-11

BURIEN—14300 1ST AVE S (AT SW 143RD ST); 206.433.6411; DAILY 7-11

KIRKLAND—12221 120TH AVE NE (AT NE 124TH ST); 425.820.3200; DAILY 7-11

RENTON—365 RENTON CTR WY SW (AT RENTON CTR); 425.204.5215; M-F 7-11; FREE PARKING

BALLARD—915 NW 45TH ST (AT 9TH AVE NW); 206.297.4300; DAILY 7-11PM

NORTH SEATTLE—100 NW 85TH ST (AT 1ST AVE NW); 206.784.9600; DAILY 7-11PM

Go To Your Room

❝...a real how-to on decorating your child's room... canopy beds, animal lamps, play tables... large selection displayed in creative ways... the staff is quite helpful and knowledgeable once you ask for assistance... competitive pricing... they will ship some items... free loaner glider available when yours is on order—now that's service... ❞

Furniture, Bedding & Decor	✓	$$$$	Prices
Gear & Equipment	✓	❹	Product availability
Nursing & Feeding	✗	❹	Staff knowledge
Safety & Babycare	✗	❹	Customer service
Clothing, Shoes & Accessories	✓	❹	Decor
Books, Toys & Entertainment	✓		

WWW.GOTOYOURROOM.COM

BELLEVUE—13000 BEL RED RD (AT 130TH AVE NE); 425.453.2990; M-SA 10-6, SU 12-5; PARKING LOT AT 130TH & BEL-RED

Gymboree

❝...beautiful clothing and great quality... colorful and stylish baby and kids wear... lots of fun birthday gift ideas... easy exchange and return policy... items usually go on sale pretty quickly... save money with Gymbucks... many stores have a play area which makes shopping with my kids fun (let alone feasible)... ❞

Furniture, Bedding & Decor	✗	$$$	Prices
Gear & Equipment	✗	❹	Product availability
Nursing & Feeding	✗	❹	Staff knowledge
Safety & Babycare	✗	❹	Customer service
Clothing, Shoes & Accessories	✓	❹	Decor
Books, Toys & Entertainment	✓		

WWW.GYMBOREE.COM

BELLEVUE—142 BELLEVUE SQ (AT NE 8TH ST); 425.450.9460; M-SA 9:30-9:30, SU 11-7

LYNNWOOD—3000 184TH ST SW (AT ALDERWOOD MALL); 425.771.4558; M-SA 10-9:30, SU 11-7; MALL PARKING

REDMOND—16432 NE 74TH (AT NE 76TH ST); 425.558.7832; M-SA 10-9, SU
11-7

DOWNTOWN—600 PINE ST (AT PACIFIC PL); 206.287.1991; M-SA 10-9, SU
11-6; FREE PARKING

MAPLE LEAF/ROOSEVELT—570 NE NORTHGATE WY (AT NORTHGATE
SHOPPING CTR); 206.366.0133; M-SA 10-9:30, SU 11-7; MALL PARKING

TUKWILA—654 SOUTHCENTER MALL (AT 28TH AVE S); 206.246.8997; M-SA
9:30-10, SU 11-7; MALL PARKING

Hanna Andersson

"...top-notch, high-quality cotton clothes for babies and kids... pricey,
but worth it for the durability and cuteness... girls clothes are
beautifully designed... some stores have a train table for kids to play
with while mom can shop... staff is always friendly... the long-john
cotton pj's are the best... Hanna's cotton has no match—it looks new
after being washed a billion times... neat kids' clothes—high-quality,
bright colors and unique... clothes are soft, gorgeous and made to
last... wonderful play dresses... **"**

Furniture, Bedding & Decor	✗	$$$$	Prices
Gear & Equipment	✗	❹	Product availability
Nursing & Feeding	✗	❹	Staff knowledge
Safety & Babycare	✗	❹	Customer service
Clothing, Shoes & Accessories	✓	❹	Decor
Books, Toys & Entertainment	✓		

WWW.HANNAANDERSSON.COM

UNIVERSITY DISTRICT/UNIVERSITY VILLAGE—2669 NE UNIVERSITY VLG (AT
UNIVERSITY VILLAGE MALL); 206.729.1099; M-SA 9:30-9, SU 11-6; MALL
PARKING

WOODINVILLE—13620 NE 175TH ST (AT 140TH AVE NE); 425.485.7998; M-SA
10-6, SU 11-5

Heaven Sent

"...one of the top consignment shops in the area... this store is a
godsend... friendly staff and the good quality stock moves quickly...
decor is adorable and while space is tight, it is kid friendly with a play
area in the center... great buying and trade in policies... great prices...
will hold items for you... Robeez shoes for way less... friendly and well
organized... **"**

Furniture, Bedding & Decor	✗	$$	Prices
Gear & Equipment	✓	❸	Product availability
Nursing & Feeding	✗	❹	Staff knowledge
Safety & Babycare	✗	❹	Customer service
Clothing, Shoes & Accessories	✓	❹	Decor
Books, Toys & Entertainment	✓		

WWW.HEAVENSENTKIDS.COM

FEDERAL WAY—1200 S 324TH ST (AT PACIFIC HWY S); 253.952.2124; M-F
10-6, SA 10-5, SU 12-5

IKEA

"...the coolest-looking and best-priced bedding, bibs and eating
utensils in town... fun, practical style and the prices are definitely
right... one of the few stores around that lets kids climb and crawl on
furniture... the kids' area has a slide, tunnels, tents... is it an indoor
playground or a store?.. unending decorating ideas for families on a
budget (lamps, rugs, beds, bedding)... it's all about organization—
cubbies, drawers, shelves, seats that double as a trunk and step stool...
arts and crafts galore... free childcare while you shop... cheap eats if
you get hungry... **"**

Furniture, Bedding & Decor	✓	$$	Prices
Gear & Equipment	✗	❹	Product availability

Nursing & Feeding	✓	❹	Staff knowledge
Safety & Babycare	✓	❹	Customer service
Clothing, Shoes & Accessories	✗	❹	Decor
Books, Toys & Entertainment	✓		

WWW.IKEA.COM

RENTON—600 SW 43RD ST (AT E VALLEY HWY); 425.656.2980; M-F 10-9:30, SA 10-9, SU 10-8; GARAGE PARKING

Inside Out Home & Garden ★★★★☆

"...boutique in historic setting... find everything from Petunia Picklebottom Diaper Bags and special-order furniture to Belly Butter and Hot Mama Books for Mom and great gifts for new grandparents... this is the place to find the perfect gift or special splurge item that everyone wants to know where you found it... **"**

Furniture, Bedding & Decor	✗	$$$	Prices
Gear & Equipment	✓	❺	Product availability
Nursing & Feeding	✗	❸	Staff knowledge
Safety & Babycare	✗	❹	Customer service
Clothing, Shoes & Accessories	✗	❸	Decor
Books, Toys & Entertainment	✓		

WWW.EINSIDEOUT.COM

SNOHOMISH—115 AVE A (AT 1ST ST); 360.563.0767; M-SAA11-5, F 11-7

Izilla Toys ★★★★★

"...the coolest toy store I've ever seen... eclectic store for parents who want funky and different toys for their kids... not a cheap tv/movie knockoff toy to be found!.. they clearly get kids (and their parents)... you're bound to find something cool... out-of-the-ordinary toys in a fun whimsical atmosphere... dolls, wooden toys, stuffed animals and most importantly the nicest staff around... a gem for local parents... **"**

Furniture, Bedding & Decor	✗	$$$	Prices
Gear & Equipment	✗	❹	Product availability
Nursing & Feeding	✗	❹	Staff knowledge
Safety & Babycare	✗	❺	Customer service
Clothing, Shoes & Accessories	✗	❹	Decor
Books, Toys & Entertainment	✓		

MADISON VALLEY/MADISON PARK—2840 E MADISON ST (AT 29TH AVE E); 206.322.8697; M-SA 10-6, SU 10-5

Janie And Jack ★★★★⯪

"...gorgeous clothing and some accessories (shoes, socks, etc.)... fun to look at, somewhat pricey, but absolutely adorable clothes for little ones... boutique-like clothes at non-boutique prices—especially on sale... high-quality infant and toddler clothes anyone would love—always good for a baby gift... I always check the clearance racks in the back of the store... their decor is darling—a really fun shopping experience... **"**

Furniture, Bedding & Decor	✗	$$$$	Prices
Gear & Equipment	✓	❹	Product availability
Nursing & Feeding	✗	❹	Staff knowledge
Safety & Babycare	✗	❹	Customer service
Clothing, Shoes & Accessories	✓	❹	Decor
Books, Toys & Entertainment	✗		

WWW.JANIEANDJACK.COM

BELLEVUE—151 BELLEVUE SQ (AT NE 4TH ST); 425.688.9879; M-SA 9:30-9:30, SU 10-7; FREE PARKING

JCPenney ★★★⯪☆

"...always a good place to find clothes and other baby basics... the registry process was seamless... staff is generally friendly but the lines

participate in our survey at

always seem long and slow... they don't have the greatest selection of toddler clothes, but their baby section is great... we had some damaged furniture delivered but customer service was easy and accommodating... a pretty limited selection of gear, but what they have is priced right... **"**

Furniture, Bedding & Decor	✓	$$ .... Prices
Gear & Equipment	✓	❸ .... Product availability
Nursing & Feeding	✓	❸ .... Staff knowledge
Safety & Babycare	✓	❸ .... Customer service
Clothing, Shoes & Accessories	✓	❸ .... Decor
Books, Toys & Entertainment	✓	

WWW.JCPENNEY.COM

BELLEVUE—300 BELLEVUE SQ (AT NE 4TH ST); 425.454.8599; M-SA 9:30-9:30, SU 11-7

LYNNWOOD—18601 33RD AVE W (AT ALDERWOOD MALL); 425.771.9555; M-SA 10-9:30, SU 11-7; MALL PARKING

MAPLE LEAF/ROOSEVELT—401 NE NORTHGATE WY (AT NORTHGATE MALL); 206.361.2500; M-SA 10-9:30, SU 11-7; MALL PARKING

TUKWILA—1200 SOUTHCENTER MALL (AT SOUTHCENTER MALL); 206.246.0850; M-SA 10-9:30, SU 11-7; MALL PARKING

Jojo Kids ★★★⯪☆

"...*I love the stuff here... colorful, funky, cute and different clothing for babies that don't break the bank... darling and trendy clothes... very unique!.. staff not always attentive... nice clearance section... lots of great girl purses and other little 'things' that make the store a fun place to stop by...* **"**

Furniture, Bedding & Decor	✗	$$$ .... Prices
Gear & Equipment	✗	❹ .... Product availability
Nursing & Feeding	✗	❸ .... Staff knowledge
Safety & Babycare	✗	❹ .... Customer service
Clothing, Shoes & Accessories	✓	❹ .... Decor
Books, Toys & Entertainment	✗	

WWW.JOJOKIDS.COM

BELLEVUE—115A BELLEVUE SQ (AT NE 4TH ST); 425.452.8787; M-SA 9:30-9, SU 11-7:30

Just Babies Baby Shop ★★★☆☆

"...*a treat to visit... unique and hard to find items... most of the products are super expensive but they do have good deals on nursing bras... way too expensive... pleasant store, but could use a broader selection... staff is not attentive...* **"**

Furniture, Bedding & Decor	✓	$$$$ .... Prices
Gear & Equipment	✓	❷ .... Product availability
Nursing & Feeding	✓	❸ .... Staff knowledge
Safety & Babycare	✗	❸ .... Customer service
Clothing, Shoes & Accessories	✗	❸ .... Decor
Books, Toys & Entertainment	✗	

WWW.JUSTBABIES.COM

MUKILTEO—11524 MUKILTEO SPEEDWAY (AT HARBOUR POINTE BLVD SW); 425.315.8888; W-SA 10:30-5

Just For Kids ★★★★☆

"...*top of my list for consignment shopping... you can get 3 shopping bags full for $75... tons and tons of used clothing for all ages... very good condition... toy selection is somewhat limited... I always walk out of there with an armload of new and used clothes for my baby... jam packed, get ready to rummage... great play area for the kids...* **"**

Furniture, Bedding & Decor	✓	$$ .... Prices
Gear & Equipment	✓	❹ .... Product availability

Nursing & Feeding	✓	❹	Staff knowledge
Safety & Babycare	✓	❹	Customer service
Clothing, Shoes & Accessories	✓	❹	Decor
Books, Toys & Entertainment	✓		

EVERETT—7510 BEVERLY BLVD (AT 75TH ST SE); 425.347.5002; M-SA 9-9,
SU 10-6 ; PARKING IN FRONT OF BLDG

KB Toys ★★★☆☆

❝...hectic and always buzzing... wall-to-wall plastic and blinking lights... more Fisher-Price, Elmo and Sponge Bob than the eye can handle... a toy super store with discounted prices... they always have some kind of special sale going on... if you're looking for the latest and greatest popular toy, then look no further—not the place for unique or unusual toys... perfect for bulk toy shopping—especially around the holidays... **❞**

Furniture, Bedding & Decor	✗	$$	Prices
Gear & Equipment	✗	❸	Product availability
Nursing & Feeding	✗	❸	Staff knowledge
Safety & Babycare	✗	❸	Customer service
Clothing, Shoes & Accessories	✗	❸	Decor
Books, Toys & Entertainment	✓		

WWW.KBTOYS.COM

LYNNWOOD—19401 ALDERWOOD MALL PKWY (AT ALDERWOOD PARKWAY
PLAZA); 425.670.8709; M-SA 9:30-9:30, SU 10-7; MALL PARKING

LYNNWOOD—3000 184TH ST SW (AT ALDERWOOD MALL); 425.778.5444; M-
SA 9:30-9:30, SU 11-7; MALL PARKING

RAINIER VALLEY—1006 SOUTHCENTER MALL (AT TUKWILA PKWY);
206.248.2215; M-SA 10-9:30, SU 11-7; MALL PARKING

Kid's Club ★★★½☆

❝...I don't need to shop anywhere else—this is one-stop baby shopping... decent selection, expensive clothing, nice decor, friendly staff... unusual toys... a fun shop that's easy to take the kids to... you'll find the latest magazine fashions here... funky clothes that are good quality... friendly staff and the feeding room is cozy and always clean... high-end prices... Bellevue location is not so desirable and University Village is hard to navigate with a stroller... Hair Chair (great place to het your kids haircut!) shares a space in both locations... **❞**

Furniture, Bedding & Decor	✗	$$$$	Prices
Gear & Equipment	✗	❹	Product availability
Nursing & Feeding	✗	❹	Staff knowledge
Safety & Babycare	✗	❹	Customer service
Clothing, Shoes & Accessories	✓	❹	Decor
Books, Toys & Entertainment	✗		

WWW.SHOPKIDSCLUB.COM

BELLEVUE—15600 NE 8TH ST (AT CROSSROADS MALL); 425.643.5437; DAILY
10-9; FREE PARKING

UNIVERSITY DISTRICT/UNIVERSITY VILLAGE—2630 NE VILLAGE LN (AT
UNIVERSITY VLG); 206.524.2553; M-SA 9:30-9, SU 11-6; GARAGE PARKING

Kid's On 45th ★★★★★

❝...what every consignment shop should be... funky little shop—about half used and half new... be ready to dig but you'll find great bargains... inventory changes quickly... staff is friendly and helpful... prices can be good and variety is great... consign your things, but beware of conditions of sale and credit limits... love the clearance and $1 racks... large selection of toys and books... **❞**

Furniture, Bedding & Decor	✗	$$	Prices
Gear & Equipment	✓	❹	Product availability
Nursing & Feeding	✓	❹	Staff knowledge

Safety & Babycare	✘	❹	Customer service
Clothing, Shoes & Accessories	✔	❸	Decor
Books, Toys & Entertainment	✔		

WALLINGFORD/FREMONT—1720 N 45TH ST (AT WALLINGFORD AVE N); 206.633.5437; M-SA 10-6, SU 11-5

Kinder Britches ★★★★☆

"...I love to browse in this store, as it has some of the cutest clothes you could imagine, but it's pricey... majority is girls' clothing, which is very high-quality... nice newborn gifts, but not a lot for practical regular baby gifts... **"**

Furniture, Bedding & Decor	✘	$$$$	Prices
Gear & Equipment	✘	❹	Product availability
Nursing & Feeding	✘	❹	Staff knowledge
Safety & Babycare	✘	❹	Customer service
Clothing, Shoes & Accessories	✔	❹	Decor
Books, Toys & Entertainment	✘		

EDMONDS—422 MAIN ST (AT 4TH AVE N); 425.778.7600; M-SA 10-6, SU 12-4

Kym's Kiddy Corner ★★★⯪☆

"...go there!.. it looks chaotic, but there is method to the madness, be ready to dig around... huge selection of baby gear and clothing... Kym is usually in the store and knows exactly what she has in stock... it's nice to be remembered when you walk in the door... be diligent and brave when you poke around... skimpy parking... keep to the merchandise inside, the stuff outside has seen better days... **"**

Furniture, Bedding & Decor	✔	$	Prices
Gear & Equipment	✔	❸	Product availability
Nursing & Feeding	✔	❹	Staff knowledge
Safety & Babycare	✘	❹	Customer service
Clothing, Shoes & Accessories	✔	❷	Decor
Books, Toys & Entertainment	✔		

WWW.KYMSKIDDYCORNER.COM

NORTH SEATTLE—11721 15TH AVE NE (AT NE 117TH ST); 206.361.5974; M-SA 10-5:30

Lakeshore Learning Store ★★★★☆

"...one of the best resources for parents in this town... amazing educational toys and tools at amazing prices... teachers use this store for practically everything they need in a classroom... frequent-buyer account... emails about specials... lots of sales... I love this store for its extraordinary variety and absence of junk... **"**

Furniture, Bedding & Decor	✘	$$$	Prices
Gear & Equipment	✘	❹	Product availability
Nursing & Feeding	✘	❹	Staff knowledge
Safety & Babycare	✘	❹	Customer service
Clothing, Shoes & Accessories	✘	❹	Decor
Books, Toys & Entertainment	✔		

WWW.LAKESHORELEARNING.COM

BELLEVUE—11027 NE 4TH ST (AT 110TH AVE); 425.462.8076; M-F 9-8, SA 9-7, SU 11-7

Lamb's Ears ★★★⯪☆

"...this is a hidden gem in Bellevue... a wonderful children's boutique that has high-end unique clothing for babies and children... definitely worth checking out... posh, and doesn't always have more than one of something... **"**

Furniture, Bedding & Decor	✘	$$$$	Prices
Gear & Equipment	✘	❸	Product availability

Nursing & Feeding	✗	❹	Staff knowledge
Safety & Babycare	✗	❸	Customer service
Clothing, Shoes & Accessories	✓	❹	Decor
Books, Toys & Entertainment	✓		

WWW.LAMBSEARS.NET

BELLEVUE—820-102ND AVE NE (ACROSS FROM BELLEVUE SQ);
425.688.1080; M-SA 10-6

Land of Nod ★★★★★

"...creative and fun decor and furnishings... lots of practical stuff with a bit more flair than your typical furnishings store... nice, helpful staff... a truly terrific place to buy gifts... lots of cool, retro stuff that you don't find elsewhere... love their book and music selection... great ideas for decorating kids' bedrooms... fabulous customer service and knowledgeable staff... adorable furniture and bedding...**"**

Furniture, Bedding & Decor	✓	$$$$	Prices
Gear & Equipment	✗	❹	Product availability
Nursing & Feeding	✗	❹	Staff knowledge
Safety & Babycare	✗	❹	Customer service
Clothing, Shoes & Accessories	✗	❺	Decor
Books, Toys & Entertainment	✓		

WWW.LANDOFNOD.COM

DOWNTOWN—2660 NE UNIVERSITY VLG (AT UNIVERSITY VLG);
206.527.9900; M-F 10-9, SA 10-7, SU 11-6; MALL PARKING

Lollipops ★★★★☆

"...children's consignment store worth going to... some designer clothing for a steal of a deal... good prices, well-organized and lots of newer clothing... you might not find cheap stuff like at a thrift store, but definitely a good price for new stuff... clean store and items are high-quality... wonderful place to shop with toddlers... great owner...**"**

Furniture, Bedding & Decor	✓	$$	Prices
Gear & Equipment	✓	❹	Product availability
Nursing & Feeding	✓	❹	Staff knowledge
Safety & Babycare	✓	❹	Customer service
Clothing, Shoes & Accessories	✓	❹	Decor
Books, Toys & Entertainment	✓		

WWW.SHOPLOLLIPOPS.COM

BURIEN—2038 SW 152ND ST (AT 21ST AVE SW); 206.243.1795; M-SA 9:30-5:30, SU 11-4; FREE PARKING

Macy's ★★★☆☆

"...Macy's has it all and I never leave empty-handed... if you time your visit right you can find some great deals... go during the week so you don't get overwhelmed with the weekend crowd... good for staples as well as beautiful party dresses for girls... lots of brand-names like Carter's, Guess, and Ralph Lauren... not much in terms of assistance... newspaper coupons and sales help keep the cost down... some stores are better organized and maintained than others... if you're going to shop at a department store for your baby, then Macy's is a safe bet...**"**

Furniture, Bedding & Decor	✓	$$$	Prices
Gear & Equipment	✗	❸	Product availability
Nursing & Feeding	✗	❸	Staff knowledge
Safety & Babycare	✗	❸	Customer service
Clothing, Shoes & Accessories	✓	❸	Decor
Books, Toys & Entertainment	✓		

WWW.MACYS.COM

BELLEVUE—400 BELLEVUE SQ (AT BELLEVUE WY NE); 425.688.6000; M-SA 9:30-9:30, SU 11-7

participate in our survey at

DOWNTOWN—1601 3RD AVE (AT PINE ST); 206.506.6000; M-SA 10-8, SU 11-7

MAPLE LEAF/ROOSEVELT—401 NE NORTHGATE WY (AT NORTHGATE SHOPPING CTR); 206.440.6671; DAILY 10-9:30

TUKWILA—500 SOUTHCENTER MALL (AT TUKWILA PKWY); 425.656.6850; M-SA 10-9:30, SU 11-7

Madrona Moose ★★★★☆

❝...store is designed with a vintage, classic feel, and contains hard-to-find lines of clothes, toys, and accessories from Europe and elsewhere... a darling, warm atmosphere with the cutest stuff...**❞**

Furniture, Bedding & Decor	✗	$$$$	Prices
Gear & Equipment	✗	❸	Product availability
Nursing & Feeding	✗	❸	Staff knowledge
Safety & Babycare	✗	❹	Customer service
Clothing, Shoes & Accessories	✓	❹	Decor
Books, Toys & Entertainment	✓		

WWW.MADRONAMOOSE.COM

MADRONA—1421 34TH AVE (AT E UNION ST); 206.320.7900; T-F 11-6, SA 11-5

Math 'n' Stuff ★★★★★

❝...I'm a huge fan... a great addition to the city... awesome array of all kinds of fun and learning items to do with kids... math, science, reading—wow... staff knows every product—for items out of the norm, this is your place... friendly staff, great selection ranging from stimulating infant toys to books on calculus... for homeschooling or educational fun, this is the place... amazing selection...**❞**

Furniture, Bedding & Decor	✗	$$	Prices
Gear & Equipment	✗	❹	Product availability
Nursing & Feeding	✗	❺	Staff knowledge
Safety & Babycare	✗	❺	Customer service
Clothing, Shoes & Accessories	✗	❹	Decor
Books, Toys & Entertainment	✓		

WWW.MATH-N-STUFF.COM

MAPLE LEAF/ROOSEVELT—8926 ROOSEVELT WAY NE (AT NE 89TH ST); 206.522.8891; T-SA 10-6; FREE PARKING

Me 'n Mom's Consignment Boutique ★★★★☆

❝...it's amazing how many outfits you can get for $20... great bargains... huge selection and prices appropriate for used items... biggest baby consignment I've ever seen... great place to get your baby gear if you are on a budget, they have everything you need... well organized and no junky clothing... toys and gear, as well... staff is always helpful...**❞**

Furniture, Bedding & Decor	✓	$$	Prices
Gear & Equipment	✓	❹	Product availability
Nursing & Feeding	✓	❹	Staff knowledge
Safety & Babycare	✓	❹	Customer service
Clothing, Shoes & Accessories	✓	❹	Decor
Books, Toys & Entertainment	✓		

WWW.MENMOMS.COM

ISSAQUAH—975 NW GILMAN BLVD (AT MAPLE ST NW); 425.427.5430; M-F 9:30-6, SA-SU 10:30-5

BALLARD—2821 NW MARKET ST (AT 28TH AVE NW); 206.781.9449; M-F 9:30-6, SA-SU 10:30-5

Merry Go Round ★★★★★

"...a wonderful, high-end store with everything you might need for your baby... a privately owned children's store with an excellent selection of strollers, cribs and other essentials... the staff is friendly and knowledgeable... look for their sales—you'll be able to pick up top of the line items on the cheap... I like that the staff was extremely honest with me about the pros and cons of the products they sell—they really tried to help fit them to my needs..."

Furniture, Bedding & Decor	✓	$$$$	Prices
Gear & Equipment	✓	❹	Product availability
Nursing & Feeding	✓	❹	Staff knowledge
Safety & Babycare	✓	❹	Customer service
Clothing, Shoes & Accessories	✓	❹	Decor
Books, Toys & Entertainment	✓		

WWW.MERRYGOROUNDKIDS.COM

BELLEVUE—1014 116TH AVE NE (AT NE 8TH ST); 425.454.1610; M-SA 10-6, SU 12-5

Mervyn's ★★★☆☆

"...wide selection of baby and kids' clothing, including OshKosh and Carter's... limited shoe selection without any real sizing assistance... lots of good sales... you might not always be able to find the size and color you want, but there's enough selection here that you're sure to find something else that will work just as well... cheap, cheap, cheap... okay for cheap basics, but don't expect anything super special..."

Furniture, Bedding & Decor	✗	$$	Prices
Gear & Equipment	✗	❹	Product availability
Nursing & Feeding	✗	❸	Staff knowledge
Safety & Babycare	✗	❸	Customer service
Clothing, Shoes & Accessories	✓	❸	Decor
Books, Toys & Entertainment	✓		

WWW.MERVYNS.COM

BELLEVUE—4126 124TH AVE SE (AT FACTORIA SQ MALL); 425.643.6554; M-SA 9-10, SU 9-9; MALL PARKING

EVERETT—1402 SE EVERETT MALL WY (AT EVERETT MALL); 425.353.8100; M-SA 9-10, SU 9-9; MALL PARKING

LYNNWOOD—3301 184TH ST SW (AT ALDERWOOD MALL); 425.672.7765; M-SA 9-10, SU 9-9; MALL PARKING

REDMOND—17601 NE UNION HILL RD (AT 178TH PL NE); 425.558.9500; M-SA 9-10, SU 9-9

TUKWILA—1100 SOUTHCENTER MALL (AT SOUTHCENTER MALL); 206.439.1919; M-SA 9-10, SU 9-9; MALL PARKING

Nordstrom ★★★★☆

"...quality service and quality clothes... awesome kids shoe department—almost as good as the one for adults... free balloons in the children's shoe area as well as drawing tables... in addition to their own brand, they carry a very nice selection of other high-end baby clothing including Ralph Lauren, Robeez, etc... adorable baby clothes—they make great shower gifts... such a wonderful shopping experience—their lounge is perfect for breastfeeding and for changing diapers... well-rounded selection of baby basics as well as fancy clothes for special events..."

Furniture, Bedding & Decor	✓	$$$$	Prices
Gear & Equipment	✓	❹	Product availability
Nursing & Feeding	✗	❹	Staff knowledge
Safety & Babycare	✗	❹	Customer service
Clothing, Shoes & Accessories	✓	❹	Decor
Books, Toys & Entertainment	✓		

participate in our survey at

WWW.NORDSTROM.COM

BELLEVUE—100 BELLEVUE SQ (AT BELLEVUE SQ); 425.455.5800; M-SA 9:30-9:30, SU 11-7

DOWNTOWN—500 PINE ST (AT 5TH AVE); 206.628.2111; M-SA 9:30-9, SU 11-7

LYNNWOOD—3200 184TH ST SW (AT ALDERWOOD MALL); 425.774.6569; M-SA 9:20-9:30, SU 11-7

MAPLE LEAF/ROOSEVELT—401 NE NORTHGATE WY (AT NORTHGATE SHOPPING CTR); 206.364.8800; M-SA 9:30-9:30, SU 11-7

TUKWILA—100 SOUTHCENTER SHOPPING CTR (AT SOUTHCENTER SHOPPING CTR); 206.246.0400; M-SA 9:30-9:30, SU 11-7

Oilily ★★★★½

"...exclusive shop with fun, colorful clothing... prices are a bit steep, but if you value unique, well-designed clothes, this is the place... better selection for girls than boys but there are special items for either sex... your tot will definitely stand out from the crowd in these unique pieces... my kids love wearing their 'cool' clothes... whimsical items for mom, too... **"**

Furniture, Bedding & Decor	✗	$$$$		Prices
Gear & Equipment	✗	❹		Product availability
Nursing & Feeding	✗	❹		Staff knowledge
Safety & Babycare	✗	❹		Customer service
Clothing, Shoes & Accessories	✓	❹		Decor
Books, Toys & Entertainment	✗			

WWW.OILILYUSA.COM

BELLEVUE—100 BELLEVUE SQ (AT NE 8TH ST); 425.688.0663; M-SA 9:30-9:30, SU 11-7

Old Navy ★★★★☆

"...hip and 'in' clothes for infants and tots... plenty of steals on clearance items... T-shirts and pants for $10 or less... busy, busy, busy—long lines, especially on weekends... nothing fancy and you won't mind when your kids get down and dirty in these clothes... easy to wash, decent quality... you can shop for your baby, your toddler, your teen and yourself all at the same time... clothes are especially affordable when you hit their sales (post-holiday sales are amazing!)... **"**

Furniture, Bedding & Decor	✗	$$		Prices
Gear & Equipment	✗	❹		Product availability
Nursing & Feeding	✗	❸		Staff knowledge
Safety & Babycare	✗	❸		Customer service
Clothing, Shoes & Accessories	✓	❸		Decor
Books, Toys & Entertainment	✗			

WWW.OLDNAVY.COM

AUBURN—1101 SUPERMALL WY (AT SUPERMALL OF THE GREAT NORTHWEST); 253.804.3470; M-SA 9-9, SU 10-6; PARKING LOT

BELLEVUE—15600 NE 8TH ST (AT 156TH AVE NE); 425.562.4252; M-SA 9-9, SU 10-6

BELLEVUE—4037 FACTORIA BLVD SE (AT FACTORIA SQ MALL); 425.957.0341; M-SA 9-9, SU 10-6; MALL PARKING

DOWNTOWN—601 PINE ST (AT 6TH AVE); 206.264.9341; M-SA 9-9, SU 10-6

FEDERAL WAY—1718 S 320TH ST (AT SEATAC MALL); 253.946.9200; M-SA 9-9, SU 10-6; MALL PARKING

LYNNWOOD 19401 ALDERWOOD MALL PKWY (AT ALDERWOOD MALL); 425.670.3660; M-SA 9-9:30, SU 11-7; MALL PARKING

TUKWILA—17470 SOUTHCENTER PKWY (AT MINKLER BLVD); 206.575.0432; M-SA 9-9, SU 11-7; MALL PARKING

Once Upon A Child

"...new and used items... the place for bargain baby items in like-new condition... a great bargain spot with a wide variety of clothes for baby... some inexpensive furniture... good selection, staff and prices... cluttered and hard to get through the store with kids... good toys and gear... some items are definitely more than 'gently used'... a kid's play area... good end-of-season sales... expect to sort through items... cash for your old items..."

Furniture, Bedding & Decor	✓	$$ .... Prices
Gear & Equipment	✓	❸ .... Product availability
Nursing & Feeding	✗	❹ .... Staff knowledge
Safety & Babycare	✗	❹ .... Customer service
Clothing, Shoes & Accessories	✓	❸ .... Decor
Books, Toys & Entertainment	✓	

WWW.OUAC.COM

KENT—26121 104TH AVE SE (AT SE 260TH ST); 253.850.7585; M-F 10-7, SA 10-6, SU 10-5; PARKING COMPLEX

OshKosh B'Gosh

"...cute, sturdy clothes for infants and toddlers... frequent sales make their high-quality merchandise a lot more affordable... doesn't every American kid have to get a pair of their overalls?.. great selection of cute clothes for boys... you can't go wrong here—their clothing is fun and worth the price... customer service is pretty hit-or-miss from store to store... we always walk out of here with something fun and colorful..."

Furniture, Bedding & Decor	✗	$$$ .... Prices
Gear & Equipment	✗	❹ .... Product availability
Nursing & Feeding	✗	❹ .... Staff knowledge
Safety & Babycare	✗	❹ .... Customer service
Clothing, Shoes & Accessories	✓	❹ .... Decor
Books, Toys & Entertainment	✗	

WWW.OSHKOSHBGOSH.COM

BELLEVUE—4092 FACTORIA MALL BLVD SE (AT MAIN ST); 425.957.7217; M-SA 10-9, SU 11-6; MALL PARKING

FEDERAL WAY—32077 PACIFIC HWY S (AT SEATAC MALL); 253.945.8268; M-SA 10-9, SU 11-6; MALL PARKING

NORTH BEND—561 S FORK AVE SW (FACTORY STORES AT NORTH BEND); 425.831.5688; M-SA 10-8, SU 12-6

WOODINVILLE—17953 GARDEN WY NE (AT NE 175TH ST); 425.483.1997; M-SA 10-9, SU 11-6

Other Mothers

"...a chain resale shop that carries maternity and kids clothes, furniture and toys... everything you may want or need without the department store prices... take the things your child outgrows in exchange for new 'used' items... great for breastfeeding mothers... my favorite place to look for gently used baby products... a hit or miss, but there are a lot more hits..."

Furniture, Bedding & Decor	✗	$$ .... Prices
Gear & Equipment	✗	❹ .... Product availability
Nursing & Feeding	✗	❹ .... Staff knowledge
Safety & Babycare	✗	❹ .... Customer service
Clothing, Shoes & Accessories	✓	❸ .... Decor
Books, Toys & Entertainment	✗	

EVERETT—13027 BOTHELL EVERETT HWY (AT 132ND ST SE); 425.357.8779; M-SA 10-6

Payless Shoe Source ★★★☆☆

66 *...a good place for deals on children's shoes... staff is helpful with sizing... the selection and prices for kids' shoes can't be beat, but the quality isn't always spectacular... good leather shoes for cheap... great variety of all sizes and widths... I get my son's shoes here and don't feel like I'm wasting my money since he'll outgrow them in 3 months anyway...* **99**

Furniture, Bedding & Decor	✗	$$	Prices
Gear & Equipment	✗	❸	Product availability
Nursing & Feeding	✗	❸	Staff knowledge
Safety & Babycare	✗	❸	Customer service
Clothing, Shoes & Accessories	✓	❸	Decor
Books, Toys & Entertainment	✗		

WWW.PAYLESS.COM

BELLEVUE—4025 FACTORIA BLVD SE (AT FACTORIA MALL); 425.401.7100; M-SA 10-8:30, SU 11-6

CENTRAL DISTRICT—2326 RAINIER AVE S (OFF WALKER ST); 206.726.1084; M-SA 9-8, SU 10-7

DOWNTOWN—1529 3RD AVE (AT PINE ST); 206.622.9557; M-SA 9-8, SU 11-6

LYNNWOOD—2701 184TH ST SW (AT ALDERWOOD MALL); 425.774.4186; M-SA 9-9, SU 10-7

RAINIER VALLEY—8824 RAINIER AVE S (OFF HENDERSON ST); 206.723.2169; M-F 9-8, SA 9-9, SU 10-7

SEATTLE—2500 SW BARTON (AT WESTWOOD SHOPPING CTR); 206.935.6787; M-SA 9-9, SU 10-7

Pinocchio's Toys ★★★★⯪

66 *...one of the best toy stores anywhere... don't miss it... fabulous options and not overrun with Barbie and pink princesses... staff is great and owner passionate about toys... sturdy, educational toys... creative and mostly non-battery operated... one of Seattle's many alternatives to Toys R Us... small trinkets to very nice toys... my favorite source for party favors... a little cramped, but great play area in back...* **99**

Furniture, Bedding & Decor	✓	$$$	Prices
Gear & Equipment	✗	❹	Product availability
Nursing & Feeding	✗	❹	Staff knowledge
Safety & Babycare	✗	❹	Customer service
Clothing, Shoes & Accessories	✗	❸	Decor
Books, Toys & Entertainment	✓		

WEDGEWOOD/RAVENNA—4540 UNION BAY PL NE (E OF UNIVERSITY VLG MALL); 206.528.1100; M-SA 10-7, SU 12-6; PARKING IN FRONT OF BLDG

Plum ★★★⯪☆

66 *...if you are in the market for high-end children's shoes this is the place... the owner is really knowledgeable and patient in working with the kids—the only drawback is the price, but the shoes are fantastic... no other store like it...* **99**

Furniture, Bedding & Decor	✗	$$$$	Prices
Gear & Equipment	✗	❸	Product availability
Nursing & Feeding	✗	❺	Staff knowledge
Safety & Babycare	✗	❺	Customer service
Clothing, Shoes & Accessories	✓	❹	Decor
Books, Toys & Entertainment	✗		

WWW.PLUMSHOES.COM

MADISON VALLEY/MADISON PARK—2913 E MADISON ST (AT 29TH AVE E); 206.322.7011; T-SA 10-5; FREE PARKING

Pop Tots ★★★★⯨

"...too cool... rock star baby gear that's far outside the usual frilly, cute stuff... a must stop for unique, punky, funky kid's clothes... high prices but worth it for something unusual... don't expect to stock up on all the necessities, but seize the chance to break out... small, but packed with retro and fun stuff for babies and kids... spendy but great fun... where you go to find 'Clash' and 'Ramones' onesies... great service... a good place for the used-to-be-cool parent... "

Furniture, Bedding & Decor	✗	$$$	Prices
Gear & Equipment	✗	❹	Product availability
Nursing & Feeding	✗	❺	Staff knowledge
Safety & Babycare	✗	❹	Customer service
Clothing, Shoes & Accessories	✓	❺	Decor
Books, Toys & Entertainment	✓		

WWW.THECRADLEROCKS.COM

MAPLE LEAF/ROOSEVELT—6505 ROOSEVELT WAY NE (AT N 65TH ST); 206.522.4322; M-SA 11-6, SU 12-4

Portage Bay Goods ★★★★☆

"...fabulous wooden toys and 'Under the Nile' brand clothing... you have to search for items on your own, but it's worth it when you find the perfect thing... good selection of high-quality and interesting clothes and gifts for baby... fun selection of toys that aren't run of the mill... the staff is why I keep going back... eco-conscious products... "

Furniture, Bedding & Decor	✗	$$$	Prices
Gear & Equipment	✓	❹	Product availability
Nursing & Feeding	✗	❹	Staff knowledge
Safety & Babycare	✗	❹	Customer service
Clothing, Shoes & Accessories	✓	❹	Decor
Books, Toys & Entertainment	✓		

WWW.PORTAGEBAYGOODS.COM

WALLINGFORD/FREMONT—706 N 34TH ST (AT AURORA AVE N); 206.547.5221; DAILY 10-7

Pottery Barn Kids ★★★★⯨

"...stylish furniture, rugs, rockers and much more... they've found the right mix between quality and price... finally a company that stands behind what they sell—their customer service is great... gorgeous baby decor and furniture that will make your nursery to-die-for... the play area is so much fun—my daughter never wants to leave... a beautiful store with tons of ideas for setting up your nursery or kid's room... bright colors and cute patterns with basics to mix and match... if you see something in the catalog, but not in the store, just ask because they often have it in the back... "

Furniture, Bedding & Decor	✓	$$$$	Prices
Gear & Equipment	✗	❹	Product availability
Nursing & Feeding	✗	❹	Staff knowledge
Safety & Babycare	✗	❹	Customer service
Clothing, Shoes & Accessories	✗	❺	Decor
Books, Toys & Entertainment	✓		

WWW.POTTERYBARNKIDS.COM

BELLEVUE—1050 BELLEVUE SQ (AT NE 8TH ST); 425.451.2966; M-SA 9:30-9:30, SU 11-7

UNIVERSITY DISTRICT/UNIVERSITY VILLAGE—4634 26TH AVE NE (AT NE 54TH ST); 206.527.5560; M-SA 9:30-9, SU 11-6

Pregnant Pause ★★★⯨☆

"...nice consignment shop full of stuff for kids and pregnant moms... store is stuffed to capacity... 'nicer' pregnancy clothes, which are priced accordingly... prices are a bit high, but the clothes are very nice... "

Furniture, Bedding & Decor	✗	$$	Prices
Gear & Equipment	✗	❸	Product availability
Nursing & Feeding	✗	❹	Staff knowledge
Safety & Babycare	✗	❸	Customer service
Clothing, Shoes & Accessories	✓	❸	Decor
Books, Toys & Entertainment	✗		

WWW.PREGNANTPAUSE.COM

MADISON VALLEY/MADISON PARK—2709 E MADISON ST (AT 27TH AVE E); 206.726.8555; T-SA 10-5

Queen Anne Dispatch/Undies & Outies ★★☆☆☆

"...interesting shoes and designer clothes in a great neighborhood... geared to skinny twentysomethings... a strange combination of shipping and fashionable accessories... interesting items and you will have fun browsing through all they have to offer... everything from clothing, to necessities, to toys, books, and music... it appears they are adding infant wear, great if you are looking for a gift with a 'label'... "

Furniture, Bedding & Decor	✗	$$$$	Prices
Gear & Equipment	✓	❷	Product availability
Nursing & Feeding	✓	❷	Staff knowledge
Safety & Babycare	✗	❷	Customer service
Clothing, Shoes & Accessories	✓	❺	Decor
Books, Toys & Entertainment	✓		

QUEEN ANNE—2212 QUEEN ANNE AVE N (AT BOSTON ST); 206.286.1024; M-F 8-8, SA 9-6, SU 11-5; STREET PARKING

REI ★★★★☆

"...a great store for outdoor/active gear and clothing for kids and their parents... this is a fun store to visit, too... they have an indoor climbing wall... the kids will be fascinated and school-age kids can even try it out themselves... good quality gear to get you outside with your baby... the gear is high-quality and the staff knows what they are talking about... "

Furniture, Bedding & Decor	✗	$$$	Prices
Gear & Equipment	✓	❹	Product availability
Nursing & Feeding	✗	❹	Staff knowledge
Safety & Babycare	✗	❹	Customer service
Clothing, Shoes & Accessories	✓	❹	Decor
Books, Toys & Entertainment	✗		

WWW.REI.COM

DOWNTOWN—222 YALE AVE N (AT JOHN ST); 206.223.1944; M-F10-9, SA-SU 10-7

LYNNWOOD—4200 194TH ST SW (AT 44TH AVE W); 425.774.1300; M-SA 10-9, SU 11-6

REDMOND—7500 166TH AVE NE (AT REDMOND TOWN CTR); 425.882.1158; M-F 10-9, SA 10-8, SU 11-6; PARKING LOT

Right Start, The ★★★★☆

"...higher-end, well selected items... Britax, Maclaren, Combi, Mustela—all the cool brands under one roof... everything from bibs to bottles and even the Bugaboo stroller... prices seem a little high, but the selection is good and the staff knowledgeable and helpful... there are toys all over the store that kids can play with while you shop... I have a hard time getting my kids out of the store because they are having so much fun... a boutique-like shopping experience but they carry most of the key brands... their registry works well... "

Furniture, Bedding & Decor	✓	$$$	Prices
Gear & Equipment	✓	❹	Product availability
Nursing & Feeding	✓	❹	Staff knowledge

Safety & Babycare .... ✓ ❹ ....Customer service
Clothing, Shoes & Accessories ...... ✓ ❹ .... Decor
Books, Toys & Entertainment .... ✓
WWW.RIGHTSTART.COM

BELLEVUE—168 BELLEVUE SQ (AT NE 2ND ST); 425.451.2445; M-SA 9:30-
9:30, SU 11-7

WEDGEWOOD/RAVENNA—4520 UNION BAY PL NE (ACROSS FROM
UNIVERSITY VLG); 206.729.7458; M-SA 10-6:30, SU 11-6

Rising Stars ★★★★☆

"...a small shop, but with a great selection... beautiful items, lots of
local handmade stuff... books, toys, and adorable clothes for baby and
children... good gift shopping, pricey for a whole wardrobe though... a
great playroom for the kids... staff is helpful and friendly... look out for
the sales, some excellent prices... good discount program... **"**

Furniture, Bedding & Decor .... ✗ $$$ ....Prices
Gear & Equipment .... ✗ ❹ .... Product availability
Nursing & Feeding .... ✗ ❹ .... Staff knowledge
Safety & Babycare .... ✗ ❹ ....Customer service
Clothing, Shoes & Accessories ...... ✓ ❺ .... Decor
Books, Toys & Entertainment .... ✓

GREENLAKE/GREENWOOD/PHINNEY RIDGE—7404 GREENWOOD AVE N (AT N
74TH ST); 206.781.0138; M-SA 10-6, SU 10-4

Robins Nest Childrens Resale ★★★☆☆

"...excellent consignment store with great products, from apparel to
toys to furniture... I feel it's just a wee bit pricey... **"**

Furniture, Bedding & Decor .... ✗ $$$ ....Prices
Gear & Equipment .... ✗ ❸ .... Product availability
Nursing & Feeding .... ✗ ❹ .... Staff knowledge
Safety & Babycare .... ✗ ❸ ....Customer service
Clothing, Shoes & Accessories ...... ✓ ❸ .... Decor
Books, Toys & Entertainment .... ✓

AUBURN—1245 AUBURN WAY N (AT AUBURN N SHOPPING CTR);
253.833.4474; M-F 10-7, SA 10-5

Ross Dress For Less ★★★☆☆

"...if you're in the mood for bargain hunting and are okay with
potentially coming up empty-handed, then Ross is for you... don't
expect to get educated about baby products here... go early on a week
day and you'll find an organized store and staff that is helpful and
available—forget weekends... their selection is pretty inconsistent, but I
have found some incredible bargains... a great place to stock up on
birthday presents or stocking stuffers... **"**

Furniture, Bedding & Decor .... ✗ $$ ....Prices
Gear & Equipment .... ✗ ❸ .... Product availability
Nursing & Feeding .... ✗ ❸ .... Staff knowledge
Safety & Babycare .... ✗ ❸ ....Customer service
Clothing, Shoes & Accessories ...... ✓ ❸ .... Decor
Books, Toys & Entertainment .... ✓
WWW.ROSSSTORES.COM

DOWNTOWN—1418 3RD AVE (AT UNION ST); 206.623.6781; M-SA 9-8, SU
10-6

NORTH SEATTLE—13201 AURORA AVE N (AT N 130TH ST); 206.367.6030; M-
SA 9:30-9:30, SU 11-7

TUKWILA—17672 SOUTHCENTER PKWY (AT MINKLER BLVD); 206.575.0110;
M-SA 9-9:30, SU 10-6; MALL PARKING

Saturday's Child Consignment ★★★½☆

❝...high-quality consignment shop... great source of hard to find used baby gear... constantly changing inventory... cute store with a great selection... packed with a lot of stuff... organized and helpful staff... a little overwhelming, but if you can find your way through the maze, you can find some good buys... check out the 99 cent room...❞

Furniture, Bedding & Decor	✗	$$ .... Prices
Gear & Equipment	✓	❹ .... Product availability
Nursing & Feeding	✗	❹ .... Staff knowledge
Safety & Babycare	✗	❹ .... Customer service
Clothing, Shoes & Accessories	✓	❸ .... Decor
Books, Toys & Entertainment	✗	

WWW.SATURDAYS-CHILD.COM

BOTHELL—18012 BOTHELL EVERETT HWY (AT 180TH ST SE); 425.486.6716; M-SA 10-5, SU 12-4

Sears ★★★☆☆

❝...a decent selection of clothes and basic baby equipment... check out the Kids Club program—it's a great way to save money... you go to Sears to save money, not to be pampered... the quality of their merchandise is better than Wal-Mart, but don't expect anything too special or different... not much in terms of gear, but tons of well-priced baby and toddler clothing...❞

Furniture, Bedding & Decor	✓	$$ .... Prices
Gear & Equipment	✓	❸ .... Product availability
Nursing & Feeding	✓	❸ .... Staff knowledge
Safety & Babycare	✓	❸ .... Customer service
Clothing, Shoes & Accessories	✓	❸ .... Decor
Books, Toys & Entertainment	✓	

WWW.SEARS.COM

EVERETT—1302 SE EVERETT MALL WAY (AT EVERETT MALL); 425.355.7070; M-SA 10-9, SU 10-6

FEDERAL WAY—1701 S 320TH ST (AT SEATAC MALL); 253.529.8200; M-SA 10-7, SU 10-9

LYNNWOOD—18600 ALDERWOOD MALL PKWY (AT ALDERWOOD MALL); 425.771.2212; M-SA 9-9:30, SU 10-7

REDMOND—2200 148TH AVE NE (AT NE 22ND ST); 425.644.6581; M-SA 10-7, SU 11-7; PARKING IN FRONT OF BLDG

NORTH SEATTLE—15711 AURORA AVE N (AT N 160TH ST); 206.440.2000; M-SA 9-9, SU 9-7

SODO—76 S LANDER ST (AT 1ST AVE S); 206.344.4893; M-F 10-9, SA 10-6, SU 11-5

TUKWILA—400 SOUTHCENTER MALL (AT SOUTHCENTER MALL); 206.241.3503; M-F 9:30-9:30, SA 8-9:30, SU 10-8; MALL PARKING

Shoe Zoo ★★★★☆

❝...I love the Shoe Zoo... these folks know children's shoes!.. they are always very kind, very helpful and very patient... my son has a wide foot, and they always have a shoe for him, or can order it quickly... they have also done a great job of helping me understand how to find appropriate shoes for him... it's rare to still find such knowledgeable, well-trained people...❞

Furniture, Bedding & Decor	✗	$$$ .... Prices
Gear & Equipment	✗	❹ .... Product availability
Nursing & Feeding	✗	❹ .... Staff knowledge
Safety & Babycare	✗	❹ .... Customer service
Clothing, Shoes & Accessories	✓	❸ .... Decor
Books, Toys & Entertainment	✗	

REDMOND—7325 164TH AVE NE (AT REDMOND TOWN CTR); 425.558.4743; DAILY 10-9

Shoefly ★★★★☆

"...super cute shoes... my favorite shoe store... not so much for kids though—they only have Robeez..., but lots for Mom!... "

Furniture, Bedding & Decor	✗	$$$$ .... Prices
Gear & Equipment	✗	❸ .... Product availability
Nursing & Feeding	✗	❹ .... Staff knowledge
Safety & Babycare	✗	❹ ....Customer service
Clothing, Shoes & Accessories	✓	❹ .... Decor
Books, Toys & Entertainment	✗	

WWW.SHOEFLY.COM

GREENLAKE/GREENWOOD/PHINNEY RIDGE—109-7900 E GREENLAKE DR N (AT WALLINGFORD AVE N); 206.729.7463; M-SA 10-7, SU 11-6

Sole Food Shoes ★★★★⯪

"...great selection of shoes for tots and moms too... shoes for baby you won't find anywhere else... most of the high-end brands available... not cheap, but one of the few places around that carries such nice merchandise... stay-on booties that actually stay on... convenient location at University Vlg Mall so you can get other shopping done too... "

Furniture, Bedding & Decor	✗	$$$$ .... Prices
Gear & Equipment	✗	❹ .... Product availability
Nursing & Feeding	✗	❹ .... Staff knowledge
Safety & Babycare	✗	❹ ....Customer service
Clothing, Shoes & Accessories	✓	❹ .... Decor
Books, Toys & Entertainment	✗	

WWW.SHOPSOLEFOOD.COM

UNIVERSITY DISTRICT/UNIVERSITY VILLAGE—2652 NORTHEAST UNIVERSITY VILLAGE (AT UNIVERSITY VILLAGE MALL); 206.526.7184; M-SA 9:30-6, SU 11-6; MALL PARKING

Spoiled by Nana ★★★★☆

"...this is a great store for buying baby shower gifts... super cute infant clothes, but a bit pricey... unique items and very friendly, knowledgeable staff... "

Furniture, Bedding & Decor	✗	$$$$ .... Prices
Gear & Equipment	✓	❹ .... Product availability
Nursing & Feeding	✗	❹ .... Staff knowledge
Safety & Babycare	✗	❹ ....Customer service
Clothing, Shoes & Accessories	✓	❹ .... Decor
Books, Toys & Entertainment	✓	

ISSAQUAH—317 NW GILMAN BLVD (AT 224TH AVE SE); 425.392.6507; M-F 10-7, SA 10-6 SU 11-6

Strasburg Children ★★★★☆

"...totally adorable special occasion outfits for babies and kids... classic baby, toddler, and kids clothes... dress-up clothes for kids... if you are looking for a flower girl or ring bearer outfit, look no further... handmade clothes that will last through multiple kids or generations... it's not cheap, but you can find great sales if you are patient... "

Furniture, Bedding & Decor	✗	$$$$ .... Prices
Gear & Equipment	✗	❹ .... Product availability
Nursing & Feeding	✗	❹ .... Staff knowledge
Safety & Babycare	✗	❹ ....Customer service
Clothing, Shoes & Accessories	✓	❹ .... Decor
Books, Toys & Entertainment	✗	

WWW.STRASBURGCHILDREN.COM

DOWNTOWN—10600 QUIL CEDA BLVD (AT 1ST AVE); 360.654.3899; M-SA 10-9 SU 10-7

Stride Rite Shoes ★★★½☆

66*...wonderful selection of baby and toddler shoes... sandals, sneakers, and even special-occasion shoes... decent quality shoes that last... they know a lot about kids' shoes and take the time to get it right—they always measure my son's feet before fittings... store sizes vary, but they always have something in stock that works... they've even special ordered shoes for my daughter... a fun 'first shoe' buying experience...* **99**

Furniture, Bedding & Decor	✗	$$$	Prices
Gear & Equipment	✗	❹	Product availability
Nursing & Feeding	✗	❹	Staff knowledge
Safety & Babycare	✗	❹	Customer service
Clothing, Shoes & Accessories	✓	❹	Decor
Books, Toys & Entertainment	✗		

WWW.STRIDERITE.COM

BELLEVUE—188 BELLEVUE SQ (AT NE 4TH ST); 425.453.0101; M-SA 9:30-9:30, SU 11-7

LYNNWOOD—446-3000 184 ST SW (AT ALDERWOOD MALL); 425.771.4969; M-SA 10-9:30, SU 11-7

NORTH BEND—461 S FORK AVE SW (AT BENDIGO BLVD S); 425.831.2004; M-SA 10-8, SU 10-6

Stuhlberg's ★★★★½

66*...they carry the cutest baby clothes around... one of my favorites for beautiful clothes, toys, blankets and other items for babies... if you are looking for something different, this is the place to go... unique decor for baby's room... great source for gifts—you'll get lots of 'oohs' and 'aahs'... lots of European, specialty clothes, toys and games... a wonderful source of gifts you can't find anywhere else...* **99**

Furniture, Bedding & Decor	✓	$$$$$	Prices
Gear & Equipment	✓	❹	Product availability
Nursing & Feeding	✗	❹	Staff knowledge
Safety & Babycare	✗	❺	Customer service
Clothing, Shoes & Accessories	✓	❺	Decor
Books, Toys & Entertainment	✓		

WWW.STUHLBERGS.COM

QUEEN ANNE—1801 QUEEN ANNE AVE N (AT W BLAINE ST); 206.352.2351; M-SA 10-6, SU 11-5

Sweet Baby Jess ★★★★☆

66*...absolutely the cutest, frilliest dresses in the world... adorable handmade clothes... great sales... reasonable prices...* **99**

Furniture, Bedding & Decor	✗	$$$$	Prices
Gear & Equipment	✗	❺	Product availability
Nursing & Feeding	✗	❸	Staff knowledge
Safety & Babycare	✗	❹	Customer service
Clothing, Shoes & Accessories	✓	❺	Decor
Books, Toys & Entertainment	✗		

PIKE MARKET—1535 1ST AVE (AT PINE); 206.340.0900; DAILY 10-6

Sweet Cheeks ★★★½☆

66*...this store is great... not the most stylish apparel, but practical, good quality, and very well priced...* **99**

Furniture, Bedding & Decor	✗	$$	Prices
Gear & Equipment	✗	❹	Product availability
Nursing & Feeding	✗	❺	Staff knowledge
Safety & Babycare	✗	❹	Customer service

Clothing, Shoes & Accessories ...... ✓		.... Decor
Books, Toys & Entertainment .... ✓		

BURIEN—13635 1ST AVE S (AT S 138TH ST); 206.241.0540; M-SA 10-5

Sweet Pea's ★★★★☆

"...little consignment store in the heart of Columbia City... a real treasure for Moms and children... incredible selection of excellent condition seconds... new items daily... I like the mix of used and new items... cute Halloween costumes... worth visiting... not overcrowded or grubby... best stock of Zooper strollers in the area... nice owner...**"**

Furniture, Bedding & Decor .... ✗	$$	.... Prices
Gear & Equipment .... ✓		.... Product availability
Nursing & Feeding .... ✗	❹	.... Staff knowledge
Safety & Babycare .... ✗	❹	...................Customer service
Clothing, Shoes & Accessories ...... ✓	❹	.... Decor
Books, Toys & Entertainment .... ✓		

COLUMBIA CITY—4820 RAINIER AVE S (AT S EDMUNDS ST); 206.722.1031;
M-T TH-SA 10-5:30, W 10-7; STREET PARKING

Talbots Kids ★★★⯪☆

"...a nice alternative to the typical department store experience... expensive, but fantastic quality... great for holiday and special occasion outfits including christening outfits... well-priced, conservative children's clothing... cute selections for infants, toddlers and kids... sales are fantastic—up to half off at least a couple times a year... the best part is, you can also shop for yourself while shopping for baby...**"**

Furniture, Bedding & Decor .... ✗	$$$$	.... Prices
Gear & Equipment .... ✗	❹	.... Product availability
Nursing & Feeding .... ✗	❹	.... Staff knowledge
Safety & Babycare .... ✗	❹	...................Customer service
Clothing, Shoes & Accessories ...... ✓	❹	.... Decor
Books, Toys & Entertainment .... ✗		

WWW.TALBOTS.COM

BELLEVUE—209 BELLEVUE SQ (AT NE 4TH ST); 425.450.3375; M-SA 9:30-
9:30, SU 11-7

Target ★★★★☆

"...our favorite place to shop for kids' stuff—good selection and very affordable... guilt-free shopping—kids grow so fast so I don't want to pay high department-store prices... everything from diapers and sippy cups to car seats and strollers... easy return policy... generally helpful staff, but you don't go for the service—you go for the prices... decent registry that won't freak your friends out with outrageous prices... easy, convenient shopping for well-priced items... all the big-box brands available—Graco, Evenflo, Eddie Bauer, etc....**"**

Furniture, Bedding & Decor .... ✓	$$	.... Prices
Gear & Equipment .... ✓		.... Product availability
Nursing & Feeding .... ✓	❸	.... Staff knowledge
Safety & Babycare .... ✓	❸	...................Customer service
Clothing, Shoes & Accessories ...... ✓	❸	.... Decor
Books, Toys & Entertainment .... ✓		

WWW.TARGET.COM

BELLEVUE—4053 FACTORIA SQ MALL SE (AT FACTORIA SQ MALL);
425.562.0830; M-SA 8-10, SU 8-9; PARKING IN FRONT OF BLDG

FEDERAL WAY—2141 S 314TH ST (AT 20TH AVE S); 253.839.3399; M-SA 8-
10, SU 8-9; PARKING IN FRONT OF BLDG

ISSAQUAH—755 NW GILMAN BLVD (AT 7TH AVE NW); 425.392.3357; M-SA 8-
10, SU 8-9; PARKING IN FRONT OF BLDG

KENT—26301 104TH AVE SE (AT SE 264TH ST); 253.850.9710; M-SA 8-10,
SU 8-9; PARKING IN FRONT OF BLDG

LYNNWOOD—18305 ALDERWOOD MALL PKWY (AT ALDERWOOD MALL); 425.670.1435; M-SA 8-10, SU 8-9; PARKING IN FRONT OF BLDG

MAPLE LEAF/ROOSEVELT—300 NE NORTHGATE WY (AT NORTHGATE SHOPPING CTR); 206.494.0897; M-SA 8-10, SU 8-9; PARKING IN FRONT OF BLDG

REDMOND—17700 NE 76TH ST (AT MERVYNS TARGET SHOPPING CPLX); 425.556.9533; M-SA 8-10, SU 8-9; PARKING IN FRONT OF BLDG

TUKWILA—301 STRANDER BLVD (AT WESTFIELD SHOPPINGTOWN CTR); 206.575.0682; M-SA 8-10, SU 8-9; PARKING IN FRONT OF BLDG

WEST SEATTLE—2800 SW BARTON ST (AT WESTWOOD TOWN CTR); 206.932.1153; M-SA 8-10, SU 8-9; PARKING IN FRONT OF BLDG

WOODINVILLE—13950 NE 178TH PL (AT 140TH AVE NE); 425.482.6410; M-SA 8-10, SU 8-9; PARKING IN FRONT OF BLDG

Teri's Toybox

"...fantastic local toy store for kids of all ages... you won't find Barbie or Pokemon, but a wealth of fun toys... a refreshing place without a bunch of plastic and noise... toys that encourage pretend play... staff is great and prices aren't too tough on the wallet... they have it all—hard to find and run of the mill toys... great wooden toys and trains... we do all of our gift shopping here... **"**

Furniture, Bedding & Decor	✗	$$$	Prices
Gear & Equipment	✗	❹	Product availability
Nursing & Feeding	✗	❹	Staff knowledge
Safety & Babycare	✗	❹	Customer service
Clothing, Shoes & Accessories	✗	❹	Decor
Books, Toys & Entertainment	✓		

EDMONDS—420 MAIN ST (AT 4TH AVE S); 425.774.3190; M-SA 10-6, TH 10-8, SU 11-4

Tin Horse

"...a lovely store... if you like the vintage look, this is the place for you... beautiful things—great for gifts... a great place for decorative ideas for your nursery... high-quality, unique furniture as well as uncommon gifts for showers... wonderful handmade bedding for your baby... **"**

Furniture, Bedding & Decor	✓	$$$$	Prices
Gear & Equipment	✓	❹	Product availability
Nursing & Feeding	✗	❹	Staff knowledge
Safety & Babycare	✗	❹	Customer service
Clothing, Shoes & Accessories	✓	❺	Decor
Books, Toys & Entertainment	✓		

WWW.THETINHORSE.COM

WALLINGFORD/FREMONT—1815 N 45TH ST (AT WALLINGFORD AVE N); 206.547.9966; M-F 10-8, SA 10-6, SU 11-5; PARKING AT 45TH & WALLINGFORD

Top Ten Toys

"...the best toy store in Seattle from infants to teens—a great store if you want quality toys that give your kids room to think for themselves... you can tell they think about what they put on their shelves... nice selection of science, math and drama type toys... well organized with a good selection... don't let the outside appearance dissuade you from checking out this gem... many, many toys at reasonable prices... toys that encourage out of the box thinking... joyful and intelligent staff... **"**

Furniture, Bedding & Decor	✗	$$$	Prices
Gear & Equipment	✗	❺	Product availability
Nursing & Feeding	✗	❺	Staff knowledge
Safety & Babycare	✗	❹	Customer service
Clothing, Shoes & Accessories	✗	❹	Decor

Books, Toys & Entertainment .... ✓

WWW.TOPTENTOYS.COM

NORTH SEATTLE—104 N 85TH ST (AT 1ST AVE NW); 206.782.0098; SA-T 9-7, W-F 9-9; PARKING IN FRONT OF BLDG

Toys R Us

"...not just toys, but also tons of gear and supplies including diapers and formula... a hectic shopping experience but the prices make it all worthwhile... I've experienced good and bad service at the same store on the same day... the stores are huge and can be overwhelming... most big brand-names available... leave the kids at home unless you want to end up with a cart full of toys... **"**

Furniture, Bedding & Decor	✓	$$$	....	Prices
Gear & Equipment	✓	❹	....	Product availability
Nursing & Feeding	✓	❸	....	Staff knowledge
Safety & Babycare	✓	❸	....	Customer service
Clothing, Shoes & Accessories	✓	❸	....	Decor
Books, Toys & Entertainment	✓			

WWW.TOYSRUS.COM

BELLEVUE—103 110TH AVE NE (AT MAIN ST); 425.453.1901; M-SA 9:30-9:30, SU 10-7

FEDERAL WAY—31510 20TH AVE S (AT S 316TH ST); 253.946.0433; M-SA 9:30-9:30, SU 10-7

LYNNWOOD—18601 ALDERWOOD MALL PKWY (AT ALDERWOOD MALL); 425.771.4748; M-SA 9:30-9:30, SU 10-7; MALL PARKING

MAPLE LEAF/ROOSEVELT—401 NE NORTHGATE WY (AT 5TH AVE NE); 206.361.1101; M-SA 9:30-9:30, SU 10-7

TUKWILA—16700 SOUTHCENTER PKWY (AT SOUTHCENTER MALL); 206.575.0780; M-SA 9:30-9:30, SU 10-7; MALL PARKING

Tree House

"...a great consignment shop with a wide range of clothing and brand-names too... a hidden treasure... lots of dance wear and dance shoes... a personal fave... very streamlined consignment process... only consign for store credit... not the easiest store to browse with a toddler in tow, but great for solo shopping trips... well-screened selection... fair prices... **"**

Furniture, Bedding & Decor	✓	$$	....	Prices
Gear & Equipment	✓	❹	....	Product availability
Nursing & Feeding	✗	❹	....	Staff knowledge
Safety & Babycare	✗	❹	....	Customer service
Clothing, Shoes & Accessories	✓	❸	....	Decor
Books, Toys & Entertainment	✗			

REDMOND—15742 REDMOND WY (AT 158TH PL NE); 425.885.1145; M-W F 9-6, TH 9-8, SA 10-5, SU 1-5; PARKING IN FRONT OF BLDG

USA Baby

"...they carry an extensive selection of high-end nursery products such as furniture, bedding, accessories and highchairs... popular place to do all the shopping for your nursery... the staff knows their products well and can help you sort through their vast selection... allow plenty of time for your products to arrive, especially the big-ticket items (they offer loaners while you wait for your order to arrive)... they have great sales a few times a year and will match competitor prices... good selection, especially if you're getting ready to set up your nursery... **"**

Furniture, Bedding & Decor	✓	$$$$	....	Prices
Gear & Equipment	✓	❹	....	Product availability
Nursing & Feeding	✓	❹	....	Staff knowledge
Safety & Babycare	✓	❹	....	Customer service
Clothing, Shoes & Accessories	✗	❹	....	Decor

Books, Toys & Entertainment .... ✓

WWW.USABABY.COM

TUKWILA—720 ANDOVER PK E (AT MINKLER BLVD); 206.575.1476; M-SA 10-8, SU 11-6

Value Village

CAPITOL HILL—1525 11TH AVE (AT E PIKE ST); 206.322.7789; M-SA 9-9, SU 10-7

Village Maternity ★★★★☆

"...a small store packed full of great stuff... they have a little bit of everything from really cute children's clothes to breast milk freezer bags and maternity clothes... the sales person was awesome and helped me find something in particular that I was looking for... usually very crowded... **"**

Furniture, Bedding & Decor .... ✗	$$$$ .... Prices
Gear & Equipment .... ✗	.... Product availability
Nursing & Feeding...................... ✗	❹ .... Staff knowledge
Safety & Babycare .... ✗	❹ .... Customer service
Clothing, Shoes & Accessories....... ✓	❹ .... Decor
Books, Toys & Entertainment .... ✓	

WWW.VILLAGEMATERNITY.COM

UNIVERSITY DISTRICT/UNIVERSITY VILLAGE—2615 NE UNIVERSITY VILLAGE ST (AT UNIVERSITY VILLAGE MALL); 206.523.5167; M-SA 9:30-9, SU 11-6; MALL PARKING

White Horse Toys ★★★★☆

"...what a fun place... one of the best toy stores in the area... they have everything for little people of all ages... fabulous selection of unusual and hard to find toys... helpful staff... not the easiest with a stroller... high-end toys you won't see at a chain... crammed with toys... **"**

Furniture, Bedding & Decor .... ✗	$$$ .... Prices
Gear & Equipment .... ✗	❹ .... Product availability
Nursing & Feeding...................... ✗	❹ .... Staff knowledge
Safety & Babycare .... ✗	❹ .... Customer service
Clothing, Shoes & Accessories....... ✗	❹ .... Decor
Books, Toys & Entertainment .... ✓	

WWW.WHITEHORSETOYS.COM

ISSAQUAH—317 NW GILMAN BLVD (AT 224TH AVE SE); 425.391.1498; M-SA 9:30-7, SA 9:30-6, SU 10-5

Tacoma

★ ★ ★ ★ ★
"lila picks"

★ Babies R Us

Babies R Us ★★★★★

❝...everything baby under one roof... they have a wide selection and carry most 'mainstream' items such as Graco, Fisher-Price, Avent and Britax... great customer service—given how big the stores are, I was pleasantly surprised at how attentive the staff was... easy return policy... super busy on weekends so try to visit on a weekday for the best service... keep an eye out for great coupons, deals and frequent sales... easy and comprehensive registry... shopping here is so easy—you've got to check it out... ❞

Furniture, Bedding & Decor	✓	$$$ .... Prices
Gear & Equipment	✓	❹ .... Product availability
Nursing & Feeding	✓	❹ .... Staff knowledge
Safety & Babycare	✓	❹ .... Customer service
Clothing, Shoes & Accessories	✓	❹ .... Decor
Books, Toys & Entertainment	✓	

WWW.BABIESRUS.COM

TACOMA—2502 S 48TH ST (AT TACOMA MALL); 253.472.4441; M-SA 9:30-9:30; FREE PARKING

Baby Depot At Burlington Coat Factory ★★★★⯪☆

❝...a large, 'super store' layout with a ton of baby gear... wide aisles, packed shelves, barely existent customer service and awesome prices... everything from bottles, car seats and strollers to gliders, cribs and clothes... I always find something worth getting... a little disorganized and hard to locate items you're looking for... the staff is not always knowledgeable about their merchandise... return policy is store credit only... ❞

Furniture, Bedding & Decor	✓	$$ .... Prices
Gear & Equipment	✓	❸ .... Product availability
Nursing & Feeding	✓	❸ .... Staff knowledge
Safety & Babycare	✓	❸ .... Customer service
Clothing, Shoes & Accessories	✓	❸ .... Decor
Books, Toys & Entertainment	✓	

WWW.BABYDEPOT.COM

TACOMA—10420 59TH AVE SW (AT MAIN ST); M-SA 10-9:30; FREE PARKING

Costco ★★★★⯪☆

❝...dependable place for bulk diapers, wipes and formula at discount prices... clothing selection is very hit-or-miss... avoid shopping there during nights and weekends if possible, because parking and checkout lines are brutal... they don't have a huge selection of brands, but the brands they do have are almost always in stock and at a great price...

lowest prices around for diapers and formula... kid's clothing tends to be picked through, but it's worth looking for great deals on name-brand items like Carter's... **"**

Furniture, Bedding & Decor .... ✓	$$ .... Prices	
Gear & Equipment .... ✓	❸ .... Product availability	
Nursing & Feeding .... ✓	❸ .... Staff knowledge	
Safety & Babycare .... ✓	❸ .... Customer service	
Clothing, Shoes & Accessories .... ✓	❷ .... Decor	
Books, Toys & Entertainment .... ✓		

WWW.COSTCO.COM

FIFE—3900 20TH ST E; 253.719.1953; M-F 8-6, SA 9:30-6

PUYALLUP—1201 39TH SW; 253.445.7543; M-F 11-8:30, SA 9:30-6, SU 10-6

TACOMA—2219 S 37TH ST; 253.475.5595; M-F 11-8:30, SA 9:30-6, SU 10-6

Gymboree ★★★★☆

"...*beautiful clothing and great quality... colorful and stylish baby and kids wear... lots of fun birthday gift ideas... easy exchange and return policy... items usually go on sale pretty quickly... save money with Gymbucks... many stores have a play area which makes shopping with my kids fun (let alone feasible)...* **"**

Furniture, Bedding & Decor .... ✗	$$$ .... Prices	
Gear & Equipment .... ✗	❹ .... Product availability	
Nursing & Feeding .... ✗	❹ .... Staff knowledge	
Safety & Babycare .... ✗	❹ .... Customer service	
Clothing, Shoes & Accessories .... ✓	❹ .... Decor	
Books, Toys & Entertainment .... ✓		

WWW.GYMBOREE.COM

PUYALLUP—3500 S MERIDAN (AT SOUTH HILL MALL); 253.845.9171; M-SA 10-9, SU 11-6; MALL PARKING

JCPenney ★★★⯪☆

"...*always a good place to find clothes and other baby basics... the registry process was seamless... staff is generally friendly but the lines always seem long and slow... they don't have the greatest selection of toddler clothes, but their baby section is great... we had some damaged furniture delivered but customer service was easy and accommodating... a pretty limited selection of gear, but what they have is priced right...* **"**

Furniture, Bedding & Decor .... ✓	$$ .... Prices	
Gear & Equipment .... ✓	❸ .... Product availability	
Nursing & Feeding .... ✓	❸ .... Staff knowledge	
Safety & Babycare .... ✓	❸ .... Customer service	
Clothing, Shoes & Accessories .... ✓	❸ .... Decor	
Books, Toys & Entertainment .... ✓		

WWW.JCPENNEY.COM

TACOMA—4502 S STEELE ST (AT S 43RD ST); 253.475.4510; M-SA 10-9:30, SU 11-6

Macy's ★★★⯪☆

"...*Macy's has it all and I never leave empty-handed... if you time your visit right you can find some great deals... go during the week so you don't get overwhelmed with the weekend crowd... good for staples as well as beautiful party dresses for girls... lots of brand-names like Carter's, Guess, and Ralph Lauren... not much in terms of assistance... newspaper coupons and sales help keep the cost down... some stores are better organized and maintained than others... if you're going to shop at a department store for your baby, then Macy's is a safe bet...* **"**

Furniture, Bedding & Decor .... ✓	$$$ .... Prices	
Gear & Equipment .... ✗	❸ .... Product availability	
Nursing & Feeding .... ✗	❸ .... Staff knowledge	

Safety & Babycare	✗	❸	Customer service
Clothing, Shoes & Accessories	✓	❸	Decor
Books, Toys & Entertainment	✓		

WWW.MACYS.COM

PUYALLUP—3500 S MERIDIAN (AT 112TH ST); 253.840.7000; M-SA 10-9, SU 11-7

TACOMA—1767 S 48TH ST (OFF 38TH ST); 253.471.5400; M-F 10-9, SA 10-7, SU 11-6

TACOMA—4502 S STEELE ST (AT S 43RD ST); 253.471.6800; M-SA 10-9, SU 11-7

Mervyn's ★★★☆☆

"...wide selection of baby and kids' clothing, including OshKosh and Carter's... limited shoe selection without any real sizing assistance... lots of good sales... you might not always be able to find the size and color you want, but there's enough selection here that you're sure to find something else that will work just as well... cheap, cheap, cheap... okay for cheap basics, but don't expect anything super special... **"**

Furniture, Bedding & Decor	✗	$$	Prices
Gear & Equipment	✗	❹	Product availability
Nursing & Feeding	✗	❸	Staff knowledge
Safety & Babycare	✗	❸	Customer service
Clothing, Shoes & Accessories	✓	❸	Decor
Books, Toys & Entertainment	✓		

WWW.MERVYNS.COM

PUYALLUP—3700 S MERIDIAN (AT 112TH ST E); 253.845.8800; M-SA 9-10, SU 9-9

TACOMA—4502 S STEELE ST (AT TACOMA MALL); 253.474.8800; M-SA 9-10, SU 9-9; MALL PARKING

Nana's Children's World ★★★★☆

"...my mom and I have been shopping here for years, we've found many great baby items for great prices... the woman who owns this shop is very picky—which means the merchandise is all top quality... nice to be able to exchange clothes as your kids grow... **"**

Furniture, Bedding & Decor	✓	$$	Prices
Gear & Equipment	✓	❹	Product availability
Nursing & Feeding	✓	❹	Staff knowledge
Safety & Babycare	✗	❺	Customer service
Clothing, Shoes & Accessories	✓	❹	Decor
Books, Toys & Entertainment	✓		

SPANAWAY—16603 PACIFIC AVE S (AT 166TH ST S); 253.531.0701; M-F 11-5, SU 12-5; PARKING IN FRONT OF BLDG

Nordstrom ★★★★☆

"...quality service and quality clothes... awesome kids shoe department—almost as good as the one for adults... free balloons in the children's shoe area as well as drawing tables... in addition to their own brand, they carry a very nice selection of other high-end baby clothing including Ralph Lauren, Robeez, etc... adorable baby clothes—they make great shower gifts... such a wonderful shopping experience—their lounge is perfect for breastfeeding and for changing diapers... well-rounded selection of baby basics as well as fancy clothes for special events... **"**

Furniture, Bedding & Decor	✓	$$$$	Prices
Gear & Equipment	✓	❹	Product availability
Nursing & Feeding	✗	❹	Staff knowledge
Safety & Babycare	✗	❹	Customer service
Clothing, Shoes & Accessories	✓	❹	Decor
Books, Toys & Entertainment	✓		

TACOMA—4502 S STEELE ST (AT TACOMA MALL); 253.475.3630; M-SA 9:30-9:30, SU 11-7

Old Navy ★★★★☆

"...hip and 'in' clothes for infants and tots... plenty of steals on clearance items... T-shirts and pants for $10 or less... busy, busy, busy—long lines, especially on weekends... nothing fancy and you won't mind when your kids get down and dirty in these clothes... easy to wash, decent quality... you can shop for your baby, your toddler, your teen and yourself all at the same time... clothes are especially affordable when you hit their sales (post-holiday sales are amazing!)... **"**

Furniture, Bedding & Decor	✗	$$ .... Prices
Gear & Equipment	✗	❹ .... Product availability
Nursing & Feeding	✗	❸ .... Staff knowledge
Safety & Babycare	✗	❸ .... Customer service
Clothing, Shoes & Accessories	✓	❸ .... Decor
Books, Toys & Entertainment	✗	

WWW.OLDNAVY.COM

LAKEWOOD—5810 LAKEWOOD TOWNE CTR BLVD SW (AT LAKEWOOD TOWN CTR); 253.588.1749; M-SA 9-9, SU 10-6; PARKING LOT AT CENTER

PUYALLUP—3500 S MERIDIAN (AT SOUTH HILL MALL); 253.435.1143; M-SA 10-9, SU 10-6; MALL PARKING

TACOMA—4502 S STEELE ST (AT TACOMA MALL); 253.471.3068; M-SA 9-9, SU 10-7; MALL PARKING

Once Upon A Child ★★★★☆

"...new and used items... the place for bargain baby items in like-new condition... a great bargain spot with a wide variety of clothes for baby... some inexpensive furniture... good selection, staff and prices... cluttered and hard to get through the store with kids... good toys and gear... some items are definitely more than 'gently used'... a kid's play area... good end-of-season sales... expect to sort through items... cash for your old items... **"**

Furniture, Bedding & Decor	✓	$$ .... Prices
Gear & Equipment	✓	❸ .... Product availability
Nursing & Feeding	✗	❹ .... Staff knowledge
Safety & Babycare	✗	❹ .... Customer service
Clothing, Shoes & Accessories	✓	❸ .... Decor
Books, Toys & Entertainment	✓	

WWW.OUAC.COM

TACOMA—7901 S HOSMER ST (AT S 80TH ST); 253.473.4555; M-F 10-7, SA 10-6, SU 12-5; PARKING COMPLEX

Other Mothers ★★★☆☆

"...a chain resale shop that carries maternity and kids clothes, furniture and toys... everything you may want or need without the department store prices... take the things your child outgrows in exchange for new 'used' items... great for breastfeeding mothers... my favorite place to look for gently used baby products... a hit or miss, but there are a lot more hits... **"**

Furniture, Bedding & Decor	✓	$$ .... Prices
Gear & Equipment	✓	❹ .... Product availability
Nursing & Feeding	✓	❹ .... Staff knowledge
Safety & Babycare	✓	❹ .... Customer service
Clothing, Shoes & Accessories	✓	❸ .... Decor
Books, Toys & Entertainment	✓	

WWW.OMTACOMA.COM

TACOMA—6409 6TH AVE (AT S MILDRED ST); 253.566.8344; M-TH 10-7, F-SA
10-6; STREET PARKING

Payless Shoe Source

❝...a good place for deals on children's shoes... staff is helpful with
sizing... the selection and prices for kids' shoes can't be beat, but the
quality isn't always spectacular... good leather shoes for cheap... great
variety of all sizes and widths... I get my son's shoes here and don't feel
like I'm wasting my money since he'll outgrow them in 3 months
anyway... **❞**

Furniture, Bedding & Decor	✗	$$	Prices
Gear & Equipment	✗	❸	Product availability
Nursing & Feeding	✗	❸	Staff knowledge
Safety & Babycare	✗	❸	Customer service
Clothing, Shoes & Accessories	✓	❸	Decor
Books, Toys & Entertainment	✗		

WWW.PAYLESS.COM

PUYALLUP—1002 A N MERIDIAN (OFF RIVER RD); 253.864.6520; M-SA 9-9,
SU 10-7

TACOMA—1601 E 72ND ST (OFF PORTLAND AVE); 253.472.6602; M-SA 9-9,
SU 10-7

TACOMA—5914 6TH AVE (OFF RT 163); 253.566.1233; M-SA 9-9, SU 10-7

TACOMA—TACOMA CENTRAL SHOPPING CTR (OFF UNION AVE);
253.572.4222; M-SA 9-9, SU 10-8

TACOMA—TACOMA MALL (AT TACOMA MALL); 253.475.3966; M-SA 10-9, SU
11-7

REI

❝...a great store for outdoor/active gear and clothing for kids and their
parents... this is a fun store to visit, too... they have an indoor climbing
wall... the kids will be fascinated and school-age kids can even try it out
themselves... good quality gear to get you outside with your baby... the
gear is high-quality and the staff knows what they are talking
about... **❞**

Furniture, Bedding & Decor	✗	$$$	Prices
Gear & Equipment	✓	❹	Product availability
Nursing & Feeding	✗	❹	Staff knowledge
Safety & Babycare	✗	❹	Customer service
Clothing, Shoes & Accessories	✓	❹	Decor
Books, Toys & Entertainment	✗		

WWW.REI.COM

TACOMA—3825 S STEELE ST (AT S 38TH ST); 253.671.1938; M-F 10-9, SA
10-7, SU 10-6

Tacoma General Hospital
(Mom & Baby Boutique)

❝...fun and practical items for your new baby... preemie clothes and
diapers, baby carriers, handmade clothes, car seats and much, much
more... conveniently located right next to the recovery ward for
postpartum... specialize in hard to find, high-quality items... prices are
steep, but I think it's well worth it... **❞**

Furniture, Bedding & Decor	✗	$$$	Prices
Gear & Equipment	✓	❹	Product availability
Nursing & Feeding	✓	❹	Staff knowledge
Safety & Babycare	✗	❹	Customer service
Clothing, Shoes & Accessories	✓	❺	Decor
Books, Toys & Entertainment	✗		

WWW.MULTICARE.ORG

TACOMA—315 MARTIN LUTHER KING JR WY (AT 3RD ST); 253.403.6081; M TH-F 9-5, T-W 9-8, SA 10-5, SU 12-5

Target ★★★★☆

❝...*our favorite place to shop for kids' stuff—good selection and very affordable... guilt-free shopping—kids grow so fast so I don't want to pay high department-store prices... everything from diapers and sippy cups to car seats and strollers... easy return policy... generally helpful staff, but you don't go for the service—you go for the prices... decent registry that won't freak your friends out with outrageous prices... easy, convenient shopping for well-priced items... all the big-box brands available—Graco, Evenflo, Eddie Bauer, etc....* **❞**

Furniture, Bedding & Decor	✓	$$	Prices
Gear & Equipment	✓	❹	Product availability
Nursing & Feeding	✓	❸	Staff knowledge
Safety & Babycare	✓	❸	Customer service
Clothing, Shoes & Accessories	✓	❸	Decor
Books, Toys & Entertainment	✓		

WWW.TARGET.COM

GIG HARBOR—11400 51ST AVE NW (AT 144TH ST NW); 253.858.9777; M-SA 8-10, SU 8-9; PARKING IN FRONT OF BLDG

PUYALLUP—3310 S MERIDIAN (AT SOUTH HILL MALL); 253.840.2900; M-SA 8-10, SU 8-9; PARKING IN FRONT OF BLDG

TACOMA—10509 GRAVELLY LAKE DR SW (AT LAKEWOOD TOWNE CTR); 253.581.7171; M-SA 8-10, SU 8-9; PARKING IN FRONT OF BLDG

TACOMA—3320 S 23RD ST (OFF S UNION AVE); 253.627.2112; M-SA 8-10, SU 8-9; PARKING IN FRONT OF BLDG

Toys R Us ★★★½☆

❝...*not just toys, but also tons of gear and supplies including diapers and formula... a hectic shopping experience but the prices make it all worthwhile... I've experienced good and bad service at the same store on the same day... the stores are huge and can be overwhelming... most big brand-names available... leave the kids at home unless you want to end up with a cart full of toys...* **❞**

Furniture, Bedding & Decor	✓	$$$	Prices
Gear & Equipment	✓	❹	Product availability
Nursing & Feeding	✓	❸	Staff knowledge
Safety & Babycare	✓	❸	Customer service
Clothing, Shoes & Accessories	✓	❸	Decor
Books, Toys & Entertainment	✓		

WWW.TOYSRUS.COM

TACOMA—4214 S TACOMA MALL BLVD (AT TACOMA MALL); 253.472.4568; M-SA 9:30-9:30, SU 10-6; MALL PARKING

Online

★★★★★

"lila picks"

★ babycenter.com   ★ babystyle.com

★ babyuniverse.com   ★ joggingstroller.com

ababy.com

Furniture, Bedding & Decor .... ✓	✓	Gear & Equipment
Nursing & Feeding .... ✗	✓	Safety & Babycare
Clothing, Shoes & Accessories ...... ✓	✗	Books, Toys & Entertainment

aikobaby.com   ★★★☆☆

❝...high end clothes that are so cute...everything from Catamini to Jack and Lily... you can find super expensive infant and baby clothes at discounted prices... amazing selection of diaper bags so you don't have to look like a frumpy mom (or dad)... ❞

Furniture, Bedding & Decor .... ✗	✓	Gear & Equipment
Nursing & Feeding .... ✗	✗	Safety & Babycare
Clothing, Shoes & Accessories ...... ✓	✗	Books, Toys & Entertainment

albeebaby.com   ★★★★☆

❝...they offer a really comprehensive selection of baby gear... their prices are some of the best online... great discounts on Maclarens before the new models come out... good product availability—fast shipping and easy transactions... the site is pretty easy to use... the prices are surprisingly great... ❞

Furniture, Bedding & Decor .... ✓	✓	Gear & Equipment
Nursing & Feeding .... ✓	✓	Safety & Babycare
Clothing, Shoes & Accessories ...... ✓	✓	Books, Toys & Entertainment

amazon.com   ★★★★½

❝...unless you've been living under a rock, you know that in addition to books, Amazon carries an amazing amount of baby stuff too... they have the best prices and offer free shipping on bigger purchases... you can even buy used items for dirt cheap... I always read the comments written by others—they're very useful in helping make my decisions... I love Amazon for just about everything, but their baby selection only carries the big box standards... ❞

Furniture, Bedding & Decor .... ✗	✓	Gear & Equipment
Nursing & Feeding .... ✓	✓	Safety & Babycare
Clothing, Shoes & Accessories ...... ✓	✓	Books, Toys & Entertainment

arunningstroller.com   ★★★★½

❝...the prices are very competitive and the customer service is great... I talked to them on the phone for a while and they totally hooked me up with the right model... if you're looking for a new stroller, look no further... talk to Marilyn—she's the best... shipping costs are reasonable and their prices overall are good... ❞

Furniture, Bedding & Decor .... ✓	✓ .... Gear & Equipment
Nursing & Feeding .... ✗	✗ .... Safety & Babycare
Clothing, Shoes & Accessories .... ✗	✗ .... Books, Toys & Entertainment

babiesinthesun.com ★★★★☆

"...one-stop shopping for cloth diapers... run by a fantastic woman who had 3 cloth diapered babies herself and is a wealth of knowledge... if you live in South Florida, the owner will let you into her home to see the merchandise and ask questions... great selection and the customer service is the best... **"**

Furniture, Bedding & Decor .... ✗	✓ .... Gear & Equipment
Nursing & Feeding .... ✗	✓ .... Safety & Babycare
Clothing, Shoes & Accessories .... ✗	✗ .... Books, Toys & Entertainment

babiesrus.com ★★★★☆

"...terrific web site with all the baby gear you'll need... registering online made it easy for my family and friends... getting the registry activated was a bit tricky... super convenient and ideal for the moms-to-be who are on bedrest... web site prices are comparable to in-store prices... shipping is usually free... a very efficient way to buy and send baby gifts... our local Babies R Us said they will accept returns if they carry the same item... not all online items are available in your local store... **"**

Furniture, Bedding & Decor .... ✓	✓ .... Gear & Equipment
Nursing & Feeding .... ✓	✓ .... Safety & Babycare
Clothing, Shoes & Accessories .... ✓	✓ .... Books, Toys & Entertainment

babiestravellite.com ★★★★½

"...caters to traveling families... they deliver baby items to your hotel room anywhere in the country... all of the different baby supplies you will need when you travel with a baby or a toddler... they sell almost every major brand for each product and their prices are sometimes cheaper than you would find at your local store... **"**

Furniture, Bedding & Decor .... ✗	✗ .... Gear & Equipment
Nursing & Feeding .... ✓	✓ .... Safety & Babycare
Clothing, Shoes & Accessories .... ✗	✓ .... Books, Toys & Entertainment

babyage.com ★★★★☆

"...fast shipping and the best prices around... flat rate shipping is great after the baby has arrived and you don't have time to go to the store... very attentive customer service... clearance items are a great deal (regular items are very competitive too)... ordering and delivery were super smooth... I usually check this web site before I purchase any baby gear... sign up for their newsletter and they'll notify you when they are having a sale... **"**

Furniture, Bedding & Decor .... ✓	✓ .... Gear & Equipment
Nursing & Feeding .... ✓	✓ .... Safety & Babycare
Clothing, Shoes & Accessories .... ✓	✓ .... Books, Toys & Entertainment

babyant.com ★★★★☆

"...wide variety of brands and products available through their site... super easy to navigate... fun, whimsical ideas... nice people and helpful... easy to return items and you can call them with questions... often has the best prices and low shipping costs... **"**

Furniture, Bedding & Decor .... ✓	✓ .... Gear & Equipment
Nursing & Feeding .... ✓	✓ .... Safety & Babycare
Clothing, Shoes & Accessories .... ✓	✓ .... Books, Toys & Entertainment

babybazaar.com

"...high-end baby stuff available on an easy-to-use web site... lots of European styles... quick processing and shipping... mom's tips, educational toys, exclusive favorites Bugaboo and Stokke..."

Furniture, Bedding & Decor ✓	✓ Gear & Equipment
Nursing & Feeding ✓	✓ Safety & Babycare
Clothing, Shoes & Accessories ✓	✓ Books, Toys & Entertainment

babybestbuy.com

Furniture, Bedding & Decor ✓	✓ Gear & Equipment
Nursing & Feeding ✓	✓ Safety & Babycare
Clothing, Shoes & Accessories ✓	✓ Books, Toys & Entertainment

babycatalog.com ★★★★☆

"...great deals on many essentials... wide selection of rockers but fewer options in other categories... the web site could be more user-friendly... customer service and delivery was fast and efficient... check out their seasonal specials... the baby club is a great way to save additional money... sign up for their wonderful pregnancy/new baby email newsletter... check this web site before you buy anywhere else..."

Furniture, Bedding & Decor ✓	✓ Gear & Equipment
Nursing & Feeding ✓	✓ Safety & Babycare
Clothing, Shoes & Accessories ✓	✓ Books, Toys & Entertainment

babycenter.com ★★★★★

"...a terrific selection of all things baby, plus quick shipping... free shipping on big orders... makes shopping convenient for new parents... web site is very user friendly... they always email you about sale items and special offers... lots of useful information for parents... carries everything you may need... online registry is simple, easy and a great way to get what you need... includes helpful products ratings by parents... they've created a nice online community in addition to their online store..."

Furniture, Bedding & Decor ✓	✓ Gear & Equipment
Nursing & Feeding ✓	✓ Safety & Babycare
Clothing, Shoes & Accessories ✓	✓ Books, Toys & Entertainment

babydepot.com ★★★☆☆

"...carries everything you'll find in a big department store but at cheaper prices and with everything all in one place... be certain you know what you want because returns can be difficult... site could be more user-friendly... online selection can differ from instore selection... love the online registry..."

Furniture, Bedding & Decor ✓	✓ Gear & Equipment
Nursing & Feeding ✓	✓ Safety & Babycare
Clothing, Shoes & Accessories ✓	✓ Books, Toys & Entertainment

babygeared.com

Furniture, Bedding & Decor ✓	✓ Gear & Equipment
Nursing & Feeding ✓	✓ Safety & Babycare
Clothing, Shoes & Accessories ✓	✓ Books, Toys & Entertainment

babyphd.com

Furniture, Bedding & Decor ✓	✗ Gear & Equipment
Nursing & Feeding ✗	✗ Safely & Babycare
Clothing, Shoes & Accessories ✓	✓ Books, Toys & Entertainment

babystyle.com ★★★★★

"...their web site is just like their stores—terrific... an excellent source for everything a parent needs... fantastic maternity and baby clothes...

participate in our survey at

they always respond quickly by email... their site seems to have even more merchandise than their stores... I started shopping on their site after receiving a gift card—very easy and convenient... wonderful selection... **"**

Furniture, Bedding & Decor ✓	✓	Gear & Equipment
Nursing & Feeding ✓	✓	Safety & Babycare
Clothing, Shoes & Accessories ✓	✓	Books, Toys & Entertainment

babysupermall.com

Furniture, Bedding & Decor ✓	✓	Gear & Equipment
Nursing & Feeding ✓	✓	Safety & Babycare
Clothing, Shoes & Accessories ✓	✓	Books, Toys & Entertainment

babyuniverse.com ★★★★★

"*...nice large selection of specialty and basic items... easy-to-use web site with decent prices... carries Carter's clothes and many other popular brands... great bedding selection - they're one of the few places with the Kidsline bedding I wanted... adorable backpacks for toddlers and preschoolers... check out the site for strollers and car seats... this was my first online shopping experience and they made it so easy, convenient and fast, I was hooked... fine customer service... flat rate (if not free) shipping takes the 'ouch' factor out of those big ticket purchases...* **"**

Furniture, Bedding & Decor ✓	✓	Gear & Equipment
Nursing & Feeding ✓	✓	Safety & Babycare
Clothing, Shoes & Accessories ✓	✓	Books, Toys & Entertainment

barebabies.com

Furniture, Bedding & Decor ✓	✓	Gear & Equipment
Nursing & Feeding ✓	✓	Safety & Babycare
Clothing, Shoes & Accessories ✓	✓	Books, Toys & Entertainment

birthandbaby.com ★★★★☆

"*...incredible site for buying a nursing bra... there is more information about different manufacturers than you can imagine... I've even received a phone call from the owner after placing an order to clarify something... free shipping, so it's easy to buy multiple sizes and send back the ones that don't fit... their selection of nursing bras is better than any other place I've found... if you are a hard to fit size, this is the place to go...* **"**

Furniture, Bedding & Decor ✗	✓	Gear & Equipment
Nursing & Feeding ✓	✓	Safety & Babycare
Clothing, Shoes & Accessories ✗	✓	Books, Toys & Entertainment

blueberrybabies.com

Furniture, Bedding & Decor ✓	✓	Gear & Equipment
Nursing & Feeding ✓	✓	Safety & Babycare
Clothing, Shoes & Accessories ✓	✓	Books, Toys & Entertainment

buybuybaby.com ★★★★☆

"*...this is the web site for the popular New York-based baby retailer... you name it, they've got it... all the items in their store can also be found on their web site... prices are fair - especially since things get shipped right to your door... we had some items that were damaged and their online customer service took care of it without any problems...* **"**

Furniture, Bedding & Decor ✓	✓	Gear & Equipment
Nursing & Feeding ✓	✓	Safety & Babycare
Clothing, Shoes & Accessories ✓	✓	Books, Toys & Entertainment

childcarriers.com

Furniture, Bedding & Decor ✗	✓	Gear & Equipment

Nursing & Feeding .... ✗   ✗ .... Safety & Babycare
Clothing, Shoes & Accessories .... ✗   ✗ .... Books, Toys & Entertainment

clothdiaper.com

Furniture, Bedding & Decor .... ✗   ✓ .... Gear & Equipment
Nursing & Feeding .... ✓   ✓ .... Safety & Babycare
Clothing, Shoes & Accessories .... ✗   ✗ .... Books, Toys & Entertainment

cocoacrayon.com

Furniture, Bedding & Decor .... ✓   ✓ .... Gear & Equipment
Nursing & Feeding .... ✓   ✓ .... Safety & Babycare
Clothing, Shoes & Accessories ...... ✓   ✓ .... Books, Toys & Entertainment

cvs.com ★★★★☆

"...super convenient web site for any 'drug store' items... items are delivered in a reasonable amount of time... decent selection of baby products... prices are competitive and ordering online definitely beats making the trip out to the drugstore... order a bunch of stuff at a time so shipping is free... I used them for my baby announcements and everyone loved them... super easy to refill prescriptions... it was a real relief to order all my formula, baby wipes and diapers online... "

Furniture, Bedding & Decor .... ✗   ✗ .... Gear & Equipment
Nursing & Feeding .... ✓   ✓ .... Safety & Babycare
Clothing, Shoes & Accessories .... ✗   ✗ .... Books, Toys & Entertainment

dreamtimebaby.com

Furniture, Bedding & Decor .... ✓   ✓ .... Gear & Equipment
Nursing & Feeding .... ✓   ✓ .... Safety & Babycare
Clothing, Shoes & Accessories ...... ✓   ✓ .... Books, Toys & Entertainment

drugstore.com ★★★★☆

Furniture, Bedding & Decor .... ✗   ✗ .... Gear & Equipment
Nursing & Feeding .... ✓   ✓ .... Safety & Babycare
Clothing, Shoes & Accessories .... ✗   ✗ .... Books, Toys & Entertainment

ebay.com ★★★★☆

"...great way to save money on everything from maternity clothes to breast pumps... be careful with whom you do business... it's always worth checking out what's available... I picked up a brand new jogger for dirt cheap... great deals to be had if you have patience to browse and be willing to resell or exchange what you don't like... baby stuff is easily found and often reasonably priced... keep an eye on shipping costs when you're bidding... "

Furniture, Bedding & Decor .... ✓   ✓ .... Gear & Equipment
Nursing & Feeding .... ✓   ✓ .... Safety & Babycare
Clothing, Shoes & Accessories ...... ✓   ✓ .... Books, Toys & Entertainment

egiggle.com ★★★★☆

"...nice selection—not overwhelming... don't expect the big box store brands here—they carry higher-end, specialty items that you won't find elsewhere... smooth shopping experience... nice site—convenient and easy to use... "

Furniture, Bedding & Decor .... ✓   ✓ .... Gear & Equipment
Nursing & Feeding .... ✓   ✓ .... Safety & Babycare
Clothing, Shoes & Accessories ...... ✓   ✓ .... Books, Toys & Entertainment

gagagifts.com ★★★★☆

"...great online store that carries fun clothes and unique gifts and toys for kids and adults... unique and special gifts like designer diaper bags, Whoozit learning toys and handmade quilts... this site makes gift buying incredibly easy—I'm done in less than 5 minutes... prices are high but products are special... "

Furniture, Bedding & Decor ....✓	✓ .... Gear & Equipment
Nursing & Feeding ....✓	✓ .... Safety & Babycare
Clothing, Shoes & Accessories.......✓	✓ .... Books, Toys & Entertainment

gap.com ★★★★☆

"...I love the Gap's online store—all the cool things in their stores available via my computer... terrific selection of boys and girls clothes plus cute shoes... you can find awesome deals and return online purchases to Gap stores... their clothes are very durable... it's easy to purchase items online and delivery is prompt... a very practical and affordable way to shop... site makes it easy to quickly find what you need... sign up for the weekly newsletter and you'll find out about online sales... **"**

Furniture, Bedding & Decor ....✓	✓ .... Gear & Equipment
Nursing & Feeding ....✗	✗ .... Safety & Babycare
Clothing, Shoes & Accessories.......✓	✓ .... Books, Toys & Entertainment

geniusbabies.com ★★★⯪☆

"...the best selection available of developmental toys and gifts... the only place to order real puppets from the Baby Einstein video series... cool place for unique baby shower and birthday gifts... their site navigation could use an upgrade... **"**

Furniture, Bedding & Decor ....✗	✗ .... Gear & Equipment
Nursing & Feeding ....✗	✗ .... Safety & Babycare
Clothing, Shoes & Accessories.......✗	✓ .... Books, Toys & Entertainment

gymboree.com ★★★★☆

"...beautiful clothing and great quality... colorful and stylish baby and kids wear... lots of fun birthday gift ideas... easy exchange and return policy... items usually go on sale pretty quickly... save money with gymbucks... many stores have a play area which makes shopping with my kids fun (let alone feasible)... **"**

Furniture, Bedding & Decor ....✗	✗ .... Gear & Equipment
Nursing & Feeding ....✗	✗ .... Safety & Babycare
Clothing, Shoes & Accessories.......✓	✓ .... Books, Toys & Entertainment

hannaandersson.com

Furniture, Bedding & Decor ....✓	✗ .... Gear & Equipment
Nursing & Feeding ....✓	✗ .... Safety & Babycare
Clothing, Shoes & Accessories.......✓	✓ .... Books, Toys & Entertainment

jcpenney.com

Furniture, Bedding & Decor ....✓	✗ .... Gear & Equipment
Nursing & Feeding ....✗	✓ .... Safety & Babycare
Clothing, Shoes & Accessories.......✓	✗ .... Books, Toys & Entertainment

joggingstroller.com ★★★★★

"...an excellent resource when you're choosing a jogging stroller... the entire site is devoted to joggers... very helpful information that's worth checking whether you plan to buy from them or not... the best online guide for researching jogging strollers... includes helpful comparisons and parent reviews on the top strollers... **"**

Furniture, Bedding & Decor ....✗	✓ .... Gear & Equipment
Nursing & Feeding ....✗	✗ .... Safety & Babycare
Clothing, Shoes & Accessories.......✗	✗ .... Books, Toys & Entertainment

kidsurplus.com

Furniture, Bedding & Decor ....✓	✗ .... Gear & Equipment
Nursing & Feeding ....✓	✗ .... Safety & Babycare
Clothing, Shoes & Accessories.......✓	✓ .... Books, Toys & Entertainment

landofnod.com

"...cool site with adorable and unique furnishings... hip kid style art work... fabulous furniture and bedding... the catalog is amusing and nicely laid out... lots of sweet selections for both boys and girls... good customer service... fun but small selection of music, books, toys and more... a great way to get ideas for putting rooms together...**"**

Furniture, Bedding & Decor..........✓	✗ ....Gear & Equipment
Nursing & Feeding ....✗	✗ ....Safety & Babycare
Clothing, Shoes & Accessories ....✗	✓ ....Books, Toys & Entertainment

landsend.com

"...carries the best quality in children's wear—their stuff lasts forever... durable and adorable clothing, shoes and bedding... they offer a huge variety of casual clothing and awesome pajamas... not as inexpensive as other sites, but you can't beat the quality... the very best diaper bags... site is easy to navigate and has great finds for the entire family... love the flannel sheets, maternity clothes and shoes for mom...**"**

Furniture, Bedding & Decor..........✓	✗ ....Gear & Equipment
Nursing & Feeding ....✗	✗ ....Safety & Babycare
Clothing, Shoes & Accessories ......✓	✗ ....Books, Toys & Entertainment

letsgostrolling.com

Furniture, Bedding & Decor..........✓	✓ ....Gear & Equipment
Nursing & Feeding ....✓	✗ ....Safety & Babycare
Clothing, Shoes & Accessories ......✓	✓ ....Books, Toys & Entertainment

llbean.com

"...high quality clothing for babies, toddlers and kids at reasonable prices... the clothes are extremely durable and stand up to wear and tear very well... a great site for winter clothing and gear shopping... wonderful selection for older kids, too... fewer options for infants... an awesome way to shop for clothing basics... you can't beat the diaper bags...**"**

Furniture, Bedding & Decor...........✗	✗ ....Gear & Equipment
Nursing & Feeding ....✗	✗ ....Safety & Babycare
Clothing, Shoes & Accessories ......✓	✗ ....Books, Toys & Entertainment

modernseed.com

"...it was fun finding many unique items for my son's nursery... I wanted a contemporary theme and they had lots of wonderful items including crib linens, wall art and lighting... the place to find super cool baby and kid stuff and the best place for modern nursery decor... they also carry children and adult clothing and furniture and toys... not cheap but one of my favorite places...**"**

Furniture, Bedding & Decor..........✓	✓......................Gear & Equipment
Nursing & Feeding ....✓	✓......................Safety & Babycare
Clothing, Shoes & Accessories ......✓	✓ ....Books, Toys & Entertainment

naturalbaby-catalog.com

"...all natural products—clothes, toys, herbal medicines, bathing, etc... fine quality and a great alternative to the usual products... site is fairly easy to navigate and has a good selection... dealing with returns is pretty painless... love the catalogue and the products... excellent customer service... lots of organic clothing made with natural materials... high quality shoes in a range of prices...**"**

Furniture, Bedding & Decor..........✓	✓......................Gear & Equipment
Nursing & Feeding ....✓	✓......................Safety & Babycare
Clothing, Shoes & Accessories ......✓	✓ ....Books, Toys & Entertainment

participate in our survey at

netkidswear.com

Furniture, Bedding & Decor .... ✓	✓ .... Gear & Equipment	
Nursing & Feeding .... ✓	✓ .... Safety & Babycare	
Clothing, Shoes & Accessories .... ✓	✓ .... Books, Toys & Entertainment	

nordstrom.com ★★★★☆

❝...*just like their stores, the site carries a great selection of high-quality items... you can't go wrong with Nordstrom—even online... quick shipping and easy site navigation... a little pricey, but great quality items... I've purchased a bunch of baby stuff from their website and have never had a problem... a great shoe selection for all ages...* **❞**

Furniture, Bedding & Decor .... ✓	✓ .... Gear & Equipment	
Nursing & Feeding .... ✗	✓ .... Safety & Babycare	
Clothing, Shoes & Accessories .... ✓	✓ .... Books, Toys & Entertainment	

oldnavy.com ★★★★☆

❝...*shopping online with Old Navy makes it easy to find incredible bargains... site was easy to use and my products arrived quickly... site carries items that aren't necessarily available in their stores... an inexpensive way to get trendy baby clothes... you can return items directly to any store... check out the sale page of this web site for deep discounts on current season clothing... I signed up for the email savings and get free shipping several times a year...* **❞**

Furniture, Bedding & Decor .... ✗	✗ .... Gear & Equipment	
Nursing & Feeding .... ✗	✗ .... Safety & Babycare	
Clothing, Shoes & Accessories .... ✓	✗ .... Books, Toys & Entertainment	

oliebollen.com ★★★★⯪

❝...*perfect for the busy mom looking for a fun baby shower gift... this online-only store has all the best brands—Catamini and Tea Collection to name a couple... great for gifts and home stuff, too... lots of style... very easy to use... 30 days full refund, 60 days store credit...* **❞**

Furniture, Bedding & Decor .... ✓	✗ .... Gear & Equipment	
Nursing & Feeding .... ✓	✗ .... Safety & Babycare	
Clothing, Shoes & Accessories .... ✓	✓ .... Books, Toys & Entertainment	

onestepahead.com ★★★★⯪

❝...*one stop shopping site with everything parents are looking for... huge variety of items to choose from... I bought everything from a crib to a nursery bottle... high quality items, many of which are developmental in nature... great line of safety equipment... easy to order and fast delivery but you will pay for shipping... web site has helpful reviews... great site for hard to find items...* **❞**

Furniture, Bedding & Decor .... ✓	✓ .... Gear & Equipment	
Nursing & Feeding .... ✓	✓ .... Safety & Babycare	
Clothing, Shoes & Accessories .... ✓	✓ .... Books, Toys & Entertainment	

peapods.com

Furniture, Bedding & Decor .... ✓	✓ .... Gear & Equipment	
Nursing & Feeding .... ✗	✓ .... Safety & Babycare	
Clothing, Shoes & Accessories .... ✓	✓ .... Books, Toys & Entertainment	

pokkadots.com

Furniture, Bedding & Decor .... ✓	✓ .... Gear & Equipment	
Nursing & Feeding .... ✓	✗ .... Safety & Babycare	
Clothing, Shoes & Accessories .... ✓	✓ .... Books, Toys & Entertainment	

poshtots.com ★★★★☆

❝...*incredible selection of whimsical and out-of-the-ordinary nursery decor... beautiful, unique designer room sets in multiple styles... they do boys and girls bedrooms... great for the baby that has everything—*

including parents with an unlimited cash account... you can get great ideas about decor just from browsing the site, even if you don't buy... **"**

Furniture, Bedding & Decor..........✓	✓ ....Gear & Equipment
Nursing & Feeding ....✓	✗ ....Safety & Babycare
Clothing, Shoes & Accessories ......✓	✓ ....Books, Toys & Entertainment

potterybarnkids.com ★★★★⯪

"...*beautiful high end furniture and bedding... they have a way with matching everything perfectly and I am always a sucker for that look... adorable merchandise of great quality... you will get what you pay for: high quality furniture at high prices... web site is easy to navigate... items like hooded towels and plush blankets make this place special... if I could afford it I would buy everything in the store...* **"**

Furniture, Bedding & Decor..........✓	✓ ....Gear & Equipment
Nursing & Feeding ....✗	✗ ....Safety & Babycare
Clothing, Shoes & Accessories ....✗	✓ ....Books, Toys & Entertainment

preemie.com

Furniture, Bedding & Decor..........✗	✓ ....Gear & Equipment
Nursing & Feeding ....✓	✓ ....Safety & Babycare
Clothing, Shoes & Accessories ......✓	✓ ....Books, Toys & Entertainment

rei.com

Furniture, Bedding & Decor..........✗	✓ ....Gear & Equipment
Nursing & Feeding ....✗	✗ ....Safety & Babycare
Clothing, Shoes & Accessories ......✓	✓ ....Books, Toys & Entertainment

royalnursery.com ★★★⯪☆

"...*this used to be a store in San Diego and now it is only online... if you need a silver rattle, luxury baby blanket or shower gift—this is the place... a beautiful site with elegant baby clothes, jewelry, and gifts...love the hand print kits—they are my current favorite gift... high end baby wear and gear... be sure to check out the sale items...* **"**

Furniture, Bedding & Decor..........✓	✗ ....Gear & Equipment
Nursing & Feeding ....✗	✓ ....Safety & Babycare
Clothing, Shoes & Accessories ......✓	✓ ....Books, Toys & Entertainment

showeryourbaby.com

Furniture, Bedding & Decor..........✓	✓ ....Gear & Equipment
Nursing & Feeding ....✓	✓ ....Safety & Babycare
Clothing, Shoes & Accessories ......✓	✓ ....Books, Toys & Entertainment

snipsnsnails.com ★★★★⯪

"...*a great boys clothing store for infants to 14 years old... clothes for every occasion, from casual to special occasion... pajamas and swimsuits, too... pricey, but upscale and fun... items on the web site are not always in stock ...* **"**

Furniture, Bedding & Decor..........✓	✗ ....Gear & Equipment
Nursing & Feeding ....✗	✗ ....Safety & Babycare
Clothing, Shoes & Accessories ......✓	✗ ....Books, Toys & Entertainment

strollerdepot.com

Furniture, Bedding & Decor..........✗	✓ ....Gear & Equipment
Nursing & Feeding ....✗	✗ ....Safety & Babycare
Clothing, Shoes & Accessories ....✗	✓ ....Books, Toys & Entertainment

strollers4less.com ★★★⯪☆

"...*some of the best prices on strollers... I love this site... we purchased our stroller online for a lot less than it costs locally... online ordering went smoothly—from ordering through receiving... wide*

participate in our survey at

selection and some incredible deals... shipping is relatively fast... free shipping if you spend $100, which isn't hard to do... **99**

Furniture, Bedding & Decor	✗	✓	Gear & Equipment
Nursing & Feeding	✗	✗	Safety & Babycare
Clothing, Shoes & Accessories	✗	✓	Books, Toys & Entertainment

target.com ★★★★☆

66*...our favorite place to shop for kids stuff—good selection and very affordable... guilt free shopping—kids grow so fast so I don't want to pay high department store prices... everything from diapers and sippy cups to car seats and strollers... easy return policy... decent registry that won't freak your friends out with outrageous prices... easy, convenient shopping for well-priced items... all the big box brands available— Graco, Evenflo, Eddie Bauer, etc....* **99**

Furniture, Bedding & Decor	✓	✓	Gear & Equipment
Nursing & Feeding	✓	✓	Safety & Babycare
Clothing, Shoes & Accessories	✓	✓	Books, Toys & Entertainment

teddylux.com

Furniture, Bedding & Decor	✗	✗	Gear & Equipment
Nursing & Feeding	✗	✗	Safety & Babycare
Clothing, Shoes & Accessories	✗	✓	Books, Toys & Entertainment

thebabyhammock.com ★★★★☆

66*...a family owned business selling parent-tested products from morning sickness relief products to baby carriers, natural skincare, gift sets and more... fast friendly service... natural products and waldorf influenced toys...* **99**

Furniture, Bedding & Decor	✓	✓	Gear & Equipment
Nursing & Feeding	✓	✓	Safety & Babycare
Clothing, Shoes & Accessories	✓	✗	Books, Toys & Entertainment

thebabyoutlet.com

Furniture, Bedding & Decor	✗	✓	Gear & Equipment
Nursing & Feeding	✓	✓	Safety & Babycare
Clothing, Shoes & Accessories	✗	✓	Books, Toys & Entertainment

tinyride.com

Furniture, Bedding & Decor	✗	✓	Gear & Equipment
Nursing & Feeding	✓	✗	Safety & Babycare
Clothing, Shoes & Accessories	✗	✗	Books, Toys & Entertainment

toadsandtulips.com

Furniture, Bedding & Decor	✓	✗	Gear & Equipment
Nursing & Feeding	✗	✗	Safety & Babycare
Clothing, Shoes & Accessories	✗	✗	Books, Toys & Entertainment

toysrus.com ★★★★☆

66*...makes shopping incredibly easy... well organized site with discount prices... makes registering for gifts super simple... even more products are online than in the actual stores... check out the outlet section and coupon codes for even more discounts... I did most of my Christmas shopping here, paid no shipping and had my gifts delivered in 3 days... web site includes helpful toy reviews... use this to send your wish lists to relatives...* **99**

Furniture, Bedding & Decor	✓	✓	Gear & Equipment
Nursing & Feeding	✓	✓	Safety & Babycare
Clothing, Shoes & Accessories	✓	✓	Books, Toys & Entertainment

tuttibella.com ★★★★☆

66*...well designed web site with beautiful, original clothing, toys, bedding and accessories... cute vintage stuff for babies and kids...*

stylish designer goods from here and abroad... your child will stand out among the Baby Gap-clothed masses... gorgeous fabrics... a great place to find that perfect gift for someone special and stylish... **"**

Furniture, Bedding & Decor.......... ✓	✓.......................Gear & Equipment
Nursing & Feeding .... ✗	✗........................Safety & Babycare
Clothing, Shoes & Accessories ...... ✓	✗.........Books, Toys & Entertainment

usillygoose.com

Furniture, Bedding & Decor.......... ✓	✗.......................Gear & Equipment
Nursing & Feeding .... ✗	✗........................Safety & Babycare
Clothing, Shoes & Accessories .... ✗	✓.........Books, Toys & Entertainment

walmart.com

"*...the site is packed with information, which can be a little difficult to navigate... anything and everything you need at a huge discount... good idea to browse the site and research prices before you visit a store... my order was delivered well before the estimated delivery date... I've found cheaper deals online than in the store...* **"**

Furniture, Bedding & Decor.......... ✓	✓.......................Gear & Equipment
Nursing & Feeding .... ✓	✓........................Safety & Babycare
Clothing, Shoes & Accessories ...... ✓	✓.........Books, Toys & Entertainment

participate in our survey at

maternity clothing

Seattle

★★★★★

"lila picks"

★ A Pea In The Pod
★ Motherhood Maternity

A Pea In The Pod

★★★★★

"...excellent if you are looking for stylish maternity clothes and don't mind paying for them... start here for special occasions and business wear... the decor is lovely and most of the clothes are beautiful... stylish fashion solutions but expect to pay more than at department stores... keep your eyes open for the sale rack—the markdowns can be terrific... an upscale shop that carries everything from intimates to fancy dresses... stylish, fun and non-maternity like..."

Casual wear	✓	$$$$	Prices
Business wear	✓	❹	Product availability
Intimate apparel	✓	❹	Customer service
Nursing wear	✓	❹	Decor

WWW.APEAINTHEPOD.COM

DOWNTOWN—600 PINE ST (AT 7TH AVE IN PACIFIC PL SHOP CTR); 206.624.8088; M-SA 9:30-9, SU 11-6; PARKING LOT

Baby Depot

★★★☆☆

"...a surprisingly good selection of maternity clothes at great prices... staff can be hard to find so be prepared to dig... cute pants, skirts and sets... I wouldn't have thought that their selection would be as good as it is... not much other than casual items, but what they have is pretty good..."

Casual wear	✓	$$	Prices
Business wear	✗	❸	Product availability
Intimate apparel	✗	❸	Customer service
Nursing wear	✗	❸	Decor

WWW.BABYDEPOT.COM

AUBURN—1101 SUPERMALL WAY S1126 (AT THE SUPERMALL OF THE GREAT NORTHWEST); 253.735.9964; M-SA 10-9, SU 11-6; FREE PARKING

EDMONDS—24111 HWY 99 (AT 240TH ST SW); 425.776.2221; M-SA 10-9, SU 11-6

Gap Maternity

★★★★☆

"...the styles are very modern and attractive... the clothes are reasonably priced and wash well... comfy yet stylish basics... they have a great online resource and you can return online purchases at the store... average every day prices but catch a sale and you're golden... sizes run big so buy small... always a sale going on where you'll find hip items for a steal..."

Casual wear	✓	$$$	Prices
Business wear	✓	❸	Product availability

participate in our survey at

| Intimate apparel | ✓ | | Customer service |
| Nursing wear | ✓ | **3** | Decor |

WWW.GAP.COM

DOWNTOWN—1530 5TH AVE (AT PIKE ST); 206.254.8000; M-SA 9:30-9,SU 10-8

JCPenney ★★★☆☆

"...competitive prices and a surprisingly cute selection... they carry bigger sizes that are very hard to find at other stores... much cheaper than most maternity boutiques and they always seem to have some sort of sale going on... an especially large selection of maternity jeans for plus sizes... a more conservative collection than the smaller, hipper boutiques... good for casual basics, but not much for special occasions... **"**

Casual wear	✓	$$	Prices
Business wear	✓	**3**	Product availability
Intimate apparel	✓	**3**	Customer service
Nursing wear	✗	**3**	Decor

WWW.JCPENNEY.COM

BELLEVUE—300 BELLEVUE SQ (AT NE 4TH ST); 425.454.8599; M-SA 9:30-9:30, SU 11-7

LYNNWOOD—18601 33RD AVE W (AT ALDERWOOD MALL); 425.771.9555; M-SA 10-9:30, SU 11-7; PARKING AT MALL

MAPLE LEAF/ROOSEVELT—401 NE NORTHGATE WY (AT NORTHGATE MALL); 206.361.2500; M-SA 10-9:30, SU 11-7; PARKING AT MALL

SILVERDALE—10315 SILVERDALE WY NW (AT KITSAP MALL); 360.692.1222; M-SA 10-9, SU 11-6; PARKING AT MALL

TUKWILA—1200 SOUTHCENTER MALL (AT SOUTHCENTER MALL); 206.246.0850; M-SA 10-9:30, SU 11-7; PARKING AT MALL

Just For Kids ★★★★☆

"...consignment shop with maternity and kids clothing... I was able to get quite a few items to meet my maternity needs here... a huge selection... **"**

Casual wear	✓	$$	Prices
Business wear	✓	**4**	Product availability
Intimate apparel	✓	**3**	Customer service
Nursing wear	✗	**4**	Decor

EVERETT—7510 BEVERLY BLVD (AT 75TH ST SE); 425.347.5002; M-SA 9-9, SU 10-6 ; PARKING IN FRONT OF BLDG

Macy's ★★★⯪☆

"...if your local Macy's has a maternity section, you're in luck—call ahead!.. I bought my entire pregnancy work wardrobe at Macy's... the styles are all relatively recent and the brands are well known... you can generally find some attractive dresses at very reasonable prices on their sales rack... like other large department stores, you're bound to find something that works if you dig enough... very convenient because you can get your other shopping done at the same time... the selection isn't huge, but what they have is nice... **"**

Casual wear	✓	$$$	Prices
Business wear	✓	**3**	Product availability
Intimate apparel	✓	**3**	Customer service
Nursing wear	✗	**3**	Decor

WWW.MACYS.COM

DOWNTOWN—1601 3RD AVE (AT PINE ST); 206.506.6000; M-SA 10-8, SU 11-7

Maternity Factory ★★★☆☆

"...actually a split store—1/2 bridal and 1/2 maternity... the owner is knowledgeable and carries some of the better brands of maternity and nursing clothing such as Japanese Weekend and Olian... the store is not huge, and not much for decor, but other than the MotherWorks empire (encompassing Pea in the Pod, Mimi Maternity, and Motherhood Maternity) there are few choices for maternity wear speciality stores, and this one is not too bad... **"** ✓

Casual wear	✓	$$$$	Prices
Business wear	✓	❸	Product availability
Intimate apparel	✓	❹	Customer service
Nursing wear	✓	❷	Decor

BELLEVUE—10676 NE 8TH ST (AT BELLEVUE WAY NE); 425.451.1945; M-TH 10-7:30, F-SA 10-6; PARKING LOT

Me 'n Mom's Consignment Boutique ★★★★☆

"...great consignment maternity, baby clothes and gear... good selection of profesional and dress attire... **"**

Casual wear	✓	$	Prices
Business wear	✗	❸	Product availability
Intimate apparel	✓	❺	Customer service
Nursing wear	✓	❸	Decor

WWW.MENMOMS.COM

BALLARD—2821 NW MARKET ST (AT 28TH AVE NW); 206.781.9449; M-F 9:30-6, SA-SU 10:30-5

Mimi Maternity ★★★★☆

"...it's definitely worth stopping here if you're still working and need some good looking outfits... not cheap, but the quality is fantastic... not as expensive as A Pea In The Pod, but better quality than Motherhood Maternity... nice for basics that will last you through multiple pregnancies... perfect for work clothes, but pricey for the everyday stuff... good deals to be found on their sales racks... a good mix of high-end fancy clothes and items you can wear every day... **"**

Casual wear	✓	$$$	Prices
Business wear	✓	❹	Product availability
Intimate apparel	✓	❹	Customer service
Nursing wear	✓	❹	Decor

WWW.MIMIMATERNITY.COM

BELLEVUE—2020 BELLEVUE SQ (AT BELLEVUE SQ); 425.454.1355; M-SA 9:30-9:30, SU 10-8

DOWNTOWN—400 PINE ST (AT 4TH AVE); 206.624.9494; M-SA 10-9, SU 12-6

Motherhood Maternity ★★★★★

"...a wide variety of styles, from business to weekend wear—all at a good price... affordable and cute... everything from bras and swimsuits to work outfits... highly recommended for those who don't want to spend a fortune on maternity clothes... less fancy and pricey than their sister stores—A Pea in the Pod and Mimi Maternity... they have frequent sales, so you just need to keep dropping in—you're bound to find something good... **"**

Casual wear	✓	$$$	Prices
Business wear	✓	❹	Product availability
Intimate apparel	✓	❹	Customer service
Nursing wear	✓	❸	Decor

WWW.MOTHERHOOD.COM

participate in our survey at

AUBURN—1101 SUPER MALL WY (AT SUPER MALL OF THE GREAT NORTHWEST); 253.833.9025; M-SA 10-9, SU 11-6; PARKING AT MALL

BELLEVUE—2020 BELLEVUE SQ (AT 20TH PL); 425.454.1355; M-SA 10-9, SU 11-7

DOWNTOWN—3RD & PINE ST (AT S 108TH PL); 206.332.9510; M-SA 9:30-5:30, SU 10-6

DOWNTOWN—400 PINE ST (AT 4TH AVE); 206.624.9494; M-SA 9:30-9, SU 11-6

ISSAQUAH—775 NW GILMAN BLVD (OFF RT 90); 425.313.0604; M-F 10-8, SA 10-7, SU 11-6

LYNNWOOD—3000 184TH ST SW (AT ALDERWOOD MALL); 425.776.2095; M-SA 10-9:30, SU 11-6; PARKING AT MALL

MAPLE LEAF/ROOSEVELT—401 NE NORTHGATE WAY (AT NORTHGATE SHOPPING CTR); 206.417.9537; M-SA 10-9:30, SU 11-7

TUKWILA—1018 SOUTHCENTER MALL (AT E BIDWELL ST); 206.246.7111; M-SA 10-9:30, SU 11-7; PARKING AT MALL

TUKWILA—500 SOUTHCENTER MALL (AT SOUTHCENTER MALL); 206.246.3586; M-SA 10-9, SU 11-7; PARKING AT MALL

Old Navy ★★★★½☆

"...the best for casual maternity clothing like stretchy T-shirts with Lycra and comfy jeans... prices are so reasonable it's ridiculous... not much for the workplace, but you can't beat the prices on casual ware... not all Old Navy locations carry their maternity line... don't expect a huge or diverse selection... the staff is not always knowledgeable about maternity clothing and can't really help with questions about sizing... they have the best return policy—order online and return to the nearest store location... perfect for inexpensive maternity duds... **"**

Casual wear	✓	$$	Prices
Business wear	✗	❹	Product availability
Intimate apparel	✗	❸	Customer service
Nursing wear	✗	❸	Decor

WWW.OLDNAVY.COM

AUBURN—1101 SUPERMALL WY (AT SUPERMALL OF THE GREAT NORTHWEST); 253.804.3470; M-SA 9-9, SU 10-6; PARKING LOT

BELLEVUE—4037 FACTORIA BLVD SE (AT FACTORIA SQ MALL); 425.957.0341; M-SA 9-9, SU 10-6; PARKING AT MALL

DOWNTOWN—601 PINE ST (AT 6TH AVE); 206.264.9341; M-SA 9-9, SU 10-6

FEDERAL WAY—1718 S 320TH ST (AT SEATAC MALL); 253.946.9200; M-SA 9-9, SU 10-6; PARKING AT MALL

TUKWILA—17470 SOUTHCENTER PKWY (AT MINKLER BLVD); 206.575.0432; M-SA 9-9, SU 11-7; PARKING AT MALL

Other Mothers ★★★★½☆

"...you can find bargains on quality clothing... awesome people that know their merchandise and are willing to help... friendly and supportive atmosphere... **"**

Casual wear	✓	$	Prices
Business wear	✓	❸	Product availability
Intimate apparel	✗	❹	Customer service
Nursing wear	✓	❸	Decor

EVERETT—13027 BOTHELL EVERETT HWY (AT 132ND ST SE); 425.357.8779; M-SA 10-6

Ross Dress For Less ★★½☆☆

"...if you don't mind looking through a lot of clothes you can find some good pieces at great prices... they sometimes have larger sizes too... totally hit or miss depending on their most recent shipment... not *the most fashionable clothing, but great for that everyday, casual T shirt or stretchy pair of pants...* **"**

Casual wear	✓	$$$		Prices
Business wear	✗	❸		Product availability
Intimate apparel	✗	❷		Customer service
Nursing wear	✗	❷		Decor

WWW.ROSSSTORES.COM

DOWNTOWN—1418 3RD AVE (AT UNION ST); 206.623.6781; M-SA 9-8, SU 10-6

NORTH SEATTLE—13201 AURORA AVE N (AT N 130TH ST); 206.367.6030; M-SA 9:30-9:30, SU 11-7

TUKWILA—17672 SOUTHCENTER PKWY (AT MINKLER BLVD); 206.575.0110; M-SA 9-9:30, SU 10-6; PARKING AT MALL

Sears ★★★☆☆

"*...good place to get maternity clothes for a low price... the clearance rack always has good deals and their sales are quite frequent... not necessarily super high quality but if you just need them for 9 months, who cares... good selection of nursing bras... I love the fact that they carry maternity wear in larger sizes—I got so tired of looking in those cutesy boutiques and then being disappointed because they didn't have my size... the only place I found maternity for plus-sized women...* **"**

Casual wear	✓	$$		Prices
Business wear	✗	❸		Product availability
Intimate apparel	✓	❸		Customer service
Nursing wear	✓	❸		Decor

WWW.SEARS.COM

EVERETT—1302 SE EVERETT MALL WAY (AT EVERETT MALL); 425.355.7070; M-SA 10-9, SU 10-6

FEDERAL WAY—1701 S 320TH ST (AT SEATAC MALL); 253.529.8200; M-SA 10-7, SU 10-9

LYNNWOOD—18600 ALDERWOOD MALL PKWY (AT ALDERWOOD MALL); 425.771.2212; M-SA 9-9:30, SU 10-7

NORTH SEATTLE—15711 AURORA AVE N (AT N 160TH ST); 206.440.2000; M-SA 9-9, SU 9-7

REDMOND—2200 148TH AVE NE (AT NE 22ND ST); 425.644.6581; M-SA 10-7, SU 11-7; PARKING IN FRONT OF BLDG

SILVERDALE—10315 SILVERDALE WY NW (AT KITSAP MALL); 360.692.1515; M-F 9-9 SA-SU 8-9; PARKING AT MALL

SODO—76 S LANDER ST (AT 1ST AVE S); 206.344.4893; M-F 10-9, SA 10-6, SU 11-5

TUKWILA—400 SOUTHCENTER MALL (AT SOUTHCENTER MALL); 206.241.3503; M-F 9:30-9:30, SA 8-9:30, SU 10-8; PARKING AT MALL

Target ★★★★☆

"*...I was surprised at how fashionable their selection is—they carry Liz Lange and other really cute selections... the price is right—especially since you'll only be wearing these clothes for a few months... great for maternity basics—T-shirts, skirts, sweaters, even maternity bras... best of all, you can do some maternity shopping while you're shopping for other household basics... shirts for $10—you can't beat that... not the most exciting or romantic maternity shopping, but once you see the prices you'll get over it... as always, Target provides the perfectly priced solution...* **"**

Casual wear	✓	$$		Prices
Business wear	✓	❸		Product availability
Intimate apparel	✓	❸		Customer service
Nursing wear	✓	❸		Decor

WWW.TARGET.COM

participate in our survey at

BELLEVUE—4053 FACTORIA SQ MALL SE (AT FACTORIA SQ MALL); 425.562.0830; M-SA 8-10, SU 8-9; PARKING IN FRONT OF BLDG

FEDERAL WAY—2141 S 314TH ST (AT 20TH AVE S); 253.839.3399; M-SA 8-10, SU 8-9; PARKING IN FRONT OF BLDG

ISSAQUAH—755 NW GILMAN BLVD (AT 7TH AVE NW); 425.392.3357; M-SA 8-10, SU 8-9; PARKING IN FRONT OF BLDG

KENT—26301 104TH AVE SE (AT SE 264TH ST); 253.850.9710; M-SA 8-10, SU 8-9; PARKING IN FRONT OF BLDG

LYNNWOOD—18305 ALDERWOOD MALL PKWY (AT ALDERWOOD MALL); 425.670.1435; M-SA 8-10, SU 8-9; PARKING IN FRONT OF BLDG

MAPLE LEAF/ROOSEVELT—300 NE NORTHGATE WY (AT NORTHGATE SHOPPING CTR); 206.494.0897; M-SA 8-10, SU 8-9; PARKING IN FRONT OF BLDG

REDMOND—17700 NE 76TH ST (AT MERVYNS TARGET SHOPPING CPLX); 425.556.9533; M-SA 8-10, SU 8-9; PARKING IN FRONT OF BLDG

SILVERDALE—3201 NW RANDALL WY (AT KITSAP MALL); 360.692.3966; M-SA 8-10, SU 8-9; PARKING IN FRONT OF BLDG

TUKWILA—301 STRANDER BLVD (AT WESTFIELD SHOPPINGTOWN CTR); 206.575.0682; M-SA 8-10, SU 8-9; PARKING IN FRONT OF BLDG

WEST SEATTLE—2800 SW BARTON ST (AT WESTWOOD TOWN CTR); 206.932.1153; M-SA 8-10, SU 8-9; PARKING IN FRONT OF BLDG

WOODINVILLE—13950 NE 178TH PL (AT 140TH AVE NE); 425.482.6410; M-SA 8-10, SU 8-9; PARKING IN FRONT OF BLDG

Value Village

CAPITOL HILL—1525 11TH AVE (AT E PIKE ST); 206.322.7789; M-SA 9-9, SU 10-7

Village Maternity   ★★★★☆

❝...*great store, friendly and helpful salespeople... tends to have both traditional maternity clothes and also some fun pieces to mix in... selection including pumps and other baby products...* **❞**

Casual wear	✓	$$$$	Prices
Business wear	✓	❹	Product availability
Intimate apparel	✓	❸	Customer service
Nursing wear	✓	❹	Decor

WWW.VILLAGEMATERNITY.COM

UNIVERSITY DISTRICT/UNIVERSITY VILLAGE—2615 UNIVERSITY VILLAGE ST (AT UNIVERSITY VILLAGE MALL); 206.523.5167; M-SA 9:30-9, SU 11-6; PARKING AT MALL

Tacoma

"lila picks"

★ Motherhood Maternity

Baby Depot At Burlington Coat Factory

❝...a surprisingly good selection of maternity clothes at great prices... staff can be hard to find so be prepared to dig... cute pants, skirts and sets... I wouldn't have thought that their selection would be as good as it is... not much other than casual items, but what they have is pretty good...**❞**

Casual wear	✓	$$	Prices
Business wear	✗	❸	Product availability
Intimate apparel	✗	❸	Customer service
Nursing wear	✗	❸	Decor

WWW.BABYDEPOT.COM

TACOMA—10420 59TH AVE SW (AT MAIN ST); M-SA 10-9:30; FREE PARKING

JCPenney

❝...competitive prices and a surprisingly cute selection... they carry bigger sizes that are very hard to find at other stores... much cheaper than most maternity boutiques and they always seem to have some sort of sale going on... an especially large selection of maternity jeans for plus sizes... a more conservative collection than the smaller, hipper boutiques... good for casual basics, but not much for special occasions...**❞**

Casual wear	✓	$$	Prices
Business wear	✓	❸	Product availability
Intimate apparel	✓	❸	Customer service
Nursing wear	✗	❸	Decor

WWW.JCPENNEY.COM

TACOMA—4502 S STEELE ST (AT S 43RD ST); 253.475.4510; M-SA 10-9:30, SU 11-6

Judy's Intimate Apparel

❝...great place for maternity and nursing bras... best selection for larger cup size bras...**❞**

Casual wear	✗	$$	Prices
Business wear	✗	❹	Product availability
Intimate apparel	✓	❸	Customer service
Nursing wear	✓	❸	Decor

WWW.JUDYSINTIMATEAPPAREL.COM

TACOMA—4538 S PINE ST (AT TACOMA MALL); 253.474.4404; M-T TH-F 10-5, W 12-5; PARKING IN FRONT OF BLDG

Macy's ★★★☆☆

"...if your local Macy's has a maternity section, you're in luck... I bought my entire pregnancy work wardrobe at Macy's... the styles are all relatively recent and the brands are well known... you can generally find some attractive dresses at very reasonable prices on their sales rack... like other large department stores, you're bound to find something that works if you dig enough... very convenient because you can get your other shopping done at the same time... the selection isn't huge, but what they have is nice... "

maternity

Casual wear	✓	$$$	Prices
Business wear	✓	❸	Product availability
Intimate apparel	✓	❸	Customer service
Nursing wear	✗	❸	Decor

WWW.MACYS.COM

PUYALLUP—3500 S MERIDIAN (AT 112TH ST); 253.840.7000; M-SA 10-9, SU 11-7

TACOMA—1767 S 48TH ST (OFF 38TH ST); 253.471.5400; M-F 10-9, SA 10-7, SU 11-6

TACOMA—4502 S STEELE ST (AT S 43RD ST); 253.471.6800; M-SA 10-9, SU 11-7

Mervyn's ★★★☆☆

"...they just started carrying a maternity line—finally!.. thanks to Holly Robinson's line of clothing, they have some nice pieces that you can mix and match to create new looks... prices are great and they carry all your basics... "

Casual wear	✓	$$	Prices
Business wear	✗	❹	Product availability
Intimate apparel	✗	❹	Customer service
Nursing wear	✗	❹	Decor

WWW.MERVYNS.COM

PUYALLUP—3700 S MERIDIAN (AT 112TH ST E); 253.845.8800; M-SA 9-10, SU 9-9

TACOMA—4502 S STEELE ST (AT TACOMA MALL); 253.474.8800; M-SA 9-10, SU 9-9; MALL PARKING

Motherhood Maternity ★★★★★

"...a wide variety of styles, from business to weekend wear, all at a good price... affordable and cute... everything from bras and swimsuits to work outfits... highly recommended for those who don't want to spend a fortune on maternity clothes... less fancy and pricey than their sister stores—A Pea in the Pod and Mimi Maternity... they have frequent sales, so you just need to keep dropping in—you're bound to find something good... "

Casual wear	✓	$$$	Prices
Business wear	✓	❹	Product availability
Intimate apparel	✓	❹	Customer service
Nursing wear	✓	❸	Decor

WWW.MOTHERHOOD.COM

LAKEWOOD—5605 LAKEWOOD TWN CTR BLVD SW (AT 47TH AVE SW); 253.588.3073; M-SA 10-8, SU 12-6

TACOMA—4502 S STEELE ST (AT S 43RD ST); 253.471.2964; M-SA 10-9, SU 11-7

Other Mothers ★★★☆☆

"...you can find bargains on quality clothing... awesome people that know their merchandise and are willing to help... friendly and supportive atmosphere... "

Casual wear	✓	$	Prices

Business wear	✓	❸	Product availability
Intimate apparel	✗	❹	Customer service
Nursing wear	✓	❸	Decor

WWW.OMTACOMA.COM

TACOMA—6409 6TH AVE (AT S MILDRED ST); 253.566.8344; M-TH 10-7, F-SA 10-6; STREET PARKING

Target

★★★★☆

"...I was surprised at how fashionable their selection is—they carry Liz Lange and other really cute selections... the price is right—especially since you'll only be wearing these clothes for a few months... great for maternity basics—T-shirts, skirts, sweaters, even maternity bras... best of all, you can do some maternity shopping while you're shopping for other household basics... shirts for $10—you can't beat that... not the most exciting or romantic maternity shopping, but once you see the prices you'll get over it... as always, Target provides the perfectly priced solution..."

Casual wear	✓	$$	Prices
Business wear	✓	❸	Product availability
Intimate apparel	✓	❸	Customer service
Nursing wear	✓	❸	Decor

WWW.TARGET.COM

GIG HARBOR—11400 51ST AVE NW (AT 144TH ST NW); 253.858.9777; M-SA 8-10, SU 8-9; PARKING IN FRONT OF BLDG

PUYALLUP—3310 S MERIDIAN (AT SOUTH HILL MALL); 253.840.2900; M-SA 8-10, SU 8-9; PARKING IN FRONT OF BLDG

TACOMA—10509 GRAVELLY LAKE DR SW (AT LAKEWOOD TOWNE CTR); 253.581.7171; M-SA 8-10, SU 8-9; PARKING IN FRONT OF BLDG

TACOMA—3320 S 23RD ST (OFF S UNION AVE); 253.627.2112; M-SA 8-10, SU 8-9; PARKING IN FRONT OF BLDG

participate in our survey at

Online

★★★★★

"lila picks"

★ breastisbest.com   ★ gap.com

★ maternitymall.com   ★ naissance maternity.com

babiesrus.com ★★★★☆

"...*their online store is surprisingly plentiful for maternity wear in addition to all of the baby stuff... they carry everything from Mimi Maternity to Belly Basics... easy shopping and good return policy... the price is right and the selection is really good...* **"**

Casual wear .... ✓   ✓ ....Nursing wear
Business wear .... ✓   ✓ .... Intimate apparel

babycenter.com ★★★★☆

"...*it's babycenter.com—of course it's good... a small but well selected maternity section... I love being able to read other people's comments before purchasing... prices are reasonable and the convenience is priceless... great customer service and easy returns...* **"**

Casual wear .... ✓   ✓ ....Nursing wear
Business wear .... ✗   ✗ .... Intimate apparel

babystyle.com ★★★★☆

"...*beautiful selection of maternity clothes... very trendy, fashionable styles... take advantage of their free shipping offers to keep the cost down... items generally ship quickly... I found a formal maternity outfit for a benefit dinner, bought it on sale and received it on time... a nice variety of things and they ship in a timely manner...* **"**

Casual wear .... ✓   ✓ ....Nursing wear
Business wear .... ✓   ✓ .... Intimate apparel

bellablumaternity.com

Casual wear .... ✓   ✓ ....Nursing wear
Business wear .... ✓   ✓ .... Intimate apparel

breakoutbras.com

Casual wear .... ✗   ✓ ....Nursing wear
Business wear .... ✗   ✓ .... Intimate apparel

breastisbest.com ★★★★★

"...*by far the best resource for purchasing good quality nursing bras online... the site is easy to use and they have an extensive online fitting guide... returns are a breeze... since they are only online you may have to try a few before you get it exactly right...* **"**

Casual wear .... ✓   ✓ ....Nursing wear
Business wear .... ✗   ✓ .... Intimate apparel

childishclothing.com

| Casual wear | ✓ | ✗ | Nursing wear |
| Business wear | ✗ | ✗ | Intimate apparel |

duematernity.com ★★★★☆

"...refreshing styles... fun and hip clothing... the site is easy to navigate and use... I've ordered a bunch of clothes from them and never had a problem... everything from casual wear to fun, funky items for special occasions... prices are reasonable... "

| Casual wear | ✓ | ✓ | Nursing wear |
| Business wear | ✓ | ✓ | Intimate apparel |

evalillian.com

| Casual wear | ✓ | ✓ | Nursing wear |
| Business wear | ✓ | ✓ | Intimate apparel |

expressiva.com ★★★★½

"...the best site for nursing clothes... prices are good and their selection is terrific... lots of selection on dressy, casual, sleep, workout and even bathing suits... if you're going to shop for maternity online then be sure not to miss this cool site... good customer service—quite prompt in answering questions about my order... "

| Casual wear | ✓ | ✓ | Nursing wear |
| Business wear | ✗ | ✓ | Intimate apparel |

gap.com ★★★★★

"...stylish maternity clothes delivered right to your doorstep... always something worth buying... the best place for functional, comfortable and affordable maternity clothes... classic styles, not too trendy... more available online than in a store... no fancy dresses but lots of casual outfits that are cheap, look good and I don't mind parting with them after my baby is born... easy to use site and deliveries are generally prompt... you can return them to any Gap store... "

| Casual wear | ✓ | ✓ | Nursing wear |
| Business wear | ✓ | ✓ | Intimate apparel |

japaneseweekend.com ★★★★☆

"...pregnancy clothes that scream 'I am proud of my pregnant body'... a must for comfy, stylish stuff... they make the best maternity pants which cradle your belly as it grows... a little expensive but I lived in their pants my entire pregnancy—I definitely got my money's worth... really nice clothing that just doesn't look and feel like your traditional pregnancy wear—I still wear a couple of the outfits (my baby is now 6 months old)... "

| Casual wear | ✓ | ✓ | Nursing wear |
| Business wear | ✓ | ✓ | Intimate apparel |

jcpenney.com ★★★☆☆

"...competitive prices and a surprisingly cute selection... they carry bigger sizes that are very hard to find at other stores... much cheaper than most maternity boutiques and they always seem to have some sort of sale going on... an especially large selection of maternity jeans for plus sizes... a more conservative collection than the smaller, hipper boutiques... good for casual basics, but not much for special occasions... "

| Casual wear | ✓ | ✓ | Nursing wear |
| Business wear | ✓ | ✓ | Intimate apparel |

lizlange.com ★★★★½

"...well-designed and cute... the real buys on this site are definitely in the sale section... cute, hip selection of jeans, skirts, blouses and

participate in our survey at

bathing suits... their evening and dressy clothes are the best with wonderful fabrics and designs... easy and convenient online shopping... practical but not frumpy styles—their web site made my maternity shopping so easy... **"**

| Casual wear | ✓ | ✗ | Nursing wear |
| Business wear | ✓ | ✗ | Intimate apparel |

maternitymall.com ★★★★★

"...*I had great luck with maternitymall.com... a large selection of vendors in all price ranges... quick and easy without having to leave my house... found everything I needed... their merchandise tends to be true to size... site is a bit hard to navigate and cluttered with ads... sale and clearance prices are fantastic...* **"**

| Casual wear | ✓ | ✓ | Nursing wear |
| Business wear | ✓ | ✓ | Intimate apparel |

mommygear.com

| Casual wear | ✓ | ✓ | Nursing wear |
| Business wear | ✗ | ✓ | Intimate apparel |

momsnightout.com

"...*for that fashionable-not-frumpy fancy occasion dress... beautiful store with gorgeous selection of dresses from cocktail to bridal... one on one attention... expensive but worth it...* **"**

| Casual wear | ✗ | ✗ | Nursing wear |
| Business wear | ✓ | ✗ | Intimate apparel |

motherhood.com ★★★★☆

"...*a wide variety of styles, from business to weekend wear—all at a good price... affordable and cute... everything from bras and swimsuits to work outfits... highly recommended for those who don't want to spend a fortune on maternity clothes... less fancy and pricey than their sister stores—A Pea in the Pod and Mimi Maternity... they have frequent sales, so you just need to keep dropping in—you're bound to find something good...* **"**

| Casual wear | ✓ | ✓ | Nursing wear |
| Business wear | ✓ | ✓ | Intimate apparel |

motherwear.com ★★★★☆

"...*excellent selection of cute and practical nursing clothes at reasonable prices... sign up for their e-mail newsletter for great offers, including free shipping... top quality clothes... decent selection of hard to find plus sizes... golden return policy, you can return any item (even used!) you aren't 100% happy with... they sell the only nursing tops I could actually wear outside the house... cute styles that aren't frumpy... so easy... pricey but worth it for the quality... top notch customer service...* **"**

| Casual wear | ✗ | ✓ | Nursing wear |
| Business wear | ✗ | ✓ | Intimate apparel |

naissancematernity.com ★★★★★

"...*the cutest maternity clothes around... hip and funky clothes for the artsy, well-dressed mom to be... their site is easy to navigate... if you can't make it down to the actual store in LA, just go online... clothes that make you look and feel sexy... it ain't cheap but you will look marvelous and the clothes will grow with you... web site is great and their phone order service was incredible...* **"**

| Casual wear | ✓ | ✗ | Nursing wear |
| Business wear | ✓ | ✗ | Intimate apparel |

nordstrom.com ★★★☆☆

66...now that they don't carry maternity in stores anymore, this is the only way to get any maternity from Nordstrom... overpriced but nice... makes returns harder, since you have to ship everything instead of just going back to a store... they carry Cadeau, Liz Lange, Belly Basics, etc... nice stuff, not so nice prices... 99

Casual wear .... ✓   ✓ .... Nursing wear
Business wear .... ✓   ✓ .... Intimate apparel

oldnavy.com ★★★★☆

66...since not all Old Navy stores carry maternity clothes, this is the easiest way to go... just like their regular clothes, the maternity selection is great for casual wear... cheap, cheap, cheap... the quality is good and the price is definitely right... frequent sales make great prices even better... 99

Casual wear .... ✓   ✓ .... Nursing wear
Business wear .... ✗   ✗ .... Intimate apparel

onehotmama.com ★★★⯪☆

66...you'll find many things you must have... cool and very nice clothing... they carry everything from underwear and tights to formal dresses... you can find some real bargains online... super fast shipping... also, lots of choices for nursing and get-back-in-shape wear... 99

Casual wear .... ✓   ✓ .... Nursing wear
Business wear .... ✓   ✓ .... Intimate apparel

showeryourbaby.com

Casual wear .... ✓   ✓ .... Nursing wear
Business wear .... ✗   ✓ .... Intimate apparel

target.com ★★★★☆

66...lots of Liz Lange at very fair prices... the selection is great and it's so easy to shop online—we bought most of our baby gear here and I managed to slip in a couple of orders for some maternity wear too... maternity shirts for $10—where else can you find deals like that... 99

Casual wear .... ✓   ✓ .... Nursing wear
Business wear .... ✓   ✓ .... Intimate apparel

participate in our survey at

activities & outings

Seattle

★★★★★

"lila picks"

- ★ Children's Museum of Seattle
- ★ Gymboree Play & Music
- ★ Imagine Children's Museum
- ★ Pacific Science Center
- ★ Seattle Aquarium
- ★ Woodland Park Zoo

Alderwood Mall ★★★★☆

"...great place to shop... even has a family lounge and everything is very accessible... changing tables, vending machines, chairs and games... the theater has a free kids summer film series... lots of places to grab a bite to eat..."

Customer service.........................**3** $$$.......................................Prices

WWW.ALDERWOODMALL.COM

LYNNWOOD—3000 184TH ST SW (AT ALDERWOOD MALL); 425.771.1121; M-SA 10-9:30, SU 11-7; FREE PARKING

Alki Community Center ★★★★☆

"...my 3-year-old loves the music class and the tot class... not necessarily great for infants—better for older tots... a great resource for the community... children can have hours of fun on a rainy day for only $1at the open mini-gym...a great playground is outside..."

Customer service.........................**4** $ ....Prices

Age range................ 18 mths and up

WWW.CITYOFSEATTLE.NET/PARKS/CENTERS/ALKICC.HTM

WEST SEATTLE—5817 SW STEVENS ST (AT 59TH AVE SW); 206.684.7430; M-T TH 1-9, W F 10-9, SA 10-5

Auburn Gymnastics Center ★★★★☆

"...they offer recreational as well as competitive gymnastics programs... we love their tiny tots programs... they provide mom and baby classes for the tiny ones and lots more for the older kids too... a very supportive environment—I like that my baby gets to see all of these talented youths working so hard... low key classes for new parents..."

Customer service.........................**3** $$$.......................................Prices

Age range................ 12 mths and up

WWW.AUBURNGYMNASTICS.COM

AUBURN—1221 29TH ST NW (AT W VALLEY HWY N); 253.876.9991; CHECK SCHEDULE ONLINE

Ballard Community Center ★★★☆☆

❝...compared to some of the other indoor play spaces this is the worst... very small and does not have a lot for the children to play with... okay if you really need to get out on a rainy day, but there are better places to go...**❞**

Customer service .... ❸ $ .... Prices

Age range .... 6 mths and up

WWW.CITYOFSEATTLE.NET/PARKS/CENTERS/BALLARD.HTM

BALLARD—6020 28TH AVE NW (AT BALLARD PLAYGROUND); 206.684.4093;
M W F 11-9, T TH 1-9, SA 10-5

activities & outings

Ballard Pool ★★★⯪☆

❝...the indoor pool is okay, but kinda cold... they do have a spa to warm up in after a swim... very economical... locker rooms need a good cleaning and are not child friendly... our child took swim lessons here and the class size was much too large and the staff way too laid back... the family swim time is fun...**❞**

Customer service .... ❸ $ .... Prices

WWW.SEATTLE.GOV/PARKS/AQUATICS/BALLARDP.HTM

BALLARD—1471 NW 67TH ST (AT 15TH AVE NW); 206.684.4094; CHECK
SCHEDULE ONLINE

Barnes & Noble ★★★★⯪

❝...wonderful weekly story times for all ages and frequent author visits for older kids... lovely selection of books and the story times are fun and very well done... they have evening story times—we put our kids in their pjs and come here as a treat before bedtime... they read a story, and then usually have a little craft or related coloring project... times vary by location so give them a call...**❞**

Customer service .... ❹ $ .... Prices

Age range .... 6 mths to 6 yrs

WWW.BARNESANDNOBLE.COM

BELLEVUE—15600 NE 8TH AVE (AT 156TH AVE); 425.644.1650; CALL FOR
SCHEDULE

BELLEVUE—626 106TH AVE NE (AT 6TH ST); 425.451.8463; CALL FOR
SCHEDULE

DOWNTOWN—600 PINE ST (AT 6TH AVE); 206.264.0156; CALL FOR
SCHEDULE

ISSAQUAH—1530 11TH AVE NW (AT NW SAMMAMISH RD); 425.557.8808;
CALL FOR SCHEDULE

LYNNWOOD—19401 ALDERWOOD MALL PKWY (AT 193RD ST); 425.771.2220;
CALL FOR SCHEDULE

TUKWILA—300 ANDOVER PK W (AT WESTFIELD SHOPPING TOWN);
206.575.3965; CALL FOR SCHEDULE

UNIVERSITY DISTRICT/UNIVERSITY VILLAGE—206.517.4107; CALL FOR
SCHEDULE

WOODINVILLE—18025 GARDEN WAY NE (AT NE 178TH ST); 425.398.1990;
CALL FOR SCHEDULE

Bellevue Square ★★★★☆

❝...the big draw for our family is the tug boat play area... the shopping is so-so, but the kids love to go and play for hours... gets crazy busy when it's rainy outside... lots of ramps for children and a glass elevator... a mother's lounge is available at Nordstrom for bathroom breaks, breast feeding or changing baby... variety of children-friendly places to eat... several play areas throughout the mall for the kids...**❞**

Customer service .... ❸ $$ .... Prices

WWW.BELLEVUESQUARE.COM

DOWNTOWN BELLEVUE—1086 BELLEVUE SQ (AT NE 8TH ST); 425.454.8096; M-SA 9:30-9:30, SU 11-7; FREE PARKING

Bitter Lake Community Center

Age range.................. 6 mths and up

WWW.SEATTLE.GOV/PARKS/CENTERS/BITTERLK.HTM

NORTH SEATTLE—13035 LINDEN AVE N (AT BITTER LAKE PARK); 206.684.7524; M-T 1-9, W-F 11-9, SA 10-5

Borders Books

"...very popular weekly story time held in most branches (check the web site for locations and times)... call before you go since they are very popular and get extremely crowded... kids love the unique blend of songs, stories and dancing... Mr. Hatbox's appearances are a delight to everyone (unfortunately he doesn't make appearances at all locations)... large children's section is well categorized and well priced... they make it fun for young tots to browse through the board-book section by hanging toys around the shelves... the low-key cafe is a great place to have coffee with your baby and leaf through some magazines... **"**

Customer service........................**❹** $ ....Prices

Age range.................. 6 mths to 6 yrs

WWW.BORDERSSTORES.COM

DOWNTOWN—1501 FOURTH AVE (AT PIKE ST); 206.622.4599; CALL FOR SCHEDULE

EVERETT—1402 SE EVERETT MALL WY (AT CENTRAL MALL DR); CALL FOR SCHEDULE

FEDERAL WAY—1824 S 320TH ST (AT PACIFIC HWY S & SEATAC MALL); 253.946.5877; CALL FOR SCHEDULE

LYNNWOOD—3000 184TH ST SW (AT ALDERWOOD MALL PKWY); 425.776.7530; CALL FOR SCHEDULE

REDMOND—REDMOND TOWN CENTER (AT 166TH AVE NE); 425.869.1907; CALL FOR SCHEDULE

TUKWILA—17501 SOUTHCENTER PKWY (AT S 180TH ST); 206.575.4506; CALL FOR SCHEDULE

Build-A-Bear Workshop

"...design and make your own bear—it's a dream come true... the most cherished toy my daughter owns... they even come with birth certificates... the staff is fun and knows how to play along with the kids' excitement... the basic stuffed animal is only about $15, but the extras add up quickly... great for field trips, birthdays and special occasions... how darling—my nephew is 8 years old now, and still sleeps with his favorite bear... **"**

Customer service........................**❹** $$$..Prices

Age range.....................3 yrs and up

WWW.BUILDABEAR.COM

DOWNTOWN BELLEVUE—144 BELLEVUE SQ (AT BELLEVUE WY NE); 425.467.5944; M-SA 9:30-9:30, SU 11-7; FREE

LYNNWOOD—3000 184TH ST SW (AT ALDERWOOD MALL); 425.778.3606; M-SA 10-9:30, SU 11-7; MALL PARKING

Chuck E Cheese's

"...lots of games, rides, playrooms and very greasy food... the kids can play and eat and parents can unwind a little... a good rainy day activity... the kids love the food, but it's a bit greasy for adults... always crowded and crazy—but that's half the fun... can you ever go wrong with pizza, games and singing?.. although they do have a salad bar for adults, remember, you're not going for the food—you're going because *your kids will love it... just about the easiest birthday party around—just pay money and show up...* **"**

Customer service .... ❸ $$ .... Prices
Age range .... 12 mths to 7 yrs

WWW.CHUCKECHEESE.COM

BELLEVUE—2239 148TH AVE NE (AT NE 24TH ST); 425.957.7665; SU-TH 9-10, F-SA 9-11

KENT—25817 104TH AVE SE (AT SE 256TH ST); 253.813.9000; SU-TH 9-10, F-SA 9-11

LYNNWOOD—3717 196TH ST SW (AT 36TH AVE W); 425.771.1195; SU-TH 9-10, F-SA 9-11

Colman Pool   ★★★★☆

"...*gorgeous saltwater pool... gets very crowded... amazing Olympic Mountain views and no chlorine to deal with...open during the summer only...have to park far away and walk through Lincoln Park to get to pool...* **"**

Customer service .... ❸ $$ .... Prices
Age range .... 3 mths and up

WWW.SEATTLE.GOV/PARKS/AQUATICS/COLMAN.HTM

WEST SEATTLE—8603 FAUNTLEROY WY SW (AT 46TH AVE SW (LINCOLN PARK)); 206.684.7494; CALL FOR SCHEDULE

Creative Dance Center   ★★★★★

"...*fantastic dance studio... plenty of classes for infants through adults... their emphasis is on movement and creativity and kids just have a blast... no recitals, which is a plus... a great place to take your kids... i've loved the nurturing baby and creative dance classes for toddlers... an afternoon of dance and celebration, nothing more and nothing less... wonderful...* **"**

Customer service .... ❺ $$$ .... Prices
Age range .... 2 mths and up

WWW.CREATIVEDANCE.ORG

NORTH SEATTLE—12577 DENSMORE AVE N (AT N 128TH ST); 206.363.7281; CHECK SCHEDULE ONLINE; PARKING LOT

Delridge Community Center   ★★★☆☆

"...*the community center is great for children... my kids love the wading pool... their indoor mini-gym is a great place to take toddlers on rainy days...* **"**

Customer service .... ❸ $$$ .... Prices
Age range .... 3 mths and up

HTTP://SEATTLE.GOV/PARKS

WEST SEATTLE—4501 DELRIDGE WY SW (AT 23RD AVE SW); 206.684.7423; M-F 1-9, T-TH 11-9, SA 10-5

Evans Pool   ★★★★★

"...*the infant swim class rocks... teachers are friendly and enthusiastic... interacted with all the kids... we started when our son was six months old, so most of the time was spent getting him used to being in the pool, but it was perfect... great price, great quality—clean pool and locker rooms...* **"**

Customer service .... ❺ $ .... Prices
Age range .... 3 mths and up

WWW.CITYOFSEATTLE.NET/PARKS/AQUATICS/EVANSPOOL.HTM

GREENLAKE/GREENWOOD/PHINNEY RIDGE—7201 E GREEN LAKE DR N (AT NE 72ND ST); 206.684.4961; CALL FOR SCHEDULE

Funtasia

"...good for older kids... ages 8 and up would probably be just right... a little large and exhausting with little ones... the ball pit is fun, but I'm always a little worried about how clean it is... your basic arcade with rides for older kids... **"**

Customer service........................ ❸ $$$.. Prices
Age range..................... 3 yrs and up

WWW.FAMILYFUNPARK.COM

EDMONDS—7212 220TH ST SW (AT 70TH AVE W); 425.775.2174; SU-TH 10-9:30 F-SA 10-11:30

Garfield Community Center

Age range.................. 3 mths and up

WWW.SEATTLE.GOV/PARKS/CENTERS/GARFIELDCC.HTM

CENTRAL DISTRICT—2323 E CHERRY ST (AT 23RD AVE); 206.684.4788; M W F 1-9, T TH 10-9, SA 10-5, SU 12-5

Green Lake Community Center

"...lots of activities for toddlers, plus a playroom... ideal for long rainy days... drop in and play as long as you like... age-appropriate toys, safe room, fun environment... they also have a pool... slides, mats, things to crawl through, and cars to push with your feet... great place to hook up with other moms... so cheap—$2... we take our son on a regular basis and we always have a blast... **"**

Customer service........................ ❸ $$... Prices
Age range............... 18 mths and up

WWW.CITYOFSEATTLE.NET/PARKS/CENTERS/GRNLAKCC.HTM

GREENLAKE/GREENWOOD/PHINNEY RIDGE—7201 E GREEN LAKE DR N (AT NE 72ND ST); 206.684.0780; CHECK SCHEDULE ONLINE

Gymagine Gymnastics

"...they offer several sessions for little ones, including a free play period... instructors are good with kids and pay attention to make sure everyone is included in the activities... obstacle course, balancing, climbing, rolling... good fun... $10 per session... **"**

Customer service........................ ❸ $$$.. Prices
Age range............... 18 mths and up

WWW.GYMAGINE.COM

MUKILTEO—3616 SOUTH RD (AT MUKILTEO SPEEDWAY); 425.513.8700; CALL FOR SCHEDULE

Gymboree Play & Music ★★★★★

"...we've done several rounds of classes with our kids and they absolutely love it... colorful, padded environment with tons of things to climb and play on... a good indoor place to meet other families and for kids to learn how to play with each other... the equipment and play areas are generally neat and clean... an easy birthday party spot... a guaranteed nap after class... costs vary, so call before showing up... **"**

Customer service........................ ❹ $$$.. Prices
Age range..................... birth to 5 yrs

WWW.GYMBOREE.COM

BALLARD—2622 NW MARKET ST (AT 26TH AVE NW); 206.783.3741; CHECK SCHEDULE ONLINE

ISSAQUAH—1175 NW GILMAN BLVD (AT TOWN & COUNTRY SQUARE); 425.392.8438; CHECK SCHEDULE ONLINE

LAURELHURST/SANDPOINT—7400 SANDPOINT WY NE (AT NE 74TH ST); 206.522.2045; CHECK SCHEDULE ONLINE

REDMOND—17625 NE 65TH ST (AT REDMOND TOWN CTR); 425.702.8811; CHECK SCHEDULE ONLINE

Gymnastics East

"...a local institution for fun toddler activities... we love their recreational movement class (Tiny Tot Fitness)—fun for toddlers... teaches good movement skills... the floors are padded and everyone is always smiling... a pleasure to come here... "

Customer service .... ❸ $$$ .... Prices
Age range .... 18 mths to 3 yrs

WWW.GYMNASTICSEAST.COM

BELLEVUE—13425 SE 30TH ST (AT RICHARDS RD SE); 425.644.8117; CALL FOR SCHEDULE

WOODINVILLE—19510 144TH AVE NE (AT N WOODINVILLE WAY); 425.486.8836; CHECK SCHEDULE ONLINE

Helene Madison Pool

Age range ....3 mths and up

WWW.CITYOFSEATTLE.NET/PARKS/AQUATICS/MADISONPOOL.HTM

NORTH SEATTLE—13401 MERIDIAN AVE N (AT N 130TH ST); 206.684.4979; CHECK SCHEDULE ONLINE

Hiawatha Community Center

Age range ....3 mths and up

WWW.SEATTLE.GOV/PARKS/CENTERS/HIAWATHA.HTM

WEST SEATTLE—2700 CALIFORNIA AVE SW (AT SW LANDER ST); 206.684.7441; M-T 1-9, W-F 11-9, SA 10-5, SU 12-5

High Point Community Center

Age range ....3 mths and up

WWW.SEATTLE.GOV/PARKS/CENTERS/HIGHPT.HTM

WEST SEATTLE—6920 34TH AVE SW (AT SW WILLOW ST); 206.684.7422; CHECK SCHEDULE ONLINE

Highland Community Center

"...for $2.50 your toddler can run around a gym filled with great toys for 2 to 3 hours... a must for the winter months... "

Customer service .... ❸ $$$ .... Prices
Age range ....6 mths and up

WWW.CITYOFBELLEVUE.ORG/PAGE.ASP?VIEW=32481

BELLEVUE—14224 BEL RED RD (AT 140TH AVE NE); 425.452.7686; CHECK SCHEDULE ONLINE

Hiram M Chittenden Locks

"...great place to take walks with small children... no tricycles allowed... the fish run during the spring and summer months is a lot of fun... fenced in area keeps children safe... lots of boats to watch... don't forget to take a walk through the gardens... it's free... "

Customer service .... ❸ $ .... Prices
Age range .... 2 yrs and up

WWW.NWS.USACE.ARMY.MIL/PUBLICMENU/MENU.CFM?SITENAME=LWSC&PAGENAME=MAINPAGE

BALLARD—3015 NW 54TH ST (AT 32ND AVE NW); 206.783.7059; CHECK SCHEDULE ONLINE

Imagine Children's Museum

"...a large indoor play space that lets kids play 'pretend' on so many different levels... the props are absolutely fantastic... very educational and encourages creativity and learning... plenty of things to play in—an airplane, a water area and a tree house... the 'Wiggles, Giggles, and Fun' class is a blast and great value for your money... "

Customer service .... ❺ $$ .... Prices

Age range................12 mths to 8 yrs

WWW.IMAGINECM.ORG

EVERETT—1502 WALL ST (AT HOYT AVE); 425.258.1006; T W SA 10-4, TH-F
10-5:30, SU 12-4

Jefferson Community Center

Age range.................. 3 mths and up

WWW.SEATTLE.GOV/PARKS/CENTERS/JEFFERCC.HTM

BEACON HILL—3801 BEACON AVE S (AT JEFFERSON PARK GOLF COURSE);
206.684.7481; CHECK SCHEDULE ONLINE

Jewish Community Center

"*...programs vary from facility to facility, but most JCCs have
outstanding early childhood programs... everything from mom and me
music classes to arts and crafts for older kids... a wonderful place to
meet other parents and make new friends... class fees are cheaper (if
not free) for members, but still quite a good deal for nonmembers... a
superb resource for new families looking for fun...* **"**

Customer service......................**❹** $$$..Prices

Age range.................. 3 mths and up

WWW.SJCC.ORG

MERCER ISLAND—3801 E MERCER WAY (AT SE 40TH ST); 206.232.7115;
CHECK SCHEDULE ONLINE

WEDGWOOD—8606 35TH AVE NE (AT NE 86TH ST); 206.526.8073; M-TH
7:30-6, F 7:30-5

Kelsey Creek Farm

"*...my young toddler loves visiting the animals at Kelsey Creek and
running up and down the pathways... free entertainment is always a
good thing... beautiful farm with pigs, sheep and ponies... the two play
areas are great... bring a picnic... free outdoor petting zoo... this was
my favorite when I was a kid and now I take my child here... perfect for
an outdoor birthday party...* **"**

Customer service......................**❹** $ ....Prices

Age range................ 12 mths and up

WWW.CITYOFBELLEVUE.ORG/PAGE.ASP?VIEW=2035

BELLEVUE—13204 SE 8TH ST (AT 140TH AVE S); 425.452.6885; CALL FOR
SCHEDULE

Kindermusik

"*...a wonderful intro to music and group play... well-trained
professionals make it both educational and fun for all ages... we started
with the mom & baby class and now my boy feels confident enough to
play without me... they have hundreds of programs nationwide... class
quality definitely varies from location to location, and teacher to
teacher... different classes for different ages... singing, movement,
dancing and rhythm—what's not to like?...* **"**

Customer service......................**❹** $$$..Prices

Age range.................. 2 mths to 7 yrs

WWW.KINDERMUSIK.COM

BELLEVUE—15241 NE 20TH ST (AT BEL-RED RD); 425.427.0984; CALL FOR
SCHEDULE

BELLEVUE—411 156TH AVE NE (AT NE 6TH ST); 425.868.5118; CHECK
SCHEDULE ONLINE

EVERETT—921 126TH ST SE (AT WALTHAM DR); 425.337.5328; CALL FOR
SCHEDULE; STREET PARKING

Laurelhurst Community Center ★★★★☆

"...set on top of the hill with wonderful views... a very spacious park is adjacent to the center... classes are fabulous—especially ballet and karate... the staff is nice and engaging with the kids... a wonderful resource for local parents...**"**

Customer service .... ❹ $$ .... Prices
Age range .... 2 yrs to 12 yrs

WWW.CITYOFSEATTLE.NET/PARKS/CENTERS/LAURELCC.HTM

LAURELHURST/SANDPOINT—4554 NE 41ST ST (AT 48TH AVE NE);
  206.684.7529; M W F 11-9, T TH 1-9

Little Artist, The ★★★★★

"...art classes in a wonderfully creative setting... the owner is super fun, and my daughter took to her immediately... lots of creative activities that I really enjoy doing with my child... my daughter loves the summer art camp... check the schedule for open art times... great for rainy days...**"**

Customer service .... ❺ $$ .... Prices
Age range .... 12 mths and up

WWW.LITTLEARTISTSTUDIO.COM

WEST SEATTLE—4740 CALIFORNIA AVE SW (AT SW ALASKA ST);
  206.935.4185; CHECK SCHEDULE ONLINE

Little Gym, The ★★★★☆

"...a well thought-out program of gym and tumbling geared toward different age groups... a clean facility, excellent and knowledgeable staff... we love the small-sized gym equipment and their willingness to work with kids with special needs... activities are fun and personalized to match the kids' age... great place for birthday parties with a nice party room—they'll organize and do everything for you...**"**

Customer service .... ❹ $$$ .... Prices
Age range .... 4 mths to 12 yrs

WWW.THELITTLEGYM.COM

BELLEVUE—1800 130TH AVE NE (AT NE 20TH ST); 425.885.3866; CALL FOR
  SCHEDULE

EVERETT—7207 EVERGREEN WY (AT MADISON ST); 425.348.4848; CHECK
  SCHEDULE ONLINE

KENMORE—6748 NE 181ST ST (AT 68TH AVE NE); 425.481.5889; CALL FOR
  SCHEDULE; FREE PARKING

KENT—18437 E VALLEY HWY (AT S 180TH ST); 425.656.0737; CALL FOR
  SCHEDULE

MAPLE LEAF/ROOSEVELT—7777 15TH AVE NE (AT NE 80TH ST);
  206.524.2623; CALL FOR SCHEDULE

Lowery C Mounger Pool ★★★★☆

"...the best pool—it's kept at a nice warm temp and offers an outdoor swimming experience... family swims are very popular and can get crowded, so try to get there early to stand in line and get a chair... the tots class wasn't very structured, it was taught by teenagers... i took a parent and me swim class and the teachers weren't as involved as I would have hoped... lots of cute splashing babies in the toddler pool...**"**

Customer service .... ❹ $$ .... Prices

WWW.CITYOFSEATTLE.NET/PARKS/AQUATICS/MOUNGER.HTM

QUEEN ANNE—2535 32ND AVE W (AT W SMITH ST); 206.684.4708; CHECK
  SCHEDULE ONLINE

Loyal Heights Community Center

"...big beautiful fields, indoor gym with weight room, and a wide selection of classes for kids and parents... great before and after school program..."

Customer service..........................❹ $$..Prices
Age range................ 18 mths and up
WWW.CITYOFSEATTLE.NET/PARKS/CENTERS/LOYALHTD.HTM
BALLARD—2101 NW 77TH ST (AT 21ST AVE NW); 206.684.4052; M W F 1-9, T TH 10-9, SA 10-5

Magnolia Community Center

"...newly renovated playground is awesome for toddlers... "

Customer service..........................❸ $$$..Prices
Age range.................. 3 mths and up
WWW.SEATTLE.GOV/PARKS/CENTERS/MAGNOLIACC.HTM
MAGNOLIA—2550 34TH AVE W (AT W SMITH ST); 206.386.4235; M-T F 1-9, W-TH 10-9, SA 10-5

Magnuson Community Center

Age range.................. 3 mths and up
WWW.SEATTLE.GOV/PARKS/CENTERS/MAGNUSON.HTM
LAURELHURST/SANDPOINT—7110 62ND AVE NE (AT NE 74TH ST); 206.684.4946; T-TH 1-9, F 10-9, SA 10-5

Market Street Music

"...we love the Kindermusik program offered here!.. both my kids have gone there since they were 5 months old—now that one is 4 1/2 and the other is 21 months, they are music fanatics, and I know Market Street Music is the reason why... lots of fun..."

Customer service..........................❺ $$$..Prices
KIRKLAND—1417 MARKET ST (AT 15TH AVE); 425.828.9841; CHECK SCHEDULE ONLINE

Meadowbrook Community Center

"...lots of programs for all ages... pool and swimming lessons... keeps the kids busy especially during the summer months... great water aerobic classes too..."

Customer service..........................❹ $ ....Prices
Age range.................. 3 mths and up
WWW.SEATTLE.GOV/PARKS/CENTERS/MEADOWBROOKCC.HTM
WEDGWOOD—10517 35TH AVE NE (AT NE 105TH ST); 206.684.7522; M W F 1-9, T TH 10-9, SA 10-5

Meadowbrook Pool

"...great pool for older kids... rope swing and two diving boards... wish the shallow end was bigger for the little ones... great deal on swim lessons and the instructors are great... changing area is a bit challenging as there is only one changing table... best pool in Seattle..."

Customer service..........................❹ $$..Prices
Age range.................. 6 mths and up
WWW.CI.SEATTLE.WA.US/PARKS/AQUATICS/MEADOWBROOKPOOL.HTM
WEDGWOOD—10515 35TH AVE NE (AT NE 105TH ST); 206.684.4989; CALL FOR SCHEDULE

Medgar Evers Pool

Age range .... 3 mths and up

WWW.SEATTLE.GOV/PARKS/AQUATICS/EVERSPOOL.HTM

CENTRAL DISTRICT—500 23RD AVE (AT E JEFFERSON ST); 206.684.4766;
  CHECK SCHEDULE ONLINE

Miller Community Center

"...fun toddler play groups... a wonderful neighborhood community center with lots of diversity... great facility... excellent selection of toys and climbing equipment...outdoor playground is great for kids and toddlers... "

Customer service .... ❸ $ .... Prices

Age range .... 3 yrs and up

WWW.CITYOFSEATTLE.NET/PARKS/CENTERS/MILLER.HTM

CAPITOL HILL—330 19TH AVE E (AT E THOMAS ST); 206.684.4753; M W F 1-9, T TH 10-9, SA 10-5, SU 12-5; PARKING LOT

Montlake Community Center

"...great indoor playground... tons of toys to play with... this community center is open six days a week and has later hours so it's a great option if your child is a morning napper... "

Customer service .... ❹ $ .... Prices

Age range .... 3 yrs and up

WWW.CITYOFSEATTLE.NET/PARKS/CENTERS/MONTLAKECC.HTM

MONTLAKE—1618 E CALHOUN ST (AT MONTLAKE PLAYFIELD);
  206.684.4736; M W F 11-9, T TH 1-9, SA 10-5

Mountlake Terrace Community Center

"...we took our baby to the recreational swim and had a blast... gets a bit crowded so get there early... great community center with tons of stuff for the kids to do... indoor playground, swimming lessons and a toddler pool for the little ones... pool is kept at a toasty 88 degrees... "

Customer service .... ❹ $$$ .... Prices

WWW.CI.MOUNTLAKE-TERRACE.WA.US/DEPARTMENTS/PARKS/

MOUNTLAKE TERRACE—5303 228TH ST SW (AT 53RD AVE); 425.776.9173;
  CHECK SCHEDULE ONLINE

Museum of Flight

"...wonderful museum with a great hands on exhibit for children... my 3-year-old was enthralled by the airplanes suspended from the ceiling... strollers recommended for younger children who have a tendency to wander off... they even have flight simulators... the cafe is great with a view of the runway and child appropriate food... great outing and if you go enough, get a membership—it's definitely worth it... "

Customer service .... ❹ $$ .... Prices

WWW.MUSEUMOFFLIGHT.ORG

TUKWILA—9404 E MARGINAL WY S (AT BOEING FIELD/KING CO INT'L AIRPORT); 206.764.5720; DAILY 10-5; PARKING AVAILABLE

Museum Of History & Industry

WWW.SEATTLEHISTORY.ORG

MONTLAKE—2700 24TH AVE E (AT WASHINGTON PARK); 206.324.1126;
  CHECK SCHEDULE ONLINE; PARKING AVAILABLE

Music Center of the Northwest ★★★☆☆

"...they offer Music Together programs for parents and tots... very fun environment in a serious music school setting... group classes as well as private instruction offered for older, more advanced kids... not cheap,

but just about the best music experience kids can experience... the staff is engaged and attentive... **"**

Customer service.........................❸ $$$...Prices

Age range................. 3 mths and up

WWW.MCNW.ORG

GREENLAKE/GREENWOOD/PHINNEY RIDGE—901 N 96TH ST (AT LINDEN AVE N); 206.526.8443; CALL FOR SCHEDULE

Music Together   ★★★★⯪

"*...the best mom and baby classes out there... music, singing, dancing—even instruments for tots to play with... liberal make-up policy, great venues, take home books, CDs and tapes which are different each semester... it's a national franchise so instructors vary and have their own style... different age groups get mixed up which makes it a good learning experience for all involved... the highlight of our week—grandma always comes along... be prepared to have your tot sing the songs at home, in the car—everywhere...* **"**

Customer service.........................❹ $$$...Prices

Age range................. 2 mths to 5 yrs

WWW.MUSICTOGETHER.COM

KENT—253.630.1453; CALL FOR SCHEDULE

MERCER ISLAND—206.525.3546; CALL FOR SCHEDULE

GREENLAKE/GREENWOOD/PHINNEY RIDGE—206.782.1010; CALL FOR SCHEDULE

NORTH SEATTLE—206.526.8443; CALL FOR SCHEDULE

Musik Nest, The   ★★★★☆

"*...my child has been taking music classes since she was a baby and has continued to love it... fabulous, colorful and fun... provides so much musical stimulation... the teachers are wonderful... they offer KinderMusik classes and more...classes are offered in Issaquah, Bellevue, and Federal Way...* **"**

Customer service.........................❹ $$...Prices

Age range....................birth to 7 yrs

ISSAQUAH—317 NW GILMAN BLVD (AT 224TH AVE SE); 425.427.0984; CALL FOR SCHEDULE; STREET PARKING

Musik Place, The   ★★★★☆

"*...a small, intimate setting for enjoying some quality time with my baby... the classes are fun and definitely educational... we love coming here to play and sing with all the other families... you get a CD and song book and before you know it, you're humming the songs all day long... such a positive experience for all involved...* **"**

Customer service.........................❸ $$$...Prices

Age range................. 3 mths to 7 yrs

WWW.THEMUSIKPLACE.COM

REDMOND—2503 152ND AVE NE (AT NE 24TH ST); 425.556.5990; CALL FOR SCHEDULE

New Eden Music Academy   ★★★★⯪

"*...music and fun for babies and older kids... classes are organized around ability and children's age... Nancy (the owner) is great and really knows how to get the kids engaged—singing and touching/playing different instruments... I like that kids can continue to 'study' music with her as they get older... a wonderful introduction to music....* **"**

Customer service.........................❺ $$$...Prices

Age range....................birth to 9 yrs

WWW.NEWEDENMUSIC.ORG

MAGNOLIA—3007 22ND AVE W (AT W BARRETT ST); 206.691.0621; CHECK
   SCHEDULE ONLINE; FREE PARKING

Northwest Aerials School

66...gymnastics, swimming and dance for children ages 12 months and
up... they also do birthday parties... drop-in parent-child gymnastics
classes that are great for busy toddlers on a wet day... in-ground
trampoline for running and bouncing... **99**

Customer service .... ❸ $$$ .... Prices
Age range .... 15 mths to 5 yrs
WWW.NWAERIALS.COM

KIRKLAND—12440 128TH LN NE (AT NE 124TH ST); 425.823.2665; CALL FOR
   SCHEDULE; FREE PARKING

Northwest Puppet Center

66...a cool theater with a great outdoor play area... the museum is
extremely small, but worth a peek... the marionettes are fun!.. great
stories for kids 2 years and up... always creative and fun... get there
early for good seats... the puppet center puts on the best shows...
friendly staff... parking could be better... **99**

Customer service .... ❺ $$ .... Prices
Age range .... 3 yrs to 11 yrs
WWW.NWPUPPET.ORG

MAPLE LEAF/ROOSEVELT—9123 15TH AVE NE (AT NE 91ST ST);
   206.523.2579; CHECK SCHEDULE ONLINE

Odyssey Maritime Discovery
Center

66...a waterfront gem... best for kids that are old enough to ask
questions about things like fishing and the ocean... rarely crowded...
highly hands-on and interactive... fun way for your little mariner to act
out fanta-seas... a little more 'grown up' than the aquarium... **99**

Customer service .... ❹ $$ .... Prices
WWW.ODY.ORG

WATERFRONT—2205 ALASKAN WAY (AT WALL ST); 206.374.4000; CHECK
   SCHEDULE ONLINE; FREE PARKING

Orca Swim School

66...I love their approach to swimming lessons... multiple locations
throughout the Seattle area make it easy to find a class that works for
you... warm water in several nice facilities... their small class sizes are
the best—you really feel like you're getting your money's worth...
classes held in Bellevue, Redmond, and Seattle... **99**

Customer service .... ❸ $$$ .... Prices
Age range .... 3 mths and up
WWW.ORCASWIMSCHOOL.COM

BELLEVUE—601 143RD AVE (AT NE 8TH ST); 425.793.9870; CHECK
   SCHEDULE ONLINE

REDMOND—23301 REDMOND-FALL CITY RD; 425.793.9870; CHECK
   SCHEDULE ONLINE

QUEEN ANNE—11 W ALOHA ST (AT BAYVIEW MANOR); 425.793.9870; CHECK
   SCHEDULE ONLINE

Pacific Science Center

66...toddler town with a water table, an area with rabbits and other
small mammals, a marine animal touch tank, a bug exhibit, a butterfly
exhibit (similar to the one in the zoo, but indoors and with no extra
cost)... lots of science exhibits to occupy older children... best bet is to
buy a membership to the Science Center... get one combined one with

the Children's Museum... worth a yearly pass just for the train show and the Imax movies... perfect on a rainy day... **99**

Customer service.......................**4** $$$.. Prices
Age range.....................2 yrs and up
WWW.PACSCI.ORG

SEATTLE CENTER—200 2ND AVE N (AT JOHN ST); 206.443.2001; DAILY 10-6

Pike Place Market   ★★★★⯪

66...a place where eclectic artisans sell their wares... great selection of eats... skip the stroller (too many stairs and gets very crowded)... check out the fish throwers... spectacular on a sunny day... great views... the vendors are generally kid friendly... lots of eye candy... curious kids love it here... bring some cash not all vendors take credit cards... a delightful cartoonist will create a family portrait at a reasonable price... a wonderful and free way to expose your children to the sights, sounds and smells of an outdoor market... **99**

Customer service.......................**3** $$.. Prices
Age range.................. 6 mths and up
WWW.PIKEPLACEMARKET.ORG

PIKE PLACE MARKET—1531 WESTERN AVE (AT PIKE ST); 206.682.7453; M-
SA 9-6, SU 11-5

Pratt Park Water Spray

Age range.................. 3 mths and up
WWW.CITYOFSEATTLE.NET/PARKS/PARKSPACES/PRATTPARK/WADINGPOOL.H
TM

CENTRAL DISTRICT—1800 S MAIN ST (AT S JACKSON ST); 206.684.7796;
CHECK SCHEDULE ONLINE

Pump It Up   ★★★★☆

66...huge warehouse type buildings filled with a variety of bounce houses and inflatable obstacle courses... colorful, padded slides and bouncers... the birthday party I went to was a blast—kids and adults were having way too much fun... they have an open gym a couple of days a week for $5 per tot—a great way to jump around and burn off some energy... $200-$250 for a really easy party that will have everybody smiling... **99**

Customer service.......................**4** $$.. Prices
Age range.................. 2 yrs to 12 yrs
WWW.PUMPITUPPARTY.COM

KIRKLAND—11605 NE 116TH ST (OFF HWY 405); 425.820.2297; CHEKC
SCHEDULE ONLINE

Queen Anne Community Center   ★★★★⯪

66...great toys... Tuesday and Thursday mornings on bad-weather days the gym is open for kids (1 to 4-years-old) to come and run around from 10 am-noon... it's fantastic... kids get to know each other in the neighborhood and from all over town... a great place to meet other moms in the area... **99**

Customer service.......................**4** $ .... Prices
Age range................12 mths to 4 yrs
WWW.SEATTLE.GOV/PARKS/CENTERS/QUEENANNECC.HTM

QUEEN ANNE—1901 1ST AVE W (AT W HOWE ST); 206.386.4240; M-T F 1-9,
W-TH 10-9; STREET PARKING

Queen Anne Pool   ★★★★☆

66...swimming lessons beginning at six months all the way to adult... the staff is great and seem to really care about the kids... a very good competitive swim program and diving classes... reasonable prices... the *pool is very clean... can be a bit cold at times especially for little ones... lessons are taught as a group...* **"**

Customer service .... **⑤** $$ .... Prices

WWW.SEATTLE.GOV/PARKS/AQUATICS/QUEENANNEPOOL.HTM

QUEEN ANNE—1920 1ST AVE W (AT W HOWE ST); 206.386.4282; CHECK
  SCHEDULE ONLINE

Rainier Beach Community Center

Age range .... 3 mths and up

WWW.CITYOFSEATTLE.NET/PARKS/CENTERS/RAINIERBEACH.HTM

RAINIER BEACH—8825 RAINIER AVE S (AT S HENDERSON ST);
  206.386.1925; M 1-9, T-F 11:30-9, SA 10-5, SU 12-5

Rainier Beach Pool ★★★☆☆

" *...a nice indoor facility that offers an inexpensive place to swim... lessons are good and our kids always have a fun time here—first the lesson, then family swim... the changing area can get really crowded at times... lots of different programs for kids and adults...* **"**

Customer service .... **❷** $ .... Prices

Age range .... 6 mths and up

WWW.SEATTLE.GOV/PARKS/AQUATICS/RAINIERBEACHPOOL.HTM

RAINIER BEACH—8825 RAINIER AVE S (AT S HENDERSON ST);
  206.386.1944; CHECK SCHEDULE ONLINE

Rainier Community Center ★★★☆☆

" *...perfect on a rainy day... indoor gym with lots of toys for toddlers... great place to meet other parents in the neighborhood... $10 punch card buys five visits per family...* **"**

Customer service .... **❸** $ .... Prices

Age range .... 6 mths and up

WWW.SEATTLE.GOV./PARKS/CENTERS/RAINIERCC.HTM

COLUMBIA CITY—4600 38TH AVE S (AT S ALASKA ST); 206.386.1919; M F 1-
  9, T-TH 11-9, SA 10-5, SU 12-5

Ravenna Eckstein Community Center ★★★★½

" *...programs are well thought out and the staff tries hard to meet all demands... lots of toys and very safe indoor playroom... open gym for children over three years old and well stocked play room for those under three... limited parking... gets crowded on a rainy day, but still a great place to go...* **"**

Customer service .... **❹** $ .... Prices

Age range .... 2 yrs and up

WWW.CITYOFSEATTLE.NET/PARKS/CENTERS/RAVENNAECKSTEINCC.HTM

WEDGEWOOD/RAVENNA—6535 RAVENNA AVE NE (AT NE 65TH ST);
  206.684.7535; M W 10-9, T TH-F 1-9, SA 10-5

Redmond Town Center ★★★★☆

" *...great place to go for a stroll in the summer... there are water fountains that the kids can play in... also a lot of kid-friendly shops and restaurants... the kids love it, and it gives the parents something to do as well...* **"**

Customer service .... **❹** $ .... Prices

WWW.SHOPREDMONDTOWNCENTER.COM

REDMOND—16495 NE 74TH ST (AT 166TH AVE NE); 425.867.0808

Reel Moms (Loews Theatres) ★★★★☆

"...not really an activity for kids, but rather something you can easily do with your baby... first-run movies for people with babies... the sound is low, the lights turned up and no one cares if your baby cries... packed with moms changing diapers all over the place... so nice to be able to go see current movies... don't have to worry about baby noise... relaxed environment with moms, dads and babies wandering all over... the staff is very friendly and there is a real community feel... a great idea and very well done... "

Customer service.........................❹ $$..Prices
Age range.................. 3 mths to 2 yrs
WWW.ENJOYTHESHOW.COM/REELMOMS

DOWNTOWN—1501 7TH AVE (AT PIKE ST); 206.622.2434; CHECK SCHEDULE
   ONLINE

WOODINVILLE—17640 GARDEN WY (AT 138TH AVE NE); 425.482.6538;
   CHECK SCHEDULE ONLINE

Safe N Sound Swimming ★★★★☆

"...lovely setting... the staff is very accommodating and the pool is nice and warm... pricey, but well worth it... changing rooms are a bit cold... my kids made rapid strides once they started swimming lessons here... only downfall is the parent/tot classes are only offered on weekday mornings... "

Customer service.........................❹ $$$..Prices
Age range................... 7 mths and up
WWW.SNSSWIM.COM

QUEEN ANNE—2040 WESTLAKE AVE N (AT CROCKETT ST); 206.285.9279;
   CHECK SCHEDULE ONLINE; STREET PARKING

Seattle Aquarium ★★★★★

"...hands-on tide pools... you even get a chance to feed the sea urchins... children and young babies are mesmerized by this place... beautiful representation of Pacific Northwest sea life... arts and crafts— we made an octopus windsock the last time we were there... step into the dome and surround yourself with fish... kids and adults get a kick out of this—be prepared to do a lot of lifting for toddlers to see the tanks... if you go enough get a membership, it's worth it... "

Customer service.........................❹ $$..Prices
Age range.................. 6 mths and up
WWW.SEATTLEAQUARIUM.ORG

WATERFRONT—1483 ALASKAN WY (AT FOOT OF PIKE ST); 206.386.4300;
   DAILY 9:30-7; PARKING AVAILABLE

Seattle Center House

Age range................ 12 mths and up
WWW.SEATTLECENTER.COM

SEATTLE CENTER—305 HARRISON ST (AT 5TH AVE N); 206.684.7200; SU-TH
   11-6, F-SA 11-8

Seattle Central Community College (Parent Child Center) ★★★★☆

"...there is a whole preschool co-op system that is run through the college—it starts with an infant co-op class, then has toddler, pre-3 and 3-5 yr programs at different sites in the community... the co-op programs are fun and affordable... a great way to have fun with your child while meeting other new parents... very educational... "

Customer service.........................❸ $$$..Prices
Age range.....................birth to 3 yrs
WWW.SEATTLECENTRAL.ORG/PARENTCHILDCENTER

CAPITOL HILL—1700 BROADWAY (AT E PINE ST); 206.587.6902; CHECK
   SCHEDULE ONLINE; STREET & GARAGE @ HARVARD & PINE

Seattle Gymnastics Academy

"...wonderful parent & tot gymnastics and tumbling classes... classes
are about 45 minutes long and very fun... they also have drop in
classes, but you should call to check the schedule before showing up...
a seven week session is about $80... **"**

Customer service .... ❸ $$$ .... Prices
Age range ....12 mths and up

WWW.SEATTLEGYMNASTICS.COM

NORTH SEATTLE—12535 26TH AVE NE (AT NE 125TH ST); 206.362.7447;
   CALL FOR SCHEDULE

Seattle Symphony / Benaroya
Hall

"...great opportunity for your preschooler to experience the symphony
during 'kids symphony days'... a bit pricey... general admission
seating... if you'd like a specific day or time buy tickets ASAP, they sell
out fast... check out Tiny Tots half hour music session for smaller
children... the Tiny Tots program is short and they understand that kids
are going to be squirmy... they make an effort to have it be
interactive... **"**

Customer service .... ❹ $$$ .... Prices
Age range ....6 mths and up

WWW.SEATTLESYMPHONY.ORG

DOWNTOWN—200 UNIVERSITY ST (AT 2ND AVE); 206.215.4747; CALL FOR
   HOURS

Soundbridge

"...wonderful music classes designed for tots and their parents...
check out the musical story time, and the music and movement
classes... there is a big room with lots of instruments and the kids love
to play with them... interactive displays as well... my son can't get
enough of it... a program of the Seattle Symphony and located in the
same building... **"**

Customer service .... ❺ $$ .... Prices
Age range ....3 mths to 7 yrs

WWW.SEATTLESYMPHONY.ORG/SOUNDBRIDGE

DOWNTOWN—200 UNIVERSITY ST (AT 2ND AVE); 206.336.6600; T-SU 10-4

South 47 Farm

"...the u-pick is a blast for everyone... lost of veggies, berries, herbs
and flowers... the staff is super friendly and seem to love the kids...
during the fall months there is a corn maze, hay rides, pumpkin patch,
and a small petting zoo... we go every year, sometimes more than
once... reasonable prices... beautiful location tucked into the
Sammammish River Valley... **"**

Customer service .... ❺ $$ .... Prices
Age range .... 2 yrs and up

WWW.FARMLLC.COM

REDMOND—15410 NORTHEAST 124TH ST (AT RTE 202); 425.869.9777;
   DAILY 10-5:30

South Park Community Center

Age range ....3 mths and up

WWW.SEATTLE.GOV/PARKS/CENTERS/SOUTHPARK.HTM

SOUTH PARK—8319 8TH AVE S (AT S THISTLE ST); 206.684.7451; M-TH 12-
9, F 11-9, SA 1-5

Southwest Community Center

WWW.SEATTLE.GOV/PARKS/CENTERS/SWCC.HTM

WEST SEATTLE—2801 SW THISTLE ST (AT 28TH AVE SW); 206.684.7438; M W
10-9, T TH-F 1-9, SA 10-4

Southwest Pool

Age range................. 3 mths and up

WWW.SEATTLE.GOV/PARKS/AQUATICS/SWPOOL.HTM

WEST SEATTLE—2801 SW THISTLE ST (AT 28TH AVE SW); 206.684.7440;
CHECK SCHEDULE ONLINE

Spectrum Dance Studio ★★★★☆

"...excellent classes for children of all ages... they offer everything
from drama to ballet and jazz dance... the teachers are fun and
patient... they offer a great movement class for parents and tots... sign
up for a class series to reduce the cost of individual classes... **"**

Customer service........................❺ $$...Prices
Age range.....................3 yrs and up

WWW.SPECTRUMDANCE.ORG

MADRONA—800 LAKE WASHINGTON BLVD (AT 38TH AVE); 206.325.4161;
CHECK SCHEDULE ONLINE; FREE PARKING

The Children's Museum Of
Seattle ★★★★★

"...lots to do for all ages... encourages creativity, gives exposure to
other cultures and traditions and is a safe place for kids to play...
perfect activity for dark, wet Seattle winters... parking is far away...
changing exhibits and tons of hands on opportunities for kids... can get
a membership for frequent visits... staff were friendly and helpful.. a bit
pricey... my son can't get enough of this place, I practically have to
drag him away when we have to go... wonderful variety of activities for
children... wish they would bring in new stuff, can get a little boring for
adults... gets crowded so keep a close eye on your little ones—there are
all sorts of nooks and crannies to lose them in... **"**

Customer service........................❹ $$...Prices
Age range................... 2 yrs to 12 yrs

WWW.THECHILDRENSMUSEUM.ORG

LOWER QUEEN ANNE/SEATTLE CENTER—305 HARRISON ST (AT 5TH AVE N);
206.441.1768; M-F 10-5, SA-SU 10-6

University Village ★★★★☆

"...open-air shopping center... very stroller friendly and there is a
playground in the center... parking is next to impossible if you go at
peak times... I find it difficult to navigate, it's always packed... lots of
shops... my son loves the outdoor playground and they even have little
cars and bikes... stores seem overpriced... **"**

Customer service........................❹ $$$.......................................Prices

WWW.UVILLAGE.COM

UNIVERSITY DISTRICT/UNIVERSITY VILLAGE—2623 NE UNIVERSITY VILLAGE
(AT 25TH AVE NE); 206.523.0622; M-F 8-6, SA-SU 11-4; PARKING
AVAILABLE

Wading Pools ★★★★☆

"...the wading pools are the perfect spot for us during the hot
summer months... nice venue for toddlers to meet other toddlers... did I
mention that they're free!.. sometimes the older kids need to tone it
down a bit but you can usually find a quiet corner for your little one to
play... pools are generally located in or near parks so you can always
take a picnic with you... wading pool hotline (updated each day) gives

daily weather report and information on pool hours of operation... they do get crowded, but all-in-all they're a wonderful resource for families with young children... **"**

Customer service .... ❹ $ .... Prices
Age range .... 3 mths to 10 yrs

WWW.CI.SEATTLE.WA.US/PARKS/AQUATICS/WADINGPOOLS.HTM

BEACON HILL—1820 13TH AVE S (AT BEACON HILL PLAYFIELD); 206.684.7796; CALL FOR SCHEDULE

BEACON HILL—2820 S MYRTLE ST (AT BEACON AVE S); 206.684.7796; CHECK SCHEDULE ONLINE

CAPITOL HILL—1247 15TH AVE E (AT E GALER ST); 206.684.7796; CHECK SCHEDULE ONLINE

CAPITOL HILL—330 19TH AVE E (AT E THOMAS ST); 206.684.7796; CHECK SCHEDULE ONLINE

CENTRAL DISTRICT—2150 S NORMAN ST (AT 21ST AVE S); 206.684.7796; CHECK SCHEDULE ONLINE

FIRST HILL—1635 11TH AVE (AT BOBBY MORRIS PLAYFIELD); 206.684.7796; CHECK SCHEDULE ONLINE

GEORGETOWN—750 S HOMER ST (AT GEORGETOWN PLAYFIELD); 206.684.7796; CHECK SCHEDULE ONLINE

GREENLAKE/GREENWOOD/PHINNEY RIDGE—923 NW 54TH ST (AT 9TH AVE NW); 206.684.7796; CHECK SCHEDULE ONLINE

GREENLAKE—N 73RD ST (AT W GREEN LAKE); 206.684.7796; CHECK SCHEDULE ONLINE

LAURELHURST/SANDPOINT—7400 SAND POINT WAY NE (AT NE 74TH ST); 206.684.7796; CHECK SCHEDULE ONLINE

LESCHI—3233 E SPRUCE ST (AT 32ND AVE); 206.684.7796; CHECK SCHEDULE ONLINE

LESCHI—352 MARTIN LUTHER KING WAY (AT E ALDER ST); 206.684.7796; CHECK SCHEDULE ONLINE

NORTH SEATTLE—12800 1ST AVE NE (AT NORTHACRES PARK); 206.684.7796; CHECK SCHEDULE ONLINE

NORTH SEATTLE—13035 LINDEN AVE N (AT N 130TH ST); 206.684.7796; CHECK SCHEDULE ONLINE

NORTH SEATTLE—1590 NW 90TH (AT 15TH AVE NW); 206.684.7796; CHECK SCHEDULE ONLINE

NORTH SEATTLE—9053 1ST AVE NW (AT NW 90TH ST); 206.684.7796; CHECK SCHEDULE ONLINE

QUEEN ANNE—160 HOWE ST (AT WARREN AVE N); 206.684.7796; CHECK SCHEDULE ONLINE

SOUTH PARK—8319 8TH AVE S (AT S THISTLE ST); 206.684.7796; CHECK SCHEDULE ONLINE

WALLINGFORD/FREMONT—4219 WALLINGFORD AVE N (AT N 42ND ST); 206.684.7796; CHECK SCHEDULE ONLINE

WEDGEWOOD/RAVENNA—4408 NE 70TH ST (AT 45TH AVE NE); 206.684.7796; CHECK SCHEDULE ONLINE

WEDGEWOOD/RAVENNA—5520 RAVENNA AVE NE (AT 55TH ST); 206.684.7796; CHECK SCHEDULE ONLINE

WEDGEWOOD/RAVENNA—7700 25TH AVE NE (AT NE 77TH ST); 206.684.7796; CHECK SCHEDULE ONLINE

WEST SEATTLE—1100 SW CLOVERDALE ST (AT HIGHLAND PARK PLAYGROUND); 206.684.7796; CHECK SCHEDULE ONLINE

WEST SEATTLE—2700 CALIFORNIA AVE SW (AT SW LANDER ST); 206.684.7796; CHECK SCHEDULE ONLINE

WEST SEATTLE—2805 SW HOLDEN ST (AT 28TH AVE SW); 206.684.7796; CHECK SCHEDULE ONLINE

WEST SEATTLE—4501 DELRIDGE WY SW (AT 23RD AVE SW); 206.684.7796; CHECK SCHEDULE ONLINE

WEST SEATTLE—8011 FAUNTLEROY WAY SW (AT 46TH AVE SW); 206.684.7796; CALL FOR HOURS; FREE PARKING

Waterbabies

"...*a guided water experience for children which uses songs, games and toys to build confidence, develop motor skills and water safety... you can take class at a private pool... our daughter started at nine months and now is a terrific swimmer and loves the water... one of the best activities we signed up for...* **"**

Customer service...........................❹ $$$..Prices
Age range.................3 mths to 12 yrs
WWW.WATERBABIES.NET

BELLEVUE—10001 NE 1ST ST (AT 100TH AVE NE); 425.643.3533; CHECK SCHEDULE ONLINE; STREET PARKING

BELLEVUE—16702 SE 11TH ST (BTWN 166TH AND 167TH AVES SE); 425.643.3533; CHECK SCHEDULE ONLINE

EVERETT—505 128TH ST SE (AT 4TH DR SE); 425.643.3533; CHECK SCHEDULE ONLINE

ISSAQUAH—4221 228TH AVE SE (AT SE 40TH ST); 425.643.3533; CHECK SCHEDULE ONLINE

KIRKLAND—6601 132ND AVE NE (NE 70TH PL); 425.643.3533; CHECK SCHEDULE ONLINE

Wild Waves & Enchanted Village

"...*expensive and crowded with long lines... they won't let you bring in any of your own food... filthy children's changing room... really not for young children, best for the 8-17 year olds...* **"**

Customer service...........................❸ $$$..Prices
Age range................ 12 mths and up
WWW.SIXFLAGS.COM/PARKS/ENCHANTEDVILLAGE

FEDERAL WAY—36201 ENCHANTED PKWY S (AT HWY 5); 253.661.8029; CALL FOR HOURS

Woodland Park Zoo ★★★★★

"...*animals are happy, they have room to roam... most exhibits are free of bars or cages... docents are informative... you can spend an hour or an entire day at the zoo... pony rides on the weekends... even in the rain there's lots to do... they rent strollers and wagons for a few dollars... elephants, Siamang monkeys, orangutans, gorillas, wild African dogs and African Savannah critters are favorites for our toddler... nice field to have a picnic...* **"**

Customer service...........................❹ $$..Prices
Age range..................6 mths and up
WWW.ZOO.ORG

GREENLAKE/GREENWOOD/PHINNEY RIDGE—601 N 59TH ST (AT FREMONT AVE N); 206.684.4800; DAILY 9:30-6

Yesler Community Center

Age range.................. 3 mths and up
WWW.SEATTLE.GOV/PARKS/CENTERS/YESLERCC.HTM

CENTRAL DISTRICT—835 E YESLER WY (AT INTERSTATE HWY 5); 206.386.1245; M W F 1-9, T TH 10-9, SA 10-5

YMCA

"...*most of the Ys in the area have classes and activities for kids... swimming, gym classes, dance—even play groups for the really little*

ones... ... some facilities are nicer than others, but in general their programs are worth checking out... prices are more than reasonable for what is offered... the best bang for your buck... they have it all—great programs that meet the needs of a diverse range of families... check out their camps during the summer and school breaks... **"**

Customer service .... ❹ $$ .... Prices
Age range ....3 mths and up

WWW.SEATTLEYMCA.ORG

AUBURN—1620 PERIMETER RD SW (AT 15TH ST SW); 253.833.2770; M-F 5-9, SA 8-6, SU 11-6; FREE PARKING

BELLEVUE—14230 BEL-RED RD (AT 140TH ST); 425.746.9900; CALL FOR SCHEDULE; FREE PARKING

BELLEVUE—5225 119TH AVE SE (AT SE 52ND ST); 425.644.8417; M-F 6:30-8:30, F 6:30-6:30, SA 9-3; PARKING LOT

BELLEVUE—777 108TH AVE NE (AT NE 8TH ST); 425.451.2422; M-F 6-8; PARKING LOT

BOTHELL—11811 NE 195TH ST (AT 120TH AVE NE); 425.485.9797; CALL FOR SCHEDULE; PARKING LOT

CENTRAL DISTRICT—1700 23RD AVE (AT E MADISON ST); 206.322.6969; CHECK SCHEDULE ONLINE

DOWNTOWN—909 4TH AVE (AT MARION ST); 206.382.5000; CALL FOR SCHEDULE; STREET PARKING

ISSAQUAH—4221 228TH SE AVE (AT SE 40TH ST); 425.391.4840; M-F 6-9, SA 8-4, SU 12-4; PARKING LOT

REDMOND—10315 CEDAR PARK CRES NE (AT NE ALDER CREST DR); 425.868.4399; CHECK SCHEDULE ONLINE

SHORELINE—1220 NE 175TH ST (AT 15TH AVE NE); 206.364.1700; M-F 6-10, SA 8-5, SU 12-5; PARKING LOT

UNIVERSITY DISTRICT/UNIVERSITY VILLAGE—5003 12TH AVE NE (AT NE 50TH ST); 206.524.1400; M-F 6-10, SA 8-5, SU 12-5

WEST SEATTLE—4515 36TH AVE SW (AT SW OREGON ST); 206.382.5003; CALL FOR SCHEDULE

WEST SEATTLE—9260 CALIFORNIA AVE SW (AT SW ROXBURY ST); 206.937.1000; M-F 7:30-9:30, SA 8-5, SU 1-5; PARKING LOT

Tacoma

"lila picks"

- ★ Northwest Trek Wildlife Park
- ★ Point Defiance Zoo & Aquarium
- ★ The Little Gym

Barnes & Noble ★★★★⯪

"...*wonderful weekly story times for all ages and frequent author visits for older kids... lovely selection of books and the story times are fun and very well done... they have evening story times—we put our kids in their pjs and come here as a treat before bedtime... they read a story, and then usually have a little craft or related coloring project... times vary by location so give them a call...* **"**

Customer service.........................❹ $ ....Prices
Age range................. 6 mths to 6 yrs
WWW.BARNESANDNOBLE.COM
LAKEWOOD—5711 MAIN ST SW (AT 108TH ST SW); 253.983.0852; CALL FOR SCHEDULE

Borders Books ★★★★☆

"...*very popular weekly story time held in most branches (check the web site for locations and times)... call before you go since they are very popular and get extremely crowded... kids love the unique blend of songs, stories and dancing... Mr. Hatbox's appearances are a delight to everyone (unfortunately he doesn't make appearances at all locations)... large children's section is well categorized and well priced... they make it fun for young tots to browse through the board-book section by hanging toys around the shelves... the low-key cafe is a great place to have coffee with your baby and leaf through some magazines...* **"**

Customer service.........................❹ $ ....Prices
Age range................. 6 mths to 6 yrs
WWW.BORDERSSTORES.COM
PUYALLUP—3829 S MERIDIAN (AT 112TH ST E); 253.845.8751; CALL FOR SCHEDULE
TACOMA—2508 S 38TH ST (AT S PINE ST); 253.473.9111; CALL FOR SCHEDULE

Build-A-Bear Workshop ★★★⯪☆

"...*design and make your own bear—it's a dream come true... the most cherished toy my daughter owns... they even come with birth certificates... the staff is fun and knows how to play along with the kids' excitement... the basic stuffed animal is only about $15, but the extras add up quickly... great for field trips, birthdays and special occasions... how darling—my nephew is 8 years old now, and still sleeps with his favorite bear...* **"**

Customer service.........................❹ $$$.......................................Prices

Age range .... 3 yrs and up

WWW.BUILDABEAR.COM

TACOMA—4502 S STEELE ST (AT TACOMA MALL); 253.671.2327; M-SA 10-9,
SU 11-7; MALL PARKING

Chuck E Cheese's

"...lots of games, rides, playrooms and very greasy food... the kids can play and eat and parents can unwind a little... a good rainy day activity... the kids love the food, but it's a bit greasy for adults... always crowded and crazy—but that's half the fun... can you ever go wrong with pizza, games and singing?.. although they do have a salad bar for adults, remember, you're not going for the food—you're going because your kids will love it... just about the easiest birthday party around—just pay money and show up..."

Customer service .... ❸ $$ .... Prices

Age range .... 12 mths to 7 yrs

WWW.CHUCKECHEESE.COM

TACOMA—4911 TACOMA MALL BLVD (AT TACOMA MALL); 253.473.3078; SU-
TH 9-10, F-SA 9-11; MALL PARKING

Gymboree Play & Music

"...we've done several rounds of classes with our kids and they absolutely love it... colorful, padded environment with tons of things to climb and play on... a good indoor place to meet other families and for kids to learn how to play with each other... the equipment and play areas are generally neat and clean... an easy birthday party spot... a guaranteed nap after class... costs vary, so call before showing up..."

Customer service .... ❹ $$$ .... Prices

Age range .... birth to 5 yrs

WWW.GYMBOREE.COM

UNIVERSITY PLACE—3617 BRIDGEPORT WAY W (AT 35TH ST W);
253.589.5126; CHECK SCHEDULE ONLINE

Little Gym, The

★★★★★

"...a well thought-out program of gym and tumbling geared toward different age groups... a clean facility, excellent and knowledgeable staff... we love the small-sized gym equipment and their willingness to work with kids with special needs... activities are fun and personalized to match the kids' age... great place for birthday parties with a nice party room—they'll organize and do everything for you..."

Customer service .... ❹ $$$ .... Prices

Age range .... 4 mths to 12 yrs

WWW.THELITTLEGYM.COM

PUYALLUP—3850 S MERIDIAN (AT 112TH ST E); 253.435.7400; CALL FOR
SCHEDULE

Northwest Trek Wildlife Park

★★★★★

"...go when it's sunny and bring a picnic (food is limited)... Northwest Trek is a wonderful way to introduce children to wildlife in a safe and comfortable way... staff and volunteers are a wealth of info... tram ride is 45 minutes... hands-on materials available if you ask ahead of time... walking trails are easy to follow and offer easy viewing of most animals... beaver den was a favorite for my troop... brand new outdoor play area and exhibit designed for young children ..."

Customer service .... ❹ $$ .... Prices

Age range .... 2 yrs and up

WWW.NWTREK.ORG

EATONVILLE—11610 TREK DR (AT HORSESHOE DR E); 360.832.6117; CHECK
SCHEDULE ONLINE

activities & outings

Point Defiance Zoo & Aquarium

"...animal shows, marine lab, tiny tales are some the many special events at this local zoo... for children of all ages... trails are easily accessible with a stroller... dress warmly in the fall/winter... ride bikes and scooters, play at Owens Beach and check out all the animals... don't miss the zoo lights around Christmas time... beautiful location... **"**

Customer service........................**❹** $$..Prices

Age range.................. 3 mths and up

WWW.PDZA.ORG

TACOMA—5400 N PEARL ST (AT N PARK AVE); 253.591.5337; DAILY 9:30-5; PARKING LOT

YMCA

"...most of the Ys in the area have classes and activities for kids... swimming, gym classes, dance—even play groups for the really little ones... ... some facilities are nicer than others, but in general their programs are worth checking out... prices are more than reasonable for what is offered... the best bang for your buck... they have it all—great programs that meet the needs of a diverse range of families... check out their camps during the summer and school breaks... **"**

Customer service........................**❹** $$..Prices

Age range.................. 3 mths and up

WWW.YMCA.COM

PUYALLUP—302 43RD AVE SE (OFF MERIDIAN E); 253.841.9622; CALL FOR SCHEDULE

TACOMA—1002 S PEARL ST (AT S 12TH ST); 253.564.9622; CALL FOR SCHEDULE

TACOMA—1144 MARKET ST (AT S 13TH ST); 253.597.6444; M-F 5-9:30, SA 7-8, SU 10-5; PARKING LOT

TACOMA—9715 LAKEWOOD DR SW (AT 100TH ST SW); 253.584.9622; CALL FOR SCHEDULE

parks & playgrounds

Seattle

★★★★★

"lila picks"

- ★ Carkeek Park
- ★ Gas Works Park Play Barn
- ★ Green Lake Park
- ★ Sand Point Magnuson Park
- ★ Seward Park

Alki Beach Park ★☆☆☆☆

"...great place to enjoy a day at the beach on a warm sunny day... paved path is perfect for strolls with baby... super place to look for little water critters when the tide is low... Alki Community Center playground nearby... great restaurants across the street from beach... the water is pretty chilly, but if you're brave go for it... campfires are allowed in the designated fire pits... plenty of picnic tables too... **"**

Equipment/play structures............❸　❸..............................Maintenance

WWW.SEATTLE.GOV/PARKS

WEST SEATTLE—1702 ALKI AVE SW (AT HARBOR AVE SW); 206.684.4075;
  DAILY 4AM-11:30PM

American Legion Memorial
Park ★★★★☆

"...very beautiful park, grab some take-out and watch the sun go down... the playground is wonderful... **"**

Equipment/play structures............❺　❺..............................Maintenance

WWW.EVERETTWA.ORG

EVERETT—145 ALVERSON BLVD (AT LEGION MEMORIAL GOLF COURSE)

Ballard Playfield ★★★★☆

"...adjacent to Ballard Community Center and Adams Elementary School... a multipurpose play field featuring a children's play area and a soccer/baseball/softball field... **"**

Equipment/play structures............❹　❸..............................Maintenance

WWW.CI.SEATTLE.WA.US/PARKS

BALLARD—2644 NW 60TH ST (AT 28TH AVE NW); 206.684.4075

Bellevue Downtown Park ★★★⯪☆

"...pretty sweet for a downtown park... nice walking paths make taking the stroller for a spin fun and enjoyable... brand new playground... fountain and restrooms... lots of benches and shade...across the street from Bellevue Square... **"**

Equipment/play structures............❹　❹..............................Maintenance

WWW.CI.BELLEVUE.WA.US

BELLEVUE—10201 NE 4TH ST (AT 100TH AVE NE); 425.452.6881

BF Day Playground

"...park has a children's play area that is accessible to youngsters with disabilities, a grass soccer/baseball field, and a shelter house built in 1911, making it one of the oldest in the system... **"**

Equipment/play structures .... **5**   **5** .... Maintenance

WWW.CI.SEATTLE.WA.US/PARKS

WALLINGFORD/FREMONT—4020 FREMONT AVE N (AT N 41ST ST); 206.684.4075

Bitter Lake Playground

"...a wading pool close to the playground is a big hit with my daughter... big grassy area to spread a blanket and have a picnic... free lunches served to children at noon and 50 cent sno-cones offered at 2 pm during the summer... **"**

Equipment/play structures .... **4**   **5** .... Maintenance

WWW.CI.SEATTLE.WA.US/PARKS

NORTH SEATTLE—13035 LINDEN AVE N (AT N 130TH ST); 206.684.4075

Blyth Park

"...a good sized playground for toddlers... a tire mountain to climb, swings and a big open grassy area for running and tossing a ball... right off the Sammaish River Trail, there are lots of covered areas for picnics... plenty of other kids to play with, or you can find a secluded spot and have some time to yourself... **"**

Equipment/play structures .... **4**   **4** .... Maintenance

BOTHELL—16950 W RIVERSIDE DR (AT 102ND AVE NE); 425.486.7430

Bryant Playground

"...the equipment seems more suited for older tots—my 2-year-old enjoyed playing on the tennis court more than on the equipment... cool slides, decks and other contraptions to climb on and explore... lots of kids and adults all the time... **"**

Equipment/play structures .... **3**   **3** .... Maintenance

WWW.CI.SEATTLE.WA.US/PARKS

WEDGEWOOD/RAVENNA—4103 NE 65TH ST (AT 42ND AVE NE); 206.684.4075

Burke-Gilman Playground Park

"...a big park... plenty of space for walking, running around and playing frisbee... the park is usually clean and the equipment is in pretty good shape... a variety of equipment for different ages... **"**

Equipment/play structures .... **4**   **4** .... Maintenance

WWW.CI.SEATTLE.WA.US/PARKS

LAURELHURST/SANDPOINT—5201 SAND POINT WY NE (AT CHILDREN'S HOSPITAL & MEDICAL CTR); 206.684.4075

Carkeek Park

"...great urban park off the beaten path... you couldn't ask for more—a beach with a beautiful view, great playground, open field, nice picnic spots, and hiking trails to get away from it all... a good share of toddler-appropriate toys... fun for train lovers who can watch the trains go by... trails are not stroller friendly... not good on rainy days as it is a bit hilly and it gets slick and muddy... take the overpass above the trains to get to the beach... **"**

Equipment/play structures .... **4**   **4** .... Maintenance

WWW.CI.SEATTLE.WA.US/PARKS

parks & playgrounds

NORTH SEATTLE—950 NW CARKEEK PARK RD (AT NW 116TH ST); 206.684.4075

Cedar Park ★★★★☆

"...great neighborhood playground, well maintained, also has a basketball court, walking path (great if you have kids on bikes with training wheels)... not as crowded as other popular Seattle city parks like Green Lake or the Zoo ... **"**

Equipment/play structures............❹ ❺ ....Maintenance

WWW.CITYOFSEATTLE.NET/PARKS/PARKSPACES/PARKLIST.HTM

NORTH SEATTLE—3737 NE 135TH ST (AT 39TH AVE NE)

Celebration Park ★★★★☆

"...great smaller park for an afternoon out... padded and organized so that you can see your child at all times... would not recommend this park for children under 3—I find their equipment to be for slightly older children—for instance they don't have the small child swings with the bucket seats... **"**

Equipment/play structures............❹ ❹ ....Maintenance

WWW.CI.FEDERAL-WAY.WA.US

FEDERAL WAY—320TH ST (AT PACIFIC HWY S); 253.661.4050

Cottage Lake Park ★★★★☆

"...play area with bathrooms right there... some paved trails for walking... lake with a long dock and small graded pebbled area for wading... lots of water fowl... outdoor pool open in the summer... **"**

Equipment/play structures............❹ ❹ ....Maintenance

WWW5.METROKC.GOV/REPORTS/PARKINFO/GETPARKINFO.ASP

WOODINVILLE—NE WOODINVILLE—DUVALL RD (AT 188TH NE); 206.296.8687

Country Village Playground ★★★⯪☆

"...seeing the ducks is always a highlight for us... my son loves to feed the ducks and play on the playground... **"**

Equipment/play structures............❸ ❸ ....Maintenance

WWW.CI.BOTHELL.WA.US

BOTHELL—23718 7TH AVE W (AT 240TH ST); 425.483.2250

Cowen Park ★★★★⯪

"...nice, varied playground equipment... plenty of excited kids screaming and running... there's a sundial, frog sculpture and a delightful little play field... connects to Ravenna Park via a beautiful trail so bring your jogger and take the tots for a walk... quiet and cool on a hot day... **"**

Equipment/play structures............❺ ❹ ....Maintenance

WWW.CITYOFSEATTLE.NET

WEDGEWOOD/RAVENNA—5849 15TH AVE NE (AT NE RAVENNA BLVD); 206.684.4075

Discovery Park ★★★★⯪

"...the park is huge... the duck pond is worth the winding drive... the playground area is somewhat sparse, but the equipment is in good shape... it's back away from the road—some people don't even know there's a playground back there... lots of trails for relaxing walks... plenty of restrooms and port-a-potties... stop at the visitors center if it's your first visit for a map and general information... **"**

Equipment/play structures............❹ ❹ ....Maintenance

WWW.CI.SEATTLE.WA.US/PARKS

MAGNOLIA—3801 W GOVERNMENT WY (AT TEXAS WAY W); 206.386.4236

participate in our survey at

Edmonds City Park

"...right off the ferry waiting area and nicely screened by bushes... two play areas that are both stroller- and wheelchair-accessible... the restrooms are pretty clean and the water fountain works... wooded setting provides shade in the summer... my boys love to hear the ferries and trains nearby... **"**

Equipment/play structures .... ❺ ❹ .... Maintenance

WWW.CI.EDMONDS.WA.US

EDMONDS—3RD AVE S (AT PINE ST); 425.771.0230

Farrel-Mc Whirter Park

"...there isn't much playground equipment; just some swings... there is a cool silo the kids can climb up via a spiral staircase, and farm animals... it's peaceful and beautiful there... a fun place to go—they have pigs, chickens, roosters, a donkey, ponies, sheep, goats, ducks, bunnies and some other animals to watch... **"**

Equipment/play structures .... ❸ ❹ .... Maintenance

WWW.CI.REDMOND.WA.US

REDMOND—19545 NE REDMOND RD; 425.556.2300

Forest Park

"...this park has everything and then some—a huge playground and even a petting zoo... the Parks and Recreation offices are here so it's also a good place to get information about programs throughout town... lots of trails and open spaces for picnics... they even have an indoor pool... **"**

Equipment/play structures .... ❺ ❺ .... Maintenance

WWW.EVERETTWA.ORG/PARKS

EVERETT—802 MUKILTEO BLVD (AT 41ST ST); 425.257.8300

Froula Playground

"...the new playground equipment makes this little park a treat... cool contraptions for tots to climb and swing on... always crowded with families and new kids to meet and play with... parking can be a bit dicey, as it's right off 75th St ... no bathrooms ... **"**

Equipment/play structures .... ❹ ❹ .... Maintenance

WWW.CI.SEATTLE.WA.US/PARKS

MAPLE LEAF/ROOSEVELT—7200 12TH AVE NE (AT NE 75TH ST);
   206.684.4075

Garfield Playfield

"...originally named "Wall Walla" after the Indian tribe in SE Washington, which means "place of many waters (streams)"... the park is on Cherry, which is pretty busy... not as peaceful as other parks... **"**

Equipment/play structures .... ❷ ❸ .... Maintenance

WWW.CI.SEATTLE.WA.US/PARKS

CENTRAL DISTRICT—23RD AVE (AT E CHERRY ST); 206.684.4075

Gas Works Park Play Barn

"...there really isn't a playground here, but the old gas works are a hoot to climb on... kids love the artwork on the ground when climbing up the hill... fun place for kids to explore, fly kites, watch boats and run around... a unique park with plenty of open space... right on the shores of Lake Union... **"**

Equipment/play structures .... ❸ ❹ .... Maintenance

WWW.CI.SEATTLE.WA.US/PARKS

WALLINGFORD/FREMONT—2101 NORTHLAKE WY (AT MERIDIAN AVE N);
   206.684.4075

Gene Coulon Memorial Beach Park ★★★★⯪

"...this is a really pretty park with great paved paths for strollers... plus there are a couple of fast food places with good stroller accessibility... it's a fun park, easy to find and lots of parking... great place for an evening stroll..."

Equipment/play structures............❹   ❺................................Maintenance

WWW.CI.RENTON.WA.US

RENTON—1201 LAKE WASHINGTON BLVD N (AT HOUSER WAY N); 425.430.6700

Gilman Playground ★★★⯪☆

"...swings, a large play structure and a wading pool... lots of shade by the pool, but not much by the play area... there are a couple of places within walking distance to grab a bite to eat..."

Equipment/play structures............❸   ❹................................Maintenance

WWW.CI.SEATTLE.WA.US/PARKS

BALLARD—923 NW 54TH ST (BTWN 9TH AND 11TH AVE NW); 206.684.4075

Golden Gardens Park ★★★★☆

"...the playground equipment is in a shaded area... the beach is awesome... we like the beautiful view and peaceful setting... never crowded on weekdays and plenty of parking... picnic tables and grills available... a great set of stairs to climb for the mother looking to get herself back in shape..."

Equipment/play structures............❸   ❸................................Maintenance

WWW.CI.SEATTLE.WA.US/PARKS

BALLARD—8498 SEAVIEW PL NW (AT NW 85TH ST); 206.684.4075

Grass Lawn Community Park ★★★★☆

"...nice equipment and tons of parking... big grassy areas for running and playing games, in addition to a cool play set... swings for big and little tots... restrooms are functional, but not exactly pristine... nice picnic shelter makes having a party here hassle free..."

Equipment/play structures............❹   ❹................................Maintenance

WWW.CI.REDMOND.WA.US

REDMOND—7031 148 AVE NE (AT OLD REDMOND RD); 425.556.2300

Green Lake Park ★★★★★

"...much of the play area is padded... a nice playground and a wading pool in the summer... the cleanest sandbox in the city... offers a wide range of activities such as walks around the park, baseball games, viewing the docks and birdwatching... plenty of room to run around under the trees... the indoor playground in the community center is great on iffy days... the public library across the street is a real plus... convenient restrooms... amazing restaurants along the side of the lake offer meal and snack options..."

Equipment/play structures............❺   ❹................................Maintenance

WWW.CI.SEATTLE.WA.US/PARKS

GREENLAKE/GREENWOOD/PHINNEY RIDGE—7201 E GREEN LAKE DR N (AT NE 72ND ST); 206.684.4075

Hiawatha Playfield ★★★★☆

"...a very nice park with a climbing structure and baby swings in one area and regular swings in another... also has a wading pool during the summer... large sandpit area... lots of grassy spots to run and play in..."

Equipment/play structures............❹   ❹................................Maintenance

WWW.CI.SEATTLE.WA.US/PARKS

Jefferson Park

"...not much equipment, but not a bad park... lots of space to run and great views of downtown and Puget Sound..."

Equipment/play structures .... ❸   ❸ .... Maintenance

WWW.CI.SEATTLE.WA.US/PARKS

GEORGETOWN—4165 16TH AVE SW (AT SW DAKOTA ST); 206.684.4075;
DAILY 4-11:30

Jennings Memorial Park

"...has a nice playground, which gets very busy on sunny days... Jennings Nature Park is down the street which has a petting farm... lots of trails and adjacent wetlands / wetland observatory..."

Equipment/play structures .... ❹   ❺ .... Maintenance

WWW.CI.MARYSVILLE.WA.US

MARYSVILLE—6915 ARMAR RD (AT GROVE ST); 360.363.8400

Kelsey Creek Park

"...it's in an odd location and difficult to find... a wide variety of activities—a great playground, petting zoo, occasional pony rides and a big open field to run and fly kites... my daughter loves to see the animals... a fun place for a picnic... an amazing rural setting just minutes from Seattle..."

Equipment/play structures .... ❹   ❹ .... Maintenance

WWW.CI.BELLEVUE.WA.US

BELLEVUE—13204 SE 8TH ST (AT 132ND AVE NE); 425.452.7688

Kubota Garden

"...not a park with a playground, but rather a beautiful and serene setting that will calm you and enchant your toddler... many walking paths with natural hiding places... a great place to inspire the imagination of my children... quiet beautiful setting..."

Equipment/play structures .... ❸   ❺ .... Maintenance

WWW.KUBOTA.ORG

RAINIER BEACH—9817 55TH AVE S (AT RENTON AVE S); 206.684.4584

Lake Boren Park

"...one of our favorite parks... a huge play area near the water with lots of grass... the play structures are good for older children and toddlers... picnic tables and covered areas are a big plus... basketball and tennis courts... nice clean restrooms... the paved walkways are great for strollers and tricycles..."

Equipment/play structures .... ❺   ❹ .... Maintenance

WWW.CI.NEWCASTLE.WA.US

NEWCASTLE—SE 84TH AVE (OFF COAL CREEK PKWY SE); 425.649.4444

Lakewood Playfield

"...lots of open spaces for fun activities... a sandbox, swings and a large playground... soccer and baseball fields for running and letting our kite fly... there's always lots of children there and it's easy to meet others from the neighborhood..."

Equipment/play structures .... ❸   ❸ .... Maintenance

WWW.CI.SEATTLE.WA.US/PARKS

SEWARD PARK—5013 S ANGELINE ST (AT 50TH AVE S); 206.684.4075

parks & playgrounds

Laurelhurst Playfield ★★★☆☆

"...the view from the top of the hill is amazing... the play structure is designed for older tots and the little ones get the swings... always clean... we don't like the gravel surface in the play structure area...**"**

Equipment/play structures............**3**   **4**................................Maintenance

WWW.CI.SEATTLE.WA.US/PARKS

LAURELHURST/SANDPOINT—4544 NE 41ST ST (AT 48TH AVE NE); 206.684.4075

Leschi Park ★★★★☆

"...beautiful location... not recommended for toddlers... not interesting enough...**"**

Equipment/play structures............**4**   **4**................................Maintenance

WWW.CI.SEATTLE.WA.US/PARKS

LESCHI—201 LAKESIDE AVE S (AT E ALDER ST); 206.684.4075

Licton Springs Park ★★★☆☆

"...a small park in the middle of a nice neighborhood... the equipment is in great shape and the park is well kept... lots of open grass area for running, picnics and games... a little too close to a busy street for my taste, but the playground itself is nice...**"**

Equipment/play structures............**4**   **4**................................Maintenance

WWW.CI.SEATTLE.WA.US/PARKS

NORTH SEATTLE—9536 ASHWORTH AVE N (AT N 92ND ST); 206.684.4075

Lincoln Park ★★★★☆

"...tons of activities for kids of all ages... grassy area great for running around... walking trails nearby... the upper play structure has the little ride-on bouncy toys, a climbing structure, slides and baby swings... the path along the beach is great for walking or hiking... the lower level of the park is beautiful with the beach right there and the ferry docks close by... two seperate playgrounds, a wading pool, an outdoor heated saltwater pool, forest, and beach... it can't be beat!...**"**

Equipment/play structures............**4**   **4**................................Maintenance

WWW.CI.SEATTLE.WA.US/PARKS

WEST SEATTLE—8011 FAUNTLEROY WY SW (AT SW MONROE ST); 206.684.4075

Lowman Beach Park ★★★★☆

"...Lowman Beach is small, but like beaches everywhere, it has some surprises... it includes about 300 feet of rocky, saltwater shoreline a few blocks north of Lincoln Park... above the beach is an acre of grass with tennis courts, swings... view of the Olympics, Alki Point, and Williams Point spread out in three directions...**"**

Equipment/play structures............**3**   **5**................................Maintenance

WWW.CI.SEATTLE.WA.US/PARKS

WEST SEATTLE—7017 BEACH DR SW (AT 47TH AVE SW); 206.684.4075

Madison Park ★★★★☆

"...a very popular park with a lakeside setting... located near the Madison Park shopping area—easy to run errands and stop off at the park for some play time... too crowded—we always have to wait for the swings and slides...**"**

Equipment/play structures............**4**   **4**................................Maintenance

WWW.CI.SEATTLE.WA.US/PARKS

MADISON VALLEY/MADISON PARK—E MADISON ST (AT E HOWE ST); 206.684.4075

Madrona Park

WWW.CI.SEATTLE.WA.US/PARKS

MADRONA—853 LAKE WASHINGTON BLVD (AT E COLUMBIA ST);
  206.684.4075

Magnolia Park

"...not much of a playground, but beautiful area especially if your kids love to run around... beautiful view of the sound and ferries... lots of green space... somewhat enclosed... equipment consists of a swing set only but the park itself is so beautiful that kids enjoy running around the trees and watching the ferries... "

Equipment/play structures .... ❸   ❹ .... Maintenance

WWW.CI.SEATTLE.WA.US/PARKS

MAGNOLIA—1461 MAGNOLIA BLVD W (AT W EATON ST); 206.684.4075

Maple Leaf Playground

"...lots of great play equipment, especially for younger kids... no shade to speak of, so it does get hot... near a busy street... this park is a little dirty and needs new paint... the bathrooms are kind of scary too... "

Equipment/play structures .... ❹   ❸ .... Maintenance

WWW.CI.SEATTLE.WA.US/PARKS

MAPLE LEAF/ROOSEVELT—1020 NE 82ND ST (AT ROOSEVELT WY NE);
  206.684.4075

Marymoor Regional Park

"...very large and family friendly... trails with great views... in the summer, my family loves listening to concerts there... little kids love to watch the cyclists in the velodrome... watch out for those gopher holes...off-leash dog park is a hit with my toddler... "

Equipment/play structures .... ❹   ❹ .... Maintenance

WWW.CI.REDMOND.WA.US

REDMOND—6046 W LAKE SAMMAMISH PKWY NE (AT NE MARYMOOR WY);
  206.205.3661

Matthews Beach Park 1.

"...a beautiful location, but a less than average experience... goose droppings on the sidewalks and play equipment are a real turnoff... a park near the water sounds great, but the play area and beach can be disgusting... although my son enjoyed the toys and the ducks we will not be returning... "

Equipment/play structures .... ❸   ❸ .... Maintenance

WWW.CI.SEATTLE.WA.US/PARKS

NORTH SEATTLE—9300 51ST AVE NE (AT S FLETCHER ST); 206.684.4075

Meadowbrook Playfield

"...once we found the playfield it was nice... it is out of the way and takes a little exploring to find... most of the toys are wooden and designed for older children to play with... not a great play place for children under 4... "

Equipment/play structures .... ❸   ❹ .... Maintenance

WWW.CI.SEATTLE.WA.US/PARKS

NORTH SEATTLE—10533 35TH AVE NE (AT NE 105TH ST); 206.684.4075

Meridian Playground

"...the playground and landscaping are well maintained... one of the better parks in Seattle... the climbing structure includes a toddler-sized climbing wall, low monkey bars and several neat slides... look for hidden trains, apples and birds, and book themes in the stonework... "

Equipment/play structures............ **⑤**   **⑤** ....Maintenance
WWW.CI.SEATTLE.WA.US/PARKS

WALLINGFORD/FREMONT—4649 SUNNYSIDE AVE N (AT N 50TH ST);
    206.684.4075

Miller Playfield   ★★★☆☆

"...this funny little park is hidden, tucked away... the equipment is
sparse, but there's a field to run around in... the restroom isn't open
often enough, but when there's a game on the play field it's open and
staffed... the water fountains and spray are fun on hot days... **"**
Equipment/play structures............ **③**   **③** ....Maintenance
WWW.CI.SEATTLE.WA.US/PARKS

CAPITOL HILL—400 19TH AVE E (AT E HARRISON ST); 206.684.4075

Mt Baker Park   ★★★★⯨

"...this shady, green park in the Mt Baker neighborhood has some of
the best play equipment in the city... just a short walk down to the
beach... especially good for babies—not overly crowded... no climbing
structure, but plenty of other things to play on... **"**
Equipment/play structures............ **④**   **④** ....Maintenance
WWW.CI.SEATTLE.WA.US/PARKS

MOUNT BAKER—2521 LAKE PARK DR S (AT S MCCLELLAN ST); 206.684.4075

Northacres Park & Playfield
WWW.CI.SEATTLE.WA.US/PARKS

NORTH SEATTLE—12718 1ST AVE NE (AT NE 130TH ST); 206.684.4075

Peter Kirk Park   ★★★⯨☆

"...this park has a big play area, and you can walk to downtown
Kirkland's waterfront... a lovely place to play and picnic... really great
play structure and wonderful place for little kids to play... lots of
benches so bring your lunch and enjoy... **"**
Equipment/play structures............ **④**   **④** ....Maintenance
WWW.CI.KIRKLAND.WA.US

KIRKLAND—202 3RD ST (AT CENTRAL WY); 425.828.1100

Phinney Ridge Playground   ★★★★⯨

"...located right next to Woodland Park Zoo... splendid... a beautiful
setting for a playground... the tallest swings for babies I've come across
in Seattle—hilarious to see my 20 month-old thrill at how high she is
going... lots of flowers, grass to run on and playground equipment...
parking on nice days can be really tough... **"**
Equipment/play structures............ **⑤**   **④** ....Maintenance
WWW.CI.SEATTLE.WA.US/PARKS

WEDGEWOOD/RAVENNA—5420 PHINNEY AVE N (AT N 54TH ST);
    206.684.4075

Pine Lake Park   ★★★★☆

"...two play areas, restrooms and a ball field... great open grass for
kids to play on... warm summer nights feature concerts, plays and even
outdoor movies... good parking... lots of shade... people are often
swimming in the lake... restrooms are easily accessible and reasonably
clean... **"**
Equipment/play structures............ **④**   **④** ....Maintenance
WWW.CI.SAMMAMISH.WA.US

SAMMAMISH—228TH AVE SE (AT SE 24TH ST); 425.898.0660

Ravenna Park

"...the playground equipment isn't the greatest, but the wading pool and semi-secluded play field are... connects to Cowen Park via a long, lush path... parts of the park are so peaceful and gorgeous that you can forget you're in the city... great for playing hide and seek, walking the dog... restrooms at either end of the park... **"**

Equipment/play structures .... ❸   ❹ .... Maintenance

WWW.CI.SEATTLE.WA.US/PARKS

WEDGEWOOD/RAVENNA—5520 RAVENNA AVE NE (AT NE 58TH ST);
206.684.4075

Regrade Park

"...a small park tucked into the heart of the densely populated Belltown neighborhood... home to a new pilot off-leash area that will provide a playground for downtown dwellers and their canine companions... even if you don't have a dog, the people- and dog-watching are great... **"**

Equipment/play structures .... ❸   ❶ .... Maintenance

WWW.CI.SEATTLE.WA.US/PARKS

BELLTOWN—2251 3RD AVE (AT BLANCHARD ST); 206.684.4075

parks & playgrounds

Roanoke Park

"...great park... a quiet neighborhood park without a lot of crowds and waiting required for swings... the entire playground was rebuilt in 2002... landscaping is beautiful... **"**

Equipment/play structures .... ❹   ❺ .... Maintenance

WWW.CI.SEATTLE.WA.US/PARKS

PORTAGE BAY—950 E ROANOKE ST (AT BROADWAY E); 206.684.4075

Robinswood Community Park

"...great play structures for big and small kids... walking paths in the woods are a gorgeous way to burn off some extra energy... very clean and well-kept... don't forget to bring some bread for the ducks... **"**

Equipment/play structures .... ❹   ❺ .... Maintenance

WWW.CI.BELLEVUE.WA.US

BELLEVUE—2430 148TH AVE SE (AT SE 24TH ST); 425.452.6881

Ross Playfield

"...a great neighborhood park—we hope that it gets remodeled soon... **"**

Equipment/play structures .... ❷   ❸ .... Maintenance

WWW.CI.SEATTLE.WA.US/PARKS

GREENLAKE/GREENWOOD/PHINNEY RIDGE—4320 4TH AVE NW (AT NW 43RD
ST); 206.684.4075

Roxhill Park

"...my toddler loves this playground that has a fortress-like play structure made of wood... unlike typical Seattle play structures, it really is unique... **"**

Equipment/play structures .... ❹   ❸ .... Maintenance

WWW.CI.SEATTLE.WA.US/PARKS

WEST SEATTLE—2850 SW ROXBURY ST (AT 28TH AVE SW); 206.684.4075

Salmon Bay Park

"...popular place for neighborhood families, especially families with little kids... playground has a nice feel—fairly toddler friendly with all equipment close together (you can be pushing a baby in a swing while watching a preschooler)... rest of the park has some nice trees and open space—restrooms never seem to be open, though... **"**

Equipment/play structures............ **❹**   **❸** ....Maintenance

WWW.CI.SEATTLE.WA.US/PARKS

BALLARD—2001 NW CANOE PL (AT 20TH AVE NW); 206.684.4075

Sam Smith Park

WWW.CI.SEATTLE.WA.US/PARKS

CENTRAL DISTRICT—1400 MARTIN LUTHER KING JR WAY S (AT I-90); 206.684.4075

Sand Point Magnuson Park Playground ★★★★★

"...the playspace is divided into themed areas so kids with varied interests can enjoy this park... 5 different play stations geared toward different ages and abilities... only downside is the restroom is not particularly close... nearby dog park which means we could exercise everyone, including our dog... has paths in and around the playground for children to learn to ride their bikes... sets the bar high for the other parks in the city... **"**

Equipment/play structures............ **❹**   **❹** ....Maintenance

WWW.CI.SEATTLE.WA.US/PARKS

LAURELHURST/SANDPOINT—7400 SAND POINT WY NE (AT NE 74TH ST); 206.684.4946

Sandel Playground ★★★☆☆

"...not a lot for a toddler, but the slide is great... features include a children's play area, walkways, large open meadow, basketball hoops, and a wading pool... **"**

Equipment/play structures............ **❸**   **❸** ....Maintenance

WWW.CI.SEATTLE.WA.US/PARKS

MAPLE LEAF/ROOSEVELT—9053 1ST AVE NW (AT N 90TH ST); 206.684.4075

Seward Park ★★★★★

"...a lovely, level bike path runs along the water... the playground is never very crowded... the setting for a walk through the woods is unbeatable... great if you want to go for a little nature hike or just lounge on the beach and watch the kids play... **"**

Equipment/play structures............ **❺**   **❺** ....Maintenance

WWW.CI.SEATTLE.WA.US/PARKS

SEWARD PARK—5900 LAKE WASHINGTON BLVD S (AT S ORCAS ST); 206.684.4075

Soundview Playfield ★★★★☆

"...great place to spend the day with the kids... children's play area, restrooms, picnic tables, tennis courts, wading pool... great park, recently remodeled with new equipment, and set away from the street (great for watching multiple children)... fairly toddler-friendly with structures not too high ... **"**

Equipment/play structures............ **❺**   **❺** ....Maintenance

WWW.CI.SEATTLE.WA.US/PARKS

NORTH SEATTLE—1590 NW 90TH ST (AT 5TH AVE NW); 206.684.4075

Spruce Street Mini Park ★☆☆☆☆

"...park often has broken glass around the area... we have also seen cats using the sand as a litter box... there is a unique slide that has rollers that children can use, but most of the equipment is old and starting to break... **"**

Equipment/play structures............ **❷**   **❶** ....Maintenance

WWW.CI.SEATTLE.WA.US/PARKS

CENTRAL DISTRICT—160 21ST AVE (AT E FIR ST); 206.684.4075

St Edward State Park

"...an excellent park with wonderful areas for both toddlers and older kids to play... a place for kids built by kids... huge play structure with one area fenced off to one side for the younger set... sandboxes, swings, slides, and climbing areas all in one place... lots of picnic tables... there are hiking trails too... open year round for day use... **"**

Equipment/play structures .... ❺　　❺ .... Maintenance

WWW.PARKS.WA.GOV

KENMORE—14500 JUANITA DR NE (AT 109TH AVE); 425.823.2992

Steel Lake Park

"...small beach area for water play... incredible large play structure for kids, which is built like a large castle... kids can maneuver their way around the entire perimeter without touching the ground... lots of different activities... a clean park with lots of eating areas... not too crowded... **"**

Equipment/play structures .... ❺　　❹ .... Maintenance

WWW.CITYOFFEDERALWAY.COM

FEDERAL WAY—S 312TH ST (AT 24TH AVE S); 253.661.4596

parks & playgrounds

Sunset Park

"...beautiful park on the water with nice playground and swings... lots of space for children to run around and great picnic areas... ballfields and skateboard park... a great please to meet other moms—and Starbucks is a short stroller walk away—we love going there!... **"**

Equipment/play structures .... ❹　　❹ .... Maintenance

WWW.METROKC.GOV

AUBURN—1306 69TH ST SE (AT LAKELAND HILLS WY)

Thornton A Sullivan Park

"...this park has come a long way since I was a kid—fully upgraded and super cool climbing toys, nice lawns and picnic areas, and life guards on sunny days... this is a fun park, it also has a beach and swimming in the summer... **"**

Equipment/play structures .... ❹　　❹ .... Maintenance

WWW.EVERETTWA.ORG

EVERETT—11405 SILVER LAKE RD (AT 112TH ST SE); 425.257.8300

University Playfield

"...we call this 'Gorilla Park' because there's a fabulous gorilla holding up some of the play equipment... nice little play field... the restroom is clean, but not open very often... a popular neighborhood park so there usually are other kids to play with in the afternoons... the public library across the street is also a plus... **"**

Equipment/play structures .... ❸　　❸ .... Maintenance

WWW.CI.SEATTLE.WA.US/PARKS

UNIVERSITY DISTRICT/UNIVERSITY VILLAGE—9TH AVE NE (AT NE 50TH ST);
   206.684.4075

Victory Heights Playground

"...a sweet little neighborhood park... nice equipment that's in good shape... the play field is small and lower than the street, so your kids really can't run into the road... no restroom... **"**

Equipment/play structures .... ❸　　❸ .... Maintenance

WWW.CI.SEATTLE.WA.US/PARKS

NORTH SEATTLE—1737 NE 106TH ST (AT 17TH AVE NE); 206.684.4075

View Ridge Playfield ★★★½☆

"...a newly remodeled park with a variety of play areas for different ages... big bucket swings and a wading pool during the summer... lots of lawn space for picnicking... street parking can be difficult depending on the time of day ... **"**

Equipment/play structures............❹   ❹ ....Maintenance

WWW.CI.SEATTLE.WA.US/PARKS

WEDGEWOOD/RAVENNA—4408 NE 70TH ST (AT 45TH AVE NE); 206.684.4075

Volunteer Park ★★★★☆

"...tall trees, a large wading pool in summer, a wide variety of metal slides... many playfields including one with a stage and another that overlooks the reservoir... the water fountains work all year... home of the Asian Art Museum... the conservatory is a nice treat on a cold or rainy day... **"**

Equipment/play structures............❹   ❹ ....Maintenance

WWW.CI.SEATTLE.WA.US/PARKS

CAPITOL HILL—1247 15TH AVE E (AT E PROSPECT ST); 206.684.4075

W Magnolia Park

WWW.CI.SEATTLE.WA.US/PARKS

MAGNOLIA—2518 34TH AVE W (AT W SMITH ST); 206.684.4075

W Queen Anne Playfield

WWW.CI.SEATTLE.WA.US/PARKS

QUEEN ANNE—150 W BLAINE ST (AT 1ST AVE W); 206.684.4075

W Woodland Park Playground ★★★★½

"...a small, pretty playground with ample parking... lots of fun equipment and a playing field for team sports... park attracts groups from nearby daycares during the summertime... play here before you enter the zoo next door... drawback: no bathrooms, and the operators of the nearby 7-11 have no compassion for a 2 year-old who's about to wet her pants... **"**

Equipment/play structures............❹   ❹ ....Maintenance

WWW.CI.SEATTLE.WA.US/PARKS

GREENLAKE/GREENWOOD/PHINNEY RIDGE—5420 PHINNEY AVE N (AT N 54TH ST); 206.684.4075

Wallingford Playfield ★★★★½

"...my daughter calls this the 'Slide Park' because there are several neat slides... the wading pool has a shallow and deep end so big and little kids are naturally separated... not enough shade near the pool... good all-around playground—suspension bridge, sandbox and larger structure for older kids... there is a hidden picnic area on the corner which is nice and quiet... very popular in the summertime, can get very crowded... **"**

Equipment/play structures............❺   ❺ ....Maintenance

WWW.CI.SEATTLE.WA.US/PARKS

WALLINGFORD/FREMONT—4219 WALLINGFORD AVE N (AT N 42ND ST); 206.684.4075

Washington Park Arboretum ★☆☆☆☆

"...great place to watch boats and have a picnic... beautiful all year round... children can dig around and discover little critters... area is known for higher crime rates so be careful... very urban... nice place to kayak... little ones love all the different sights and smells... nice area to take pictures... **"**

Equipment/play structures............❸   ❸ ....Maintenance

participate in our survey at

WWW.DEPTS.WASHINGTON.EDU/WPA

CAPITOL HILL—2300 ARBORETUM DR E; 206.543.8800; 7-SUNSET; FREE
  PARKING

Washington Park Playfield

WWW.CI.SEATTLE.WA.US/PARKS

CAPITOL HILL—2500 LAKE WASHINGTON BLVD E (AT E MILLER ST);
  206.684.4075

Webster Playground

"...a great park for caregivers with multiple age children... there's
climbing toys, green space and an area for bike riding... designated a
"pesticide free park"... **"**

Equipment/play structures .... ❺   ❺ .... Maintenance

WWW.CI.SEATTLE.WA.US/PARKS

BALLARD—3014 NW 67TH ST (AT 30TH AVE NW); 206.684.4075

Wilburton Hill Park &
Bellevue Botanical Garden

"...very nice children's play structures and picnic tables... a great park
to go to for a walk and look at the flowers—afterward we like to have
a picnic near the parking lot... **"**

Equipment/play structures .... ❺   ❺ .... Maintenance

WWW.CI.BELLEVUE.WA.US

BELLEVUE—12001 MAIN ST (OFF 18TH AVE SE); 425.452.6881

parks & playgrounds

Tacoma

★ ★ ★ ★ ★

"lila picks"

★ Titlow Park

DeLong Park   ★★★☆☆

"...right across the street from our house... not a lot of toys, only one piece of play equipment, but a grassy field to play, run, and kick balls in..."

Equipment/play structures............ ❸   ❸ ....Maintenance

WWW.CITYOFTACOMA.ORG

TACOMA—4700 S 12TH ST (AT ORCHARD ST)

Jefferson Park   ★★★★☆

"...well-maintained... a lot of people bring their dogs here and don't seem to like children around them, but this is usually in the evenings... in the summer they have a good staff for the pool and free lunches and snacks... summer programs here are great... bathrooms aren't always open during the rest of the year... play equipment is not geared for toddlers / 2 year-olds... nice wading pool in summer, great walking track around the whole park..."

Equipment/play structures............ ❹   ❹ ....Maintenance

WWW.METROPARKSTACOMA.ORG

TACOMA—N 9TH ST (AT N MONROE ST); 253.305.1000

Kids Gig, The

GIG HARBOR—4905 ROSEDALE ST (AT PENINSULA PARK); 888.553.5428

South Hill Community Park

WWW.CO.PIERCE.WA.US

PUYALLUP—86TH AVE E (AT 144TH ST E)

Titlow Park   ★★★★★

"...not my first choice for beach parks, but we like eating at Steamers and then going for a walk on the beach... they have a kiddie pool (about 6 inches deep) that I love to take the younger kids to, while my older two swim in the big pool... the playground area is great... huge grass area to run and play in..."

Equipment/play structures............ ❸   ❸ ....Maintenance

WWW.METROPARKSTACOMA.ORG

TACOMA—8201 6TH AVE (AT S LAUREL LN); 253.305.1000

Wapato Lake Park   ★★☆☆☆

"...a fun place for a walk or run in a nice setting... not very clean—there are bird droppings everywhere, dirty... the bathrooms are rarely open and when they are, they're also quite unclean... too bad..."

Equipment/play structures .... ❸   ❸ .... Maintenance
WWW.METROPARKSTACOMA.ORG
TACOMA—6500 S SHERIDAN AVE; 253.305.1054

restaurants

Seattle

★ ★ ★ ★ ★

"lila picks"

- ★ Café Flora
- ★ California Pizza Kitchen
- ★ Elliott Bay Brewery & Pub
- ★ My Coffee House
- ★ Red Robin
- ★ Ruby's Diner

5 Spot ★★★★☆

❝...*first-rate neighborhood cafe/diner... fantastic breakfasts, good kid's menus... real family place with great food... very crowded for weekend breakfasts...* **❞**

Children's menu	✓	$$	Prices
Changing station	✓	❺	Customer service
Highchairs/boosters	✓	❸	Stroller access

WWW.CHOWFOODS.COM

QUEEN ANNE—1502 QUEEN ANNE AVE N (AT W GALER ST); 206.285.7768

Alki Bakery ★★★★☆

❝...*the view of the water can't be beat... so popular with kids, it gets a little crazy with excess strollers... awesome baked goods... best chocolate chip macaroons in town... kids menu is a big hit...* **❞**

Children's menu	✓	$$	Prices
Changing station	✓	❹	Customer service
Highchairs/boosters	✓	❸	Stroller access

WWW.ALKIBAKERY.COM

WEST SEATTLE—2738 ALKI AVE SW (AT 61ST AVE SW); 206.935.1352;
  SUMMER: SU-TH 7-9, F-SA 7-10, WINTER: SU-TH 7-8, F-SA 7-9

Angelina's Trattoria ★★☆☆☆

❝...*we took our baby here on Christmas for brunch and the were the only customers so I didn't mind that she was a little fussy...* **❞**

Children's menu	✗	$$$	Prices
Changing station	✗	❸	Customer service
Highchairs/boosters	✓	❸	Stroller access

WEST SEATTLE—2311 CALIFORNIA AVE SW (AT ADMIRAL WY); 206.932.7311

Anthony's Beach Cafe ★★★½☆

❝...*nice fun environment for kids, but good grown-up food too... reasonable prices... casual atmosphere, good grub, low prices. But once we added a baby, it further endeared itself to us... menu allows lots of choices for kid-friendly food, they offer crayons and coloring place mats, and they don't seem to mind a little bit of a mess...* **❞**

Children's menu	✓	$$	Prices
Changing station	✗	❹	Customer service

| Highchairs/boosters | ✗ | ❹ | Stroller access |

WWW.ANTHONYS.COM

EDMONDS—456 ADMIRAL WAY (AT RAILROAD AVE); 425.771.4400

Arnies Restaurant ★★★⯪☆

"...staff is very child-friendly, as is the menu... "

Children's menu	✓	$$	Prices
Changing station	✗	❹	Customer service
Highchairs/boosters	✓	❹	Stroller access

WWW.ARNIESRESTAURANT.COM

MUKILTEO—714 2ND ST (OFF MUKILTEO SPEEDWAY); 425.355.2181;
PARKING LOT LOCATED AT 2ND ST

Atlas Foods ★★★★☆

"...a great family date place... serves American standards all day long... super menu for parents and kids... keeps toys on hand for kids to play with while they wait... you don't feel like you are at a kiddie joint, but the staff and food works for all ages... 'stroller parking' zone is very helpful... "

Children's menu	✓	$$$	Prices
Changing station	✓	❹	Customer service
Highchairs/boosters	✓	❹	Stroller access

WWW.CHOWFOODS.COM

UNIVERSITY DISTRICT/UNIVERSITY VILLAGE—2820 NE UNIVERSITY VLG (AT
NE PACIFIC ST); 206.522.6025; M-F 9-10, SA 8-10, SU 9-10

Azteca Mexican Restaurant ★★★★☆

"...my kids always finish their whole meal here... quick and friendly service... very roomy, good stroller access... a colorful place that's fun for infants and children... love the food... breastfeeding in the booth isn't so easy... "

Children's menu	✓	$$	Prices
Changing station	✗	❹	Customer service
Highchairs/boosters	✓	❹	Stroller access

WWW.AZTECAMEX.COM

EVERETT—1321 SE EVERETT MALL WY (AT EVERETT MALL); 425.353.7588;
SU-M 11-10, T-TH 11-10:30, F-SA 11-11:30; MALL PARKING

MAPLE LEAF/ROOSEVELT—543 NE NORTHGATE WY (AT NORTHGATE
SHOPPING CTR); 206.362.0066; SU-M 11-10, T-TH 11-10:30, F-SA 11-11:30

TUKWILA—17555 SOUTHCENTER PKWY (AT SOUTHCENTER MALL);
206.575.0990; SU-M 11-10, T-TH 11-10:30, F-SA 11-11:30; MALL PARKING

Bagel Oasis ★★★★☆

"...perfect place for lunch after time spent at the Ravenna-Ecstein Community Center ... right around the corner from one another... bagels are great, they carry Odwallas and make great lattes—what more could you want... my only recommendation is that you order your bagel with just a 'schmear' of cream cheese, and ask for half of that if it's for the kids... "

Children's menu	✗	$$	Prices
Changing station	✗	❹	Customer service
Highchairs/boosters	✓	❺	Stroller access

WEDGEWOOD/RAVENNA—2112 NORTHEAST 65TH ST (AT 22ND AVE);
206.526.0525

Benihana ★★★★⯪

"...stir-fry meals are always prepared in front of you—it keeps everyone entertained, parents and kids alike... chefs often perform especially for the little ones... tables sit about 10 people, so it

restaurants

encourages talking with other diners... tend to be pretty loud so it's pretty family friendly... delicious for adults and fun for kids... **"**

Children's menu	✗	$$$	Prices
Changing station	✓	❹	Customer service
Highchairs/boosters	✓	❸	Stroller access

WWW.BENIHANA.COM

SEATTLE—1200 5TH AVE (AT SENECA ST); 206.682.4686

Big Time Uncommon Pizzeria ★★★★☆

"...*good pizza and salads... they give the kids a lump of pizza dough to smush around while you wait for your meal to arrive... low cost... a little loud, but this has always worked to our advantage...* **"**

Children's menu	✗	$$$	Prices
Changing station	✗	❹	Customer service
Highchairs/boosters	✓	❹	Stroller access

WWW.BIGTIMEPIZZA.COM

REDMOND—7824 LEARY WY NE (AT CLEAVELAND ST); 425.885.6425

Bing's Bodacious Burgers ★★★⯪☆

"...*very accommodating of people with children... busy and noisy so noisy children fit right in... highchairs are readily available, staff are accommodating, and the place is packed with families on the weekends... ambient level of noise is already high so no guilt-factor if the kids are screaming...* **"**

Children's menu	✓	$$	Prices
Changing station	✗	❹	Customer service
Highchairs/boosters	✓	❹	Stroller access

CAPITOL HILL—4200 E MADISON ST (AT 42ND AVE E); 206.323.8623

Brasa ★★★☆☆

"...*wood-burning oven, and co-owner Bryan Hill was chosen as the Best Sommelier in Seattle... they're always striving for the best in their menu and wine list...* **"**

Children's menu	✗	$$$	Prices
Changing station	✗	❸	Customer service
Highchairs/boosters	✓	❸	Stroller access

WWW.BRASA.COM

DOWNTOWN—2107 3RD AVE (AT LENORA ST); 206.728.4220

Buca di Beppo ★★★★☆

"...*Italian food served 'family style' which means big plates for everyone to share... loud and crazy so your screaming child fits right in... enough noise to mask the meltdown of your own child... the food is good and the waitstaff super nice and accommodating... booths are high enough to camouflage nursing moms... they offer valet parking so you can leave the stroller in the car...* **"**

Children's menu	✗	$$$	Prices
Changing station	✗	❹	Customer service
Highchairs/boosters	✓	❸	Stroller access

WWW.BUCADIBEPPO.COM

EASTLAKE/LAKE UNION—701 9TH AVE N (AT BROAD ST); 206.244.2288

Burrito Loco ★★★★☆

"...*yummy inexpensive Mexican food... very kid-friendly... accommodating staff, good food at low prices... my daughter's favorite place to eat dinner...* **"**

Children's menu	✓	$	Prices
Changing station	✗	❺	Customer service
Highchairs/boosters	✓	❸	Stroller access

UNIVERSITY DISTRICT/UNIVERSITY VILLAGE—4608 26TH AVE NE (AT
UNIVERSITY VILLAGE MALL); 206.729.2240; M-TH 10-9, F-SA 10-10, SU 10-
8; MALL PARKING

Café Besalu

"...coffee and pastries here are exceptional... small shop, and slightly
crowded, so good to take away, or sit on seats outside... **"**

Children's menu	✗	$$	Prices
Changing station	✗	❹	Customer service
Highchairs/boosters	✗	❸	Stroller access

BALLARD—5909 24TH AVE NW (AT NW 59TH ST); 206.789.1463

Cafe Flora

"...a family favorite... amazing vegetarian food... delicious and
inexpensive kids menu... the staff offered to call us in from the bamboo
garden when our lunch was ready so we didn't have to wait at the
table... very accommodating about special orders for picky eaters...
even meat eaters will enjoy the food... **"**

Children's menu	✓	$$$	Prices
Changing station	✓	❹	Customer service
Highchairs/boosters	✓	❹	Stroller access

WWW.CAFEFLORA.COM

CAPITOL HILL—2901 E MADISON ST (AT 29TH AVE E); 206.325.9100

California Pizza Kitchen

"...you can't go wrong with their fabulous pizza... always clean... the
food's great, the kids drinks all come with a lid... the staff is super
friendly to kids... crayons and coloring books keep little minds busy...
most locations have a place for strollers at the front... no funny looks or
attitude when breastfeeding... open atmosphere with friendly service...
tables are well spaced so you don't feel like your kid is annoying the
diners nearby (it's usually full of kids anyway)... **"**

Children's menu	✓	$$	Prices
Changing station	✓	❹	Customer service
Highchairs/boosters	✓	❹	Stroller access

WWW.CPK.COM

BELLEVUE—595 106TH AVE NE (AT NE 6TH ST); 425.454.2545; SU-TH 11-10,
F-SA 11-11

MAPLE LEAF/ROOSEVELT—401 NE NORTHGATE WY (AT NORTHGATE
SHOPPING CTR); 206.367.4445; M-TH 11-10, F 11-11, SA 11:30-11, SU 11-
30-10

Charlestown Street Cafe

"...great neighborhood cafe that serves breakfast, lunch and dinner...
the menu has a great variety of foods for kids and adults... one of the
best features of the staff is that they don't cringe when they see kids...
provide books, crayons and a great toy chest for kids to choose toys to
play with while dining... **"**

Children's menu	✓	$	Prices
Changing station	✗	❺	Customer service
Highchairs/boosters	✓	❹	Stroller access

WWW.CHARLESTOWNCHOWDER.COM

WEST SEATTLE—3800 CALIFORNIA AVE SW (AT SW CHARLESTOWN AVE);
206.937.3800

Cheesecake Factory, The

"...although their cheesecake is good, we come here for the kid-
friendly atmosphere and selection of good food... eclectic menu has
something for everyone... they will bring your tot a plate of yogurt,
cheese, bananas and bread free of charge... we love how flexible they

restaurants

are—they'll make whatever my kids want... lots of mommies here... always fun and always crazy... no real kids menu, but the pizza is great to share... waits can be really long... **"**

Children's menu	✗	$$$	Prices
Changing station	✓	❹	Customer service
Highchairs/boosters	✓	❸	Stroller access

WWW.THECHEESECAKEFACTORY.COM

BELLEVUE—401 BELLEVUE SQ (AT NE 4TH ST); 425.450.6000; M-TH 11-11:30, F-SA 11-12:30, SU 10-10

DOWNTOWN—700 PIKE ST (AT 7TH AVE); 206.652.5400; M-TH 11-11:30, F-SA 11-12:30, SU 10-10

Chevys Fresh Mex ★★★★☆

"...*a nice combo of good food for adults and a nice kid's menu... always a sure bet with tots in tow... tasty Mexican food with a simple kids menu (especially the quesedillas)... the tortilla making machine is sure to grab your toddler's attention until the food arrives... an occasional balloon making man... party-like atmosphere with colorful decorations... huge Margaritas for mom and dad... service generally excellent and fast, but you may have to wait for a table at peak hours... long tables can accommodate the multifamily get-together...* **"**

Children's menu	✓	$$	Prices
Changing station	✓	❹	Customer service
Highchairs/boosters	✓	❹	Stroller access

WWW.CHEVYS.COM

LYNNWOOD—44TH AVE W (AT 176TH ST SW); 425.776.2000

Chili's Grill & Bar ★★★½☆

"...*family-friendly, mild Mexican fare... delicious ribs, soups, salads... kids' menu and crayons as you sit down... on the noisy side, so you don't mind if your kids talk in their usual loud voices... service is excellent... fun night out with the family... a wide variety of menu selections for kids and their parents—all at a reasonable price... best chicken fingers on any kids' menu...* **"**

Children's menu	✓	$$	Prices
Changing station	✓	❹	Customer service
Highchairs/boosters	✓	❹	Stroller access

WWW.CHILIS.COM

BELLEVUE—15600 NE 8TH ST (AT 156TH AVE NE); 425.641.0500; SU-TH 11-11, F-SA 11-12

ISSAQUAH—715 NW GILMAN BLVD (OFF NEWPORT WY); 425.392.5600; SU-TH 11-11, F-SA 11-12

Chinook's At Salmon Bay ★★★★☆

"...*northwest seafood in a casual setting... loud and full of kids... general noise tends to drown out your kids... large room in the back is good for families with children... crayons on the tables for kids... terrific weekend brunch...* **"**

Children's menu	✓	$$$	Prices
Changing station	✗	❹	Customer service
Highchairs/boosters	✓	❹	Stroller access

WWW.ANTHONYSRESTAURANTS.COM

MAGNOLIA—1900 W NICKERSON ST (AT 20TH AVE N); 206.283.4665; M-TH 11-10, F 11-11, SA 7-11, SU 7:30-10

Claim Jumper Restaurant ★★★☆☆

"...*food is delicious and service is very child-friendly... so noisy that nobody notices a squawking baby... terrific lunch spot... huge portions are ideal for sharing... plenty of booth seating that offers privacy for breastfeeding...* **"**

Children's menu .... ✓	$$$ .... Prices
Changing station....................... ✓	❹ .... Customer service
Highchairs/boosters .... ✓	❹ ....Stroller access

WWW.CLAIMJUMPER.COM

REDMOND—7210 164TH AVE NE (AT REDMOND TOWN CTR); 425.885.1273;
SU-TH 11-10, F-SA 11-11

Coastal Kitchen ★★★★☆

"...seafood for the whole family... friendly staff was very
accommodating... I felt comfortable breast feeding here... service can
take a while sometimes and the weekend brunches tend to be busy... **"**

Children's menu .... ✓	$$$ .... Prices
Changing station....................... ✗	❹ .... Customer service
Highchairs/boosters .... ✓	❸ ....Stroller access

WWW.CHOWFOODS.COM

CAPITOL HILL—429 15TH AVE E (AT E HARRISON ST); 206.322.1145; M-F 8-
11, SA-SU 8-3

Crossroads Shopping Center
Food Court ★★★★⯪

"...a favorite—something for everyone at any age... wonderful place
to bring kids—lots of food choices (for everyone), plenty of other kids,
frequent free family-appropriate concerts on the stage, and charming
quarter-fed rides after you're done eating... variety of great ethnic
restarants... **"**

Children's menu .... ✗	$$ .... Prices
Changing station....................... ✗	❹ .... Customer service
Highchairs/boosters .... ✓	❺ ....Stroller access

WWW.CROSSROADSBELLEVUE.COM

BELLEVUE—15600 NE 8TH ST (AT 156TH AVE NE); 425.644.1111

Cucina Cucina Italian Cafe ★★★★☆

"...you wouldn't think of this as your typical 'kid-friendly' Italian
restaurant, but the staff is wonderful with children... kids are given
edible bread dough to eat, or play with, while they wait for dinner...
tables are covered with paper and crayons are available for children
(and adults) to color away... excellent food and terrific service... putting
paper under the highchairs is a smart touch... **"**

Children's menu .... ✓	$$ .... Prices
Changing station....................... ✗	❹ .... Customer service
Highchairs/boosters .... ✓	❹ ....Stroller access

WWW.CUCINACUCINA.COM

ISSAQUAH—1510 11TH AVE NW (AT NW SAMMISH RD); 425.391.3800; SU-
TH 11-10, F-SA 11-11

KIRKLAND—2220 CARILLON PT (OFF LAKE WASHINGTON BLVD NE);
425.822.4000; SU-TH 11-10, F-SA 11-11

TUKWILA—17770 SOUTHCENTER PKWY (AT 178TH ST); 206.575.0520; MALL
PARKING

Dad Watson's ★★★★☆

"...renowned burgers and brew and ok for the kids as long as you sit
in the back... the front gets very smokey... **"**

Children's menu .... ✓	$ .... Prices
Changing station....................... ✗	❹ .... Customer service
Highchairs/boosters .... ✓	❸ ....Stroller access

WWW.MCMENAMINS.COM

GREENLAKE/GREENWOOD/PHINNEY RIDGE—3601 FREMONT AVE N (AT N
36TH ST); 206.632.6505

Dish D'Lish ★★★★☆

"...this is one of our standbys when I haven't gotten around to preparing a meal—tasty, healthy, and for little appetites, not too expensive... "

Children's menu	✗	$$	Prices
Changing station	✗	❹	Customer service
Highchairs/boosters	✗	❺	Stroller access

WWW.KATHYCASEY.COM

PIKE MARKET—1505 PIKE PLACE (AT WESTERN AVE); 206.223.1848

Elliott Bay Brewery & Pub ★★★★★

"...great food in a fun, casual environment... a wonderful place to bring kids and drink beer... basic pub food that's good quality and made with love... servers are skilled at dealing with kids and bend over backwards to welcome families... crayons and ceiling fans entertain the kids... great fish and chips and good children's menu... if you have a toddler get a booth—the sides are so tall you can't see to the next table... "

Children's menu	✓	$$	Prices
Changing station	✗	❺	Customer service
Highchairs/boosters	✓	❸	Stroller access

WWW.ELLIOTTBAYBREWING.COM

WEST SEATTLE—4720 CALIFORNIA AVE SW (AT SW ALASKA ST); 206.932.8695; M-TH 11:30-11, F-SA 11:30-1AM, SU 12-10

Elysian TangleTown ★★★★☆

"...food is really good as is the beer and they have a nice kids menu. Weekend brunch is definitely our families favorite... family friendly, plenty of highchairs... this is a very kid-friendly restaurant near Greenlake... always lots of kids in there... nice food, good beer—part of Elysian Brewery... "

Children's menu	✓	$$	Prices
Changing station	✓	❹	Customer service
Highchairs/boosters	✓	❹	Stroller access

WWW.ELYSIANBREWING.COM

WALLINGFORD/FREMONT—2106 N 55TH ST (AT MERIDIAN AVE N); 206.547.5929; SU-TH 11:30-10, F-SA 11:30-11

Endolyne Joe's ★★★★☆

"...food and the staff are very kid-friendly... decor changes every 3 months with a new theme... lots of things for the kids to look at... kids menu and crayons... "

Children's menu	✓	$$$	Prices
Changing station	✓	❺	Customer service
Highchairs/boosters	✓	❺	Stroller access

CHOWFOODS.COM

WEST SEATTLE—9261 45TH AVE SW (AT SW BRACE POINT DR); 206.937.6310; PARKING LOT NEXT TO BLDG

Etta's Seafood ★★★★☆

"...good brunch spot ... staff is very kid-friendly, ready with the cup of crayons... noisy enough to hide kid noise... only downside is that tables are a little close, so if you need a highchair, you need to wait until a spot with lots of space opens up... "

Children's menu	✗	$$$$	Prices
Changing station	✗	❹	Customer service
Highchairs/boosters	✗	❹	Stroller access

WWW.TOMDOUGLAS.COM

BELLTOWN—2020 WESTERN AVE (AT VIRGINIA ST); 206.443.6000

Gordon Biersch

"...a fantastic brewery that serves delicious food... awesome beer that is brewed onsite... fun atmosphere that works well for kids... high-end bar food... staff seems to adore babies... server was very doting and attentive to my family's needs... best to go early before the after work scene gets going... the big vats and pipes provide for a fun walk-around with my tot..."

Children's menu ✓	$$$	Prices
Changing station ✓	❹	Customer service
Highchairs/boosters ✓	❹	Stroller access

WWW.GORDONBIERSCH.COM

DOWNTOWN—600 PINE ST (AT PACIFIC PLACE); 206.405.4205; DAILY 11:30-1AM

Grady's Montlake Pub & Eatery

"...back area has this 'kid pit' with toys, books, etc for the kids to play in until 9pm... similar to its sister restaurant The Madrona Ale House... menu is ok, but not great—I wish it had more basic pub like stuff, but the setting is excellent for kids... great break for quick family dinner..."

Children's menu ✓	$$$	Prices
Changing station ✓	❹	Customer service
Highchairs/boosters ✓	❹	Stroller access

MONTLAKE—2307 24TH AVE E (AT E LYNN ST); 206.726.5968

Great Harvest Bread Company

"...fabulous breads, cookies, granola, deli sandwiches... my daughter loves the breadsticks... great staff makes it kid-friendly... always giving away free samples (yum)... Not a sit down restaurant, order at the counter... good place to stop for a snack..."

Children's menu ✗	$$	Prices
Changing station ✗	❺	Customer service
Highchairs/boosters ✓	❹	Stroller access

WWW.GREATHARVESTSEA.COM

BALLARD—2218 NW MARKET ST (AT 22ND AVE NW); 206.706.3434

LAURELHURST/SANDPOINT—5408 SAND POINT WY NE (AT 47TH AVE NE); 206.524.4873

NORTH SEATTLE—17171 BOTHELL WY NE (AT LAKE FOREST PARK CTR); 206.365.4778

WEST SEATTLE—4709 CALIFORNIA AVE SW (AT SW ALASKA ST); 206.935.6882

Hi-Life, The

"...baby and adult friendly... better for brunch than dinner... the waitstaff remembers our daughter each time we go...located in the old Ballard Firehouse..."

Children's menu ✓	$$	Prices
Changing station ✗	❹	Customer service
Highchairs/boosters ✓	❹	Stroller access

WWW.CHOWFOODS.COM

BALLARD—5425 RUSSELL AVE NW (AT 20TH AVE NW); 206.784.7272

IKEA

"...Swedish meatballs and funny berry drinks—all very yummy and cheap... a clean, comfortable place to eat... the restaurant sells baby food and has bottle/jar warmers... worth visiting even if you aren't shopping—the food is cheap, but good... totally kid-friendly... lines can sometimes be long—especially during peak shopping hours..."

Children's menu	✓	$$	Prices
Changing station	✓	❹	Customer service
Highchairs/boosters	✓	❹	Stroller access

WWW.IKEA.COM

RENTON—600 SW 43RD ST (AT E VALLEY HWY); 425.656.2980; M-F 10-9:30, SA 10-9, SU 10-8; GARAGE PARKING

Il Fornaio ★★★★⯪

"...lovely place for a family date... fancy, but welcoming to the whole family... my son loves the breadsticks that come in the bread basket... my husband and I love bringing our child as she loves the veggies in the minestrone soup... nice outdoor seating on a warm night... great brunch too... their French toast is quite tasty... **"**

Children's menu	✓	$$$	Prices
Changing station	✓	❹	Customer service
Highchairs/boosters	✓	❹	Stroller access

DOWNTOWN—600 PINE ST (AT 6TH AVE); 206.264.0994

Imperial Garden Seafood Restaurant ★★★★☆

"...Best dim sum in town... family oriented place... **"**

Children's menu	✗	$$	Prices
Changing station	✗	❹	Customer service
Highchairs/boosters	✓	❹	Stroller access

WWW.IMPERIALGARDENSEAFOOD.COM

KENT—18230 E VALLEY HWY (OFF 180TH ST); 425.656.0999

Ivar's Acres of Clams ★★★☆☆

"...kind of touristy, but we love the fish bar outside...indoor and outdoor dining...great place to eat after a visit to the Seattle Aquarium...the best fish and chips in town... **"**

Children's menu	✗	$$	Prices
Changing station	✗	❸	Customer service
Highchairs/boosters	✓	❸	Stroller access

WWW.IVARS.NET

DOWNTOWN—1001 ALASKAN WY (AT MADISON ST); 206.624.6852

Ivar's Salmon House ★★★★☆

"...we went during the lunch & the waitstaff was wonderful... they were patient & understanding when my daughter yelled, threw things around and overall was messy... put us in a great place so she had a lot to look at... will go again without reservation..located on north Lake Union... **"**

Children's menu	✓	$$$	Prices
Changing station	✗	❹	Customer service
Highchairs/boosters	✓	❸	Stroller access

WWW.IVARS.NET

GREENLAKE/GREENWOOD/PHINNEY RIDGE—401 NE NORTHLAKE WY (AT 6TH AVE NE); 206.632.0767

Ixtapa Restaurant ★★★★☆

"...quality food, low prices, and VERY family friendly... family Mexican located at the retail center of the Redmond Ridge community... boisterous and kid-friendly... waitstaff always make a point of greeting the children enthusiastically... **"**

Children's menu	✗	$$	Prices
Changing station	✗	❹	Customer service
Highchairs/boosters	✓	❹	Stroller access

REDMOND—22350 NE MARKETPLACE DR (AT CEDAR PARK CRES);
425.868.8283

SNOHOMISH—515 2ND ST (AT LINCOLN AVE); 360.568.4522

Johnny Rockets

"...burgers, fries and a shake served up in a 50's style diner... we love
the singing waiters—they're always good for a giggle... my daughter is
enthralled with the juke box and straw dispenser... sit at the counter
and watch the cooks prepare the food... simple, satisfying and always a
hit with the little ones... **"**

Children's menu	✓	$$	Prices
Changing station	✗	❹	Customer service
Highchairs/boosters	✓	❸	Stroller access

WWW.JOHNNYROCKETS.COM

AUBURN—1101 SUPERMALL WY (AT SUPERMALL OF THE GREAT
NORTHWEST); 253.735.2449; FREE PARKING

DOWNTOWN—600 PINE ST (AT PACIFIC PLACE); 206.749.9803; M-TH 9-10,
F-SA 9-11, SU 9-9

Jose O'Reilly's Cantina

"...food is consistently good, but service is sometimes a bit
unpredictable... changing table in the men's room... **"**

Children's menu	✓	$$	Prices
Changing station	✓	❹	Customer service
Highchairs/boosters	✓	❹	Stroller access

WALLINGFORD/FREMONT—4401 WALLINGFORD AVE N (AT NE 44TH ST);
206.633.1175

Kanishka

"...I really love this Indian place ... staff is really patient with my
daughter; they come & talk with her & no one even blinks when she
cries or is exuberant... we like to take her there—it's a good low key
place to eat and the food is really good... **"**

Children's menu	✗	$	Prices
Changing station	✗	❹	Customer service
Highchairs/boosters	✓	❸	Stroller access

REDMOND—16101 REDMOND WAY (AT 161ST AVE); 425.869.9182

Lake Route Cafe

"...off the beaten path superb place for breakfast... fresh wholesome
breakfasts, home made muffins, whole wheat pancakes along with your
standard country potatoes, eggs and bacon stuff... during the week,
there's always a crowd of older folks around waiting to fawn over your
little ones... restaurant is small, but very homey... **"**

Children's menu	✗	$$	Prices
Changing station	✗	❸	Customer service
Highchairs/boosters	✗	❸	Stroller access

BALLARD—9261 57TH AVE S (AT RAINIER AVE); 206.723.6580

Luisa's Mexican Grill

"...our favorite family restaurant, and the only one we would dare
venture into when we had three kids under four... as you enter for
dinner, someone is making homemade tortillas... casual and the food is
good... staff adore our children and remember us even after six months
goes by... recommend it as a family friendly restaurant... **"**

Children's menu	✓	$$	Prices
Changing station	✗	❹	Customer service
Highchairs/boosters	✓	❸	Stroller access

WWW.LUISASMEXICANGRILL.COM

BALLARD—9747 4TH AVE NW (AT HOMAN RD); 206.784.4132

restaurants

Luna Park Café

★★★★☆

"...whole decor lends itself to dining with children... very kid-friendly restaurant both in terms of menu selection and decor...**"**

Children's menu...................... ✓   \$\$.. Prices
Changing station .... ✗   ❹ ....Customer service
Highchairs/boosters.................. ✓   ❹ .... Stroller access

WEST SEATTLE—2918 SW AVALON WY (AT SW SPOKANE ST); 206.935.7250

Madrona Eatery & Ale House

★★★⯪☆

"...kick back and have a beer, some grub and feel comfortable—your kid can run around, socialize and play with toys... a neighborhood haven for parents... our son loved the pizza and the hummus equally... big bucket of toys and a couch where your kids can hang out while you eat a burger and watch the game...**"**

Children's menu...................... ✓   \$\$\$.. Prices
Changing station .... ✗   ❹ ....Customer service
Highchairs/boosters.................. ✓   ❸ .... Stroller access

MADRONA—1138 34TH AVE (AT E SPRING ST); 206.323.7807

Maggie Bluff's Grill

★★★★☆

"...friendly and amazing view of Elliot bay, plus you can get the fancy Palisades deserts as they are above...located at Elliot Bay Marina...excellent food...outdoor dining in the summer...**"**

Children's menu...................... ✓   \$\$.. Prices
Changing station .... ✗   ❹ ....Customer service
Highchairs/boosters.................. ✓   ❸ .... Stroller access

MAGNOLIA—2601 W MARINA PL (AT 23RD AVE W); 206.283.8322

Maneki Restaurant

★★★★☆

"...notable Japanese food... make reservation for one of the 'tatami rooms' so the kids can roam around in the room...**"**

Children's menu...................... ✗   \$\$\$.. Prices
Changing station .... ✗   ❸ ....Customer service
Highchairs/boosters.................. ✗   ❸ .... Stroller access

DOWNTOWN—304 6TH AVE S (AT JACKSON ST); 206.622.2631

Mayas

★★★☆☆

"...one of the best places for Mexican food in the city... child-friendly...**"**

Children's menu...................... ✗   \$\$.. Prices
Changing station .... ✗   ❸ ....Customer service
Highchairs/boosters.................. ✗   ❸ .... Stroller access

RAINIER VALLEY—9447 RAINIER AVE S (AT 56TH AVE S); 206.725.5510

Mayuri Indian Cuisine

★★★★☆

"...Mayuri is very family friendly. Our kids love the Mango Lassi, the 'Chicken Nuggets' (Chicken Pakoras) and the 'Hamburger in the bread' (Keema Nan)... great way to get the food you want while still pleasing the kids, and introducing them to other foods...**"**

Children's menu...................... ✗   \$\$\$.. Prices
Changing station .... ✗   ❹ ....Customer service
Highchairs/boosters.................. ✗   ❸ .... Stroller access

WWW.MAYURISEATTLE.COM

BELLEVUE—15400 NE 20TH ST (AT 156TH AVE); 425.641.4442

McCormick & Schmicks

★★★★☆

"...steak and seafood are the mainstay but the menu is broad... terrific happy-hour menu... a little more formal than your regular 'tot-friendly' restaurant, but the staff is great and goes out of their way to make sure *you're comfortable... try to get one of the banquet rooms—it makes breastfeeding much easier... good food for adults and more than enough for the little ones too...* "

Children's menu	✓	$$$	Prices
Changing station	✓	❹	Customer service
Highchairs/boosters	✓	❹	Stroller access

WWW.MCCORMICKANDSCHMICKS.COM

EASTLAKE/LAKE UNION—1200 WESTLAKE AVE N (AT 8TH AVE N); 206.270.9052; PARKING IN FRONT OF BLDG

Mr. Villa ★★★★★

"...great little authentic Mexican Restaurant... kids meals for only $2.99... staff is child-friendly... highly recommend the tacos on homemade tortillas... also, the burrito pancho villa is great... "

Children's menu	✗	$	Prices
Changing station	✗	❹	Customer service
Highchairs/boosters	✓	❹	Stroller access

MAPLE LEAF/ROOSEVELT—8064 LAKE CITY WY NE (AT 15TH AVE NE); 206.517.5660

My Coffee House ★★★★★

"...best place for a rainy day... basic bagel and good coffee and a great play area... especially nice because you can have an adult conversation while kids play... bring your child for some fun while you get to enjoy some great coffee... a super kid-friendly coffee house with so many toys for the kids to enjoy... "

Children's menu	✓	$$	Prices
Changing station	✗	❺	Customer service
Highchairs/boosters	✗	❺	Stroller access

MADISON VALLEY/MADISON PARK—2818 E MADISON ST (AT 28TH AVE E); 206.568.7509

Noah's Bagels ★★★★☆

"...top place for breakfast with the kids... can't beat juice and bagels... kids love the variety and ability to choose their own type of bagel and cream cheese/shmear... "

Children's menu	✗	$	Prices
Changing station	✗	❹	Customer service
Highchairs/boosters	✗	❹	Stroller access

WWW.NOAHS.COM

CAPITOL HILL—220 BROADWAY E (AT E JOHN ST); 206.720.2925

Old Country Buffet ★★★★☆

"...homey comfort food... enough selections so that even the pickiest child will find something they like... get lost in the hustle and bustle... the kids can go crazy and no one will notice... does tend to get crowded at times... we have a large family and this is one of the few places where everyone can find something they like... inexpensive and kind of rough around the edges... "

Children's menu	✗	$$	Prices
Changing station	✓	❹	Customer service
Highchairs/boosters	✓	❹	Stroller access

WWW.OLDCOUNTRYBUFFET.COM

KENT—25630 104TH AVE SE (AT SE 256TH ST); 253.859.3224; M-TH 11-8:30, F 11-9, SA 8-9, SU 8-8:30; PARKING LOT AT KENT HILL PLAZA

Old Spaghetti Factory, The ★★★½☆

"...good for a fast, cheap meal if the place isn't too packed... apple sauce for kids... fun for the whole family and easy to eat for under $25 (family of four)... if you've got a hankering for spaghetti and meatballs,

look no further... relatively inexpensive and you get big portions for your money... a place with a relaxed feel... it is usually so busy that no one will notice if your toddler is crying... the staff makes it easy to hang out and have a good time... **"**

Children's menu	✓	$$	....	Prices
Changing station	✓	❹	....	Customer service
Highchairs/boosters	✓	❹	....	Stroller access

WWW.OLDSPAGHETTIFACTORY.COM

BELLTOWN—2801 ELLIOTT AVE (AT CLAY ST); 206.441.7724; M-F 11:30-9:30, F 5-10, SA 11:30-10, SU 11:30-9:30; PARKING IN FRONT OF BLDG

LYNNWOOD—2509 196TH ST SW (AT 24TH AVE W); 425.672.7006; M-F 11:30-9:30, F 5-10, SA 11:30-10, SU 11:30-9:30; PARKING IN FRONT OF BLDG

Olive Garden ★★★★☆

"*...finally a place that is both kid and adult friendly... tasty Italian chain with lot's of convenient locations... the staff consistently attends to the details of dining with babies and toddlers—minimizing wait time, highchairs offered spontaneously, bread sticks brought immediately... food is served as quickly as possible... happy to create special orders... our waitress even acted as our family photographer...* **"**

Children's menu	✓	$$	....	Prices
Changing station	✓	❹	....	Customer service
Highchairs/boosters	✓	❹	....	Stroller access

WWW.OLIVEGARDEN.COM

EVERETT—1321 SE EVERETT MALL WY (AT EVERETT MALL); 425.347.9857; SU-TH 11-10, F-SA 11-11; MALL PARKING

FEDERAL WAY—35030 ENCHANTED PKWY (AT S 351ST ST); 253.815.1375; SU-TH 11-10, F-SA 11-11

KIRKLAND—11325 NE 124TH ST (AT 113TH AVE NE); 425.820.7740; SU-TH 11-10, F-SA 11-11

Ooba's Mexican Grill ★★★★⯪

"*...great choice for lighter Mexican fare—not your typical Mexican, no cheese and tomato and refried beans here... good food with some kids choices... toy kiosk at the front with different games for kids... fast and very friendly service... really good food—mostly grilled... fresh lemonade, but eat early if you want some—they almost always run out by the end of the day...* **"**

Children's menu	✗	$$	....	Prices
Changing station	✗	❺	....	Customer service
Highchairs/boosters	✓	❹	....	Stroller access

REDMOND—15802 NE 83RD ST (OFF 164TH AVE); 425.702.1694

WOODINVILLE—17302 140TH AVE NE (AT THE ALBERTSON'S MALL); 425.481.5252

Original Pancake House ★★★★⯪

"*...consistently the best breakfast around... great flapjacks and appropriately-sized kids meals... food comes quickly... the most amazing apple pancakes ever... service is always friendly, but sometimes it can take a while to actually get the food... the highlight for my daughter is the free balloon when we leave... always a lot of families here with small children on the weekends, so you don't have to worry about being the only one...* **"**

Children's menu	✓	$$	....	Prices
Changing station	✓	❹	....	Customer service
Highchairs/boosters	✓	❸	....	Stroller access

WWW.ORIGINALPANCAKEHOUSE.COM

KIRKLAND—130 PARKPLACE CENTER (OFF MARKET ST); 425.827.7575

participate in our survey at

SEATTLE—8037 15TH AVE NW (OFF 80TH ST); 206.781.3344

Outback Steakhouse

"...*Aussie style eatery with big steaks and shrimp on the barbie... don't miss the bloomin' onion, but be prepared to share—it's huge... very understanding of our screaming infant and gave us a booth a little out of the way... gave us extra whipped cream for dessert and on occasion free ice cream... the wait for a table can get long so go early to avoid the masses... nice wide aisles makes maneuvering around with strollers easy... tables toys in the waiting area...* **"**

Children's menu	✓	$$$	Prices
Changing station	✓	❹	Customer service
Highchairs/boosters	✓	❸	Stroller access

WWW.OUTBACKSTEAKHOUSE.COM

BELLEVUE—15100 SE 38TH ST (AT 150TH AVE); 425.746.4647

BOTHELL—22606 BOTHELL EVERETT HWY (AT 228TH ST); 425.486.7340

EASTLAKE/LAKE UNION—701 WESTLAKE AVE N (AT VALLEY ST); 206.262.0326

EVERETT—10121 EVERGREEN WAY (AT 100TH AVE); 425.513.2181

FEDERAL WAY—2210 S 320TH ST (AT SEATAC MALL); 253.839.1340

KIRKLAND—12120 NE 85TH ST (AT 124TH AVE); 425.803.6880

NORTH SEATTLE—13231 AURORA AVE N (AT 130TH ST); 206.367.7780

TUKWILA—16510 SOUTHCENTER PKWY (AT STRANDER BLVD); 206.575.9705

Pagliacci Pizzeria

"...*what can one say, 'Pags' is the best... Salmon Primo features wild salmon that is lightly smoked... Pizza by the slice or entire pies...order at the counter...my toddler loves their pasta salad...best pizza in Seattle...* **"**

Children's menu	✗	$$	Prices
Changing station	✗	❹	Customer service
Highchairs/boosters	✗	❸	Stroller access

BELLEVUE—563 BELLEVUE SQ (AT NE 4TH ST); 425.453.1717; SU-TH11-11, F-SA 11-12AM

CAPITOL HILL—426 BROADWAY E (AT E HARRISON ST); 206.726.1717; SU-TH 11-11, F-SA 11-12; STREET PARKING

LOWER QUEEN ANNE/SEATTLE CENTER—550 QUEEN ANNE AVE N (AT W MERCER ST); 206.285.1232

UNIVERSITY DISTRICT/UNIVERSITY VILLAGE—4529 UNIVERSITY WAY NE (AT NE 45TH ST); 425.453.1717; SU-TH11-11, F-SA 11-12

Pallino Pastaria

"...*topflight pasta (especially the cheese sauce!) and they have lots of toys available for kids to play with... they even have disinfectant wipes to wipe down the toys before you give them to your little one... delicious pasta and sandwiches... offers discounts for kids, with deep discounts for kids on Sundays... they have a dozen different sauces and you put the sauces over the pasta of your choice, including fettucine, gemelli, cheese raviolis, etc... order at the counter ...* **"**

Children's menu	✓	$$	Prices
Changing station	✗	❹	Customer service
Highchairs/boosters	✓	❹	Stroller access

WWW.PALLINO.COM

BELLEVUE—NE 8TH ST & BELLEVUE WAY NE (AT BELLEVUE SQUARE); 425.462.7589; SU-TH 11-9:30, F-SA 11-10

DOWNTOWN—601 UNION ST (AT 6TH AVE); 206.583.8755; M-F 7-3

FIRST HILL—1221 MADISON ST (ARNOLD PAVILLION AT SWEDISH HOSPITAL); 206.382.7885; M-F 7-7

ISSAQUAH—6150 E LAKE SAMMAMISH PKWY (AT 62ND ST); 425.394.1090

SEATTLE—2626 NE 46TH ST (UNIVERSITY VILLAGE MALL); 206.522.8617;
SU-TH 11-9, F-SA 11-10

WOODINVILLE—17848 GARDEN WAY NE (AT NE 175TH ST); 425.424.0500;
SU-TH 11-9, F-SA 11-10

Pasta & Co

❝...*Pasta & Co. has great prepared foods to take home—pasta of course, but also really good, healthy salads, meats, pasta dishes... huge variety every day... you can choose a variety, a spoonful of this and that, and eat it in the shop .. ends up being a good, healthy and pretty inexpensive lunch...* **❞**

Children's menu .... ✗ $ .... Prices
Changing station .... ✗   ❸ .... Customer service
Highchairs/boosters .... ✓   ❺ .... Stroller access

WWW.PASTACO.COM

BELLEVUE—10218 NE 8TH ST (AT BELLEVUE SQUARE); 425.453.8760; M-TH
10-8, F-SA 10-8:30, SU 11-7:30

REDMOND—7425 170TH AVE NE (AT REDMOND TOWN CTR); 425.881.1992;
M-TH 10-8, F-SA 10-8:30, SU 11-7:30

QUEEN ANNE—2109 QUEEN ANNE AVE N (AT CROCKETT ST); 206.283.1182;
M-TH 10-8, F-SA 10-8:30, SU 11-7:30

UNIVERSITY DISTRICT/UNIVERSITY VILLAGE—4622 26TH AVE NE (AT
UNIVERSITY VILLAGE); 206.523.8594; M-SA 9:30-9, SU 10-6

Pasta Nova

Children's menu .... ✗ $$$ .... Prices
Changing station .... ✗   ❺ .... Customer service
Highchairs/boosters .... ✗   ❺ .... Stroller access

WOODINVILLE—17310 140TH AVE NE (AT WOODINVILLE PLAZA);
425.483.3716

Portage Bay Cafe

❝...*Portage Bay is always crowded, we have had good experiences here for brunch with our 5-month old... servers are very baby-friendly, and the food is yummy...* **❞**

Children's menu .... ✓ $$ .... Prices
Changing station .... ✗   ❺ .... Customer service
Highchairs/boosters .... ✗   ❸ .... Stroller access

WWW.PORTAGEBAYCAFE.COM

UNIVERSITY DISTRICT/UNIVERSITY VILLAGE—4140 ROOSEVELT WAY NE (AT
42ND ST); 206.547.8230; M-F 7:30-3, SA SU 8-3

Puerto Vallarta Restaurant ★★★★☆

❝...*fresh Mexican cooking... my five kids can make a mess and the folks there have never flinched... they have 99 cent kid meals on sunday and unlimited chips and salsa...* **❞**

Children's menu .... ✓ $ .... Prices
Changing station .... ✗   ❺ .... Customer service
Highchairs/boosters .... ✓   ❹ .... Stroller access

WEST SEATTLE—4727 CALIFORNIA AVE SW (AT SW ALASKA ST);
206.937.7335; DAILY 11-10:30

Queen Anne Cafe

Children's menu .... ✓   ✗ .... Changing station
Highchairs/boosters .... ✓

LOWER QUEEN ANNE/SEATTLE CENTER—2121 QUEEN ANNE AVE N (AT W
CROCKETT ST); 206.285.2060; M-F 7-2:30, 5-8, SA 8-8, SU 8-2:30

Rainforest Cafe

★★★☆☆

"...like eating in the jungle... the decor keeps the kids entertained and the food is decent... kids either love it or are terrified at first and need to ease into the wild animal thing... I get at least 20 extra minutes of hang time with my friends because my daughter is so enchanted by the setting... waiters tend to be very accommodating... they always give me (with my three kiddos) an extra-large table... watch the toy section chock full of 'but I want it' items... **"**

Children's menu .... ✓
Changing station .... ✓
Highchairs/boosters .... ✓

$$$ .... Prices
❹ .... Customer service
❹ .... Stroller access

WWW.RAINFORESTCAFE.COM

TUKWILA—290 SOUTHCENTER MALL (AT SOUTHCENTER MALL); 206.248.8882; M-TH 11-9:30, F-SA 11-10, SU 11-8; MALL PARKING

Ram Restaurant & Brewery

★★★★☆

"...lively scene with TV in the background... veggies and dip brought to the table... pub food and nice kids menu... quick service and draft beers for mom and dad... kids eat free one day a week... the servers are all very nice and the place is swarming with kids on Friday night... **"**

Children's menu .... ✓
Changing station .... ✗
Highchairs/boosters .... ✓

$$ .... Prices
❹ .... Customer service
❹ .... Stroller access

WWW.THERAM.COM

WEDGEWOOD/RAVENNA—4730 NE UNIVERSITY VILLAGE PL (AT UNIVERSITY VILLAGE MALL); 206.525.3565; MALL PARKING

Red Mill Burgers

★★★★☆

"...original Red Mill was located in the capitol hill neighborhood in Seattle and opened in 1937, it closed in 1967... was known as a diner and ice creamery with table and counter service... current Red Mills were opened first in the phinney ridge neighborhood in 1994 and the second location in the Interbay neighborhood in 1998... received honorable mention in the best burger category in the Seattle Weekly's annual Best of Seattle issue... best burger in town... inexpensive food, but when it's crowded it's hard to maneuver a stroller through the restaurant, particularly with the flight of stairs to the dining area... **"**

Children's menu .... ✗
Changing station .... ✗
Highchairs/boosters .... ✗

$ .... Prices
❹ .... Customer service
❸ .... Stroller access

WWW.REDMILLBURGERS.COM

GREENLAKE/GREENWOOD/PHINNEY RIDGE—312 N 67TH ST (AT GREENWOOD AVE N); 206.783.6362; T-SA 11-9, SU 12-8

MAGNOLIA—1613 W DRAVUS ST (AT 15TH AVE W); 206.284.6363; T-SA 11-9, SU 12-8

Red Robin

★★★★★

"...very kid-oriented—loud, balloons, bright lights, colorful decor and a cheerful staff make Red Robin a favorite among parents and children... the food is mainly burgers (beef or chicken)... loud music covers even the most boisterous of screaming... lots of kids—all the time... sometimes the wait can be long, but the arcade games and balloons help pass the time... **"**

Children's menu .... ✓
Changing station .... ✓
Highchairs/boosters .... ✓

$$ .... Prices
❹ .... Customer service
❹ .... Stroller access

WWW.REDROBIN.COM

ALGONA—1018 SUPERMALL WY (AT SUPERMALL THE GREAT NORTHWEST); 253.804.6550; M-TH 11-11, F-SA 11-12AM, SU 11-10

restaurants

AUBURN—1002 SUPER MALL WAY (AT 15TH ST SW); 253.804.6550; MALL PARKING

BELLEVUE—3909 FACTORIA BLVD SE (AT FACTORIA SQ MALL); 425.641.3989; MALL PARKING

BELLEVUE—408 BELLEVUE SQ (AT BELLEVUE WY); 425.453.9522

DES MOINES—22705 MARINE VIEW DR (AT S 227TH PL); 206.824.2214; M-SA 11-10, SU 11-9

DOWNTOWN—1101 ALASKAN WAY (AT SPRING ST); 206.623.1942; SU-TH 11-11, F-SA 11-12

EVERETT—1305 SE EVERETT MALL WAY (AT EVERETT MALL); 425.355.7330; MALL PARKING

FEDERAL WAY—2233 S 320TH ST (AT 23RD AVE S); 253.946.8646; SU-TH 11-11, F-SA 11-12:30

ISSAQUAH—1085 LAKE DR (AT 11TH AVE NW); 425.313.0950

KENT—25207 104TH AVE SE (AT SE 253RD PL); 253.850.8101; M-SA 11-11, SU 11-10

LYNNWOOD—18410 33RD AVE W (AT ALDERWOOD MALL); 425.771.6492; M-TH 11-11, F-SA 11-12, SU 11-10; MALL PARKING

MAPLE LEAF/ROOSEVELT—555 NE NORTHGATE WY (AT 3RD AVE); 206.365.0933; MALL PARKING

PORTAGE BAY—3272 FUHRMAN AVE E (AT EASTLAKE AVE E); 206.323.0918

REDMOND—2390 148TH AVE NE (AT NE 24TH ST); 425.641.3810

REDMOND—7597 170TH AVE NE (AT REDMOND TOWN CTR); 425.895.1870; SU-TH 11-11, F-SA 11-12

TUKWILA—17300 SOUTHCENTER PKWY (AT SOUTHCENTER MALL); 206.575.8382; MALL PARKING

WOODINVILLE—18029 GARDEN WAY NE (AT NE 178TH PL); 425.488.6300

Romano's Macaroni Grill ★★★★☆

"...family oriented and tasty... noisy so nobody cares if your kids make noise... the staff goes out of their way to make families feel welcome... they even provide slings by the table for infant carriers... the noise level is pretty constant so it's not too loud, but loud enough so that crying babies don't disturb the other patrons... good kids' menu with somewhat healthy items... crayons for kids to color on the paper tablecloths...**"**

Children's menu	✓	$$$	Prices
Changing station	✓	❹	Customer service
Highchairs/boosters	✓	❹	Stroller access

WWW.MACARONIGRILL.COM

LYNNWOOD—3000 184TH ST SW (OFF ALDERWOOD MALL); 425.368.2875; SU-TH 11-10, F-SA 11-11

Ruby's Diner ★★★★★

"...a fun 50's diner where they really cater to kids and their parents... decor is colorful and entertaining... always busy, so be prepared to wait... lots of visual stimulation for the little ones... healthy alternatives on the menu, so don't feel you have to eat a burger and fries... excellent milk shakes... plenty of room to park strollers...**"**

Children's menu	✓	$$	Prices
Changing station	✓	❹	Customer service
Highchairs/boosters	✓	❹	Stroller access

WWW.RUBYS.COM

LYNNWOOD—3000 184TH ST SW (AT ALDERWOOD MALL); 425.778.8729

REDMOND—16501 NE 74TH ST (AT REDMOND TOWN CTR); 425.497.8290; SU-TH 7-9, F-SA 7-10

participate in our survey a

Sahib

"...great Indian food... offers a nice buffet that is priced quite nicely (especially on weekdays)... not too crowded at lunch and there is room for strollers ... staff is very helpful and friendly. Highly recommended. Great view of the water, ferry and train too..."

Children's menu	✗	$$	Prices
Changing station	✗	❺	Customer service
Highchairs/boosters	✓	❹	Stroller access

EDMONDS—101 MAIN ST (AT SUNSET AVE); 425.775.2828

Shiki Japanese Restaurant

"...our top choice for sushi... decor and atmosphere are unassuming, the sushi chef/owner and all of the staff adore our toddler daughter... they even let her sit at the sushi bar..."

Children's menu	✗	$$$	Prices
Changing station	✗	❺	Customer service
Highchairs/boosters	✓	❺	Stroller access

QUEEN ANNE—4 W ROY ST (AT QUEEN ANNE AVE); 206.281.1352

Sip & Ship

"...you can eat at the cafe—baked items, sandwiches and coffees all while surfing the net and sending packages... there is a kid-friendly loft with toys, a swing and a playpen... the only drawback is the kid area is upstairs so getting a stroller up there is challenging if you're alone... every time I've been there, however, there have been plenty of friendly, helpful employees around to lend a hand..."

Children's menu	✗	$$	Prices
Changing station	✓	❺	Customer service
Highchairs/boosters	✗	❸	Stroller access

WWW.SIPANDSHIP.NET

BALLARD—1752 NW MARKET ST (AT 17TH AVE NW); 206.789.4488; M-F 7-7,
SA 8-7, SU 12-5; PARKING BEHIND BLDG

Space Needle Restaurant

"...get your pointing finger ready! every degree of the Observation Deck's 360° view commands your attention... lofty panorama of Seattle's natural wonders...floor of restaurant slowly spins while you eat, so you can enjoy views from all angles...pretty fancy affair-special occassion only for my toddler..."

Children's menu	✓	$$$$$	Prices
Changing station	✓	❺	Customer service
Highchairs/boosters	✓	❸	Stroller access

WWW.SPACENEEDLE.COM

LOWER QUEEN ANNE/SEATTLE CENTER—219 4TH AVE N (AT BROAD ST);
206.443.2100

St Clouds Restaurant

"...casual local restaurant with great food and very kid-friendly... they keep small toys at the hostess stand to keep toddlers happy at the table, and have a good supply of highchairs and booster seats... small outside seating area where antsy toddlers can bounce off steam while waiting for their meal..."

Children's menu	✓	$$$	Prices
Changing station	✓	❺	Customer service
Highchairs/boosters	✓	❹	Stroller access

WWW.STCLOUDS.COM

MADRONA—1131 34TH AVE (AT E UNION ST); 206.726.1522

restaurants

Stellar Pizza & Ale

"...everything at Stellar is homemade—pizza, pasta, soups and sandwiches... micro brews on tap plus a great selection of bottled beer & wine, pool tables, and good old-fashioned pinball games... family friendly—up until 9pm... **"**

Children's menu	✓	$$	Prices
Changing station	✗	❸	Customer service
Highchairs/boosters	✓	❸	Stroller access

WWW.STELLARPIZZA.COM

GEORGETOWN—5513 AIRPORT WAY S (OFF RT 5); 206.763.1660

Susan's 5100 Bistro ★★★★☆

"...ripping little cafe to hangout for a leisurely lunch/brunch... we've been going every week since our baby was 1-month-old... **"**

Children's menu	✓	$$	Prices
Changing station	✗	❸	Customer service
Highchairs/boosters	✓	❺	Stroller access

SEWARD PARK—5100 S DAWSON ST (AT S DAWSON ST); 206.721.6308

Taco Del Mar ★★★★☆

"...Mexican food made to your specifications... lots of vegetarian options... reasonable prices... small space so stroller access is not the best... always have lots of kiddie customers... food is FAST and you can watch it being prepared which makes the wait seem even shorter... **"**

Children's menu	✓	$	Prices
Changing station	✗	❹	Customer service
Highchairs/boosters	✓	❹	Stroller access

WWW.TACODELMAR.COM

BALLARD—6101 15TH AVE NW (AT NW 61ST ST); 206.297.4446

BELLEVUE—677 120TH AVE NE (AT NE 8TH ST); 425.646.9041

DOWNTOWN—1620 4TH AVE (AT PINE ST); 206.343.0400

DOWNTOWN—2136 1ST AVE (AT LENORA ST); 206.448.8877

DOWNTOWN—725 PIKE ST (AT 7TH AVE); 206.628.8982

GEORGETOWN—2932 4TH AVE S (AT S SPOKANE AVE); 206.521.8887

GREENLAKE/GREENWOOD/PHINNEY RIDGE—1815 N 45TH ST (AT WALLINGFORD AVE N); 206.545.3720

GREENLAKE/GREENWOOD/PHINNEY RIDGE—3526 FREMONT PL N (AT N 36TH ST); 206.545.8001

ISSAQUAH—730 NW GILMAN BLVD (AT MAPLE ST NW); 425.837.3755

KIRKLAND—210 MAIN ST (AT CENTRAL WAY); 425.827.0177

NORTH SEATTLE—12311 LAKE CITY WAY NE (AT NE 125TH ST); 206.363.9151

NORTH SEATTLE—8004 GREENWOOD AVE N (AT NW 80TH ST); 206.706.4063

QUEEN ANNE—1205 DEXTER AVE N (AT ALOHA ST); 206.281.9968

QUEEN ANNE—29 W MERCER ST (AT QUEEN ANNE AVE N); 206.216.5990

QUEEN ANNE—908 STEWART ST (AT 9TH AVE); 206.624.4300

REDMOND—8074 160TH AVE NE (AT CLEVELAND ST); 425.883.8822

SEATTLE—107 1ST AVE (AT LENORA ST); 206.467.5940

TUKWILA—17410 SOUTHCENTER PKWY (AT SOUTHCENTER MALL); 206.575.8587; M-SA 10:30-9, SU 11-7; MALL PARKING

WEDGEWOOD/RAVENNA—1033 65TH NE (AT 12TH AVE NE); 206.729.0670

Tall Grass Bakery ★★★★☆

"...nice bakery for kids, they love the pretzels, baguettes and cookies... staff is really friendly, too... **"**

Children's menu	✗	$$	Prices

Changing station	✗	❹	Customer service
Highchairs/boosters	✗	❹	Stroller access

BALLARD—5907 24TH AVE NW (AT 59TH ST); 206.706.0991

TGI Friday's ★★★★☆

"...good old American bar food with a reasonable selection for the healthier set as well... I love that the kids meal includes salad... my daughter requests the potato skins on a regular basis (which is good because they are also my favorite)... moderately priced... cheerful servers are used to the mess my kids leave behind... relaxed scene... I'd steer clear on a Friday night unless you don't mind waiting and watching the singles scene... "

Children's menu	✓	$$	Prices
Changing station	✓	❹	Customer service
Highchairs/boosters	✓	❸	Stroller access

WWW.TGIFRIDAYS.COM

KIRKLAND—505 PARKPLACE (AT CENTRAL WY); 425.828.3743

restaurants

Thai Ginger ★★★★★

"...pre-parent favorite spot of mine in Bellevue and Madison Park, the staff at Thai Ginger Pacific Place were HAPPY to see me wheeling in my stroller and infant... consistently child-friendly and very helpful with stroller storage... "

Children's menu	✗	$$	Prices
Changing station	✗	❺	Customer service
Highchairs/boosters	✓	❺	Stroller access

WWW.THAIGINGER.COM

DOWNTOWN—600 PINE ST (AT 6TH AVE); 206.749.9100

Tutta Bella Neapolitan Pizzera ★★★★☆

"...reasonable prices... enjoy going there with other families with babies... best pizza in town, sometimes have live music, quite child-friendly environment, very festive and somewhat loud (screaming toddlers are not a problem)... fabulous gelato ice cream ... "

Children's menu	✗	$$	Prices
Changing station	✗	❺	Customer service
Highchairs/boosters	✓	❹	Stroller access

WWW.TUTTABELLAPIZZA.COM

COLUMBIA CITY—4918 RAINIER AVE S (AT FERDINAND ST); 206.721.3501

Vios Cafe and Marketplace ★★★★☆

"...fresh food... great atmosphere... children's play area with variety of toys & the gate allows mothers to sit & enjoy a meal or cup of coffee without chasing toddlers about the restaurant... about as kid-friendly as they come. They even have a separate play area in the back of the restaurant... confined area for the kids to play... "

Children's menu	✓	$$$	Prices
Changing station	✗	❹	Customer service
Highchairs/boosters	✓	❹	Stroller access

CAPITOL HILL—903 19TH AVE EAST (AT ALOHA ST); 206.329.3236

Wasabi Bistro ★★★★☆

"...great food, pricey, but worth it... they didn't even blink and we arrived with an infant and a wheelchair... "

Children's menu	✗	$$$	Prices
Changing station	✗	❺	Customer service
Highchairs/boosters	✓	❸	Stroller access

WWW.WASABIBISTRO.COM

BELLTOWN—2311 2ND AVE (AT BELL ST); 206.441.6044

Wild Mountain Café

❝...nice spot with quality food... is in an old house, complete with steps going to the front door, so the layout is not great for a stroller... very kid-friendly, tons of toys for the little ones, plus great food...**❞**

Children's menu......................... ✓ $$$... Prices
Changing station ....✗   **❺** ....Customer service
Highchairs/boosters..................... ✓   **❷** .... Stroller access

WWW.WILDMTNCAFE.COM

BALLARD—1408 NORTHWEST 85TH ST (AT 14TH AVE); 206.297.WILD

World Wrapps

❝...a nice variety of flavorful gourmet 'meals' wrapped in a healthy tortilla or served in a bowl... a tastier, healthier alternative to your standard fast food... wrapps are popular with adults and kids... plenty of open space for strollers... kids get a fun coloring activity sheet to keep them occupied while they wait...**❞**

Children's menu......................... ✓ $$.. Prices
Changing station .... ✓   **❹** ....Customer service
Highchairs/boosters..................... ✓   **❹** .... Stroller access

WWW.WORLDWRAPPS.COM

BELLEVUE—228 BELLEVUE SQ MALL (AT NE 4TH ST); 425.635.0103; M-SA 9:30-9:30, SU 11-7; MALL PARKING

CAPITOL HILL—222 YALE AVE N (AT JOHN ST); 206.233.0222; M-F 10:30-8:30, SA-SU 10:30-6:30

DOWNTOWN—400 PINE ST (AT 4TH AVE); 206.628.6868; M-SA 10:30-9, SU 10:30-6

DOWNTOWN—601 UNION ST (AT 6TH AVE); 206.628.9601; M-F 7-4

DOWNTOWN—701 5TH AVE (AT CHERRY ST); 206.340.0810; M-F 10:30-4

FIRST HILL—1109 MADISON ST (AT BOREN AVE); 206.467.9744; M-F 10:30-8

GREENLAKE/GREENWOOD/PHINNEY RIDGE—7900 E GREEN LAKE DR N (AT STROUD AVE N); 206.524.9727; DAILY 10:30-9

KIRKLAND—124 LAKE ST S (AT KIRKLAND AVE); 425.827.9727; DAILY 10:30-9

QUEEN ANNE—528 QUEEN ANN AVE N (AT REPUBLICAN ST); 206.286.9727; DAILY 10:30-9:30

UNIVERSITY DISTRICT/UNIVERSITY VILLAGE—2750 NE UNIVERSITY VILLAGE (AT UNIVERSITY VILLAGE MALL); 206.522.7873; DAILY 10:30-9; MALL PARKING

Zao Noodle Bar

❝...pan-asian noodle place with playful yet chic decor... good place for families to get together with other families... large portions allow for sharing and trying all the tasty dishes... kid-size chopsticks are always a hit... kids love the funny fish they give out after the meal... large spaces allow you to bring your stroller in...**❞**

Children's menu......................... ✓ $$.. Prices
Changing station .... ✓   **❹** ....Customer service
Highchairs/boosters..................... ✓   **❸** .... Stroller access

WWW.ZAO.COM

WEDGEWOOD/RAVENNA—2590 NE UNIVERSITY VLG (AT UNIVERSITY VILLAGE MALL); 206.529.8278; DAILY 11-10; MALL PARKING

Zeek's Pizza

❝...fabulous weekday deals make this a favorite outing... kids love the pizza, the waitstaff are great about bringing dough balls or small plates of topping for our kids to enjoy before dinner arrives... outdoor deck is great kids are always able to go outside and run off some energy without bothering anyone in the restaurant...**❞**

Children's menu	✗		$$	Prices
Changing station	✓	❹		Customer service
Highchairs/boosters	✓	❹		Stroller access

WWW.ZEEKSPIZZA.COM

GREENLAKE/GREENWOOD/PHINNEY RIDGE—6000 PHINNEY AVE N (AT N 60TH ST); 206.285.TOGO; STREET PARKING

restaurants

Tacoma

★★★★★
"lila picks"

★Red Robin

Azteca Mexican Restaurant ★★★★☆

"...my kids always finish their whole meal here... quick and friendly service... very roomy, good stroller access... a colorful place that's fun for infants and children... love the food... breastfeeding in the booth isn't so easy ... **"**

Children's menu	✓	$$	Prices
Changing station	✗	❹	Customer service
Highchairs/boosters	✓	❹	Stroller access

WWW.AZTECAMEX.COM

TACOMA—4801 TACOMA MALL BLVD (AT TACOMA MALL); 253.472.0246; SU-M 11-10, T-TH 11-10:30, F-SA 11-11:30; MALL PARKING

Casa Mia ★★★★☆

"...superior food at reasonable prices... kid-friendly... **"**

Children's menu	✗	$$	Prices
Changing station	✗	❸	Customer service
Highchairs/boosters	✗	❸	Stroller access

PUYALLUP—505 N MERIDIAN (AT 5TH AVE); 253.770.0400

Chevys Fresh Mex ★★★★☆

"...a nice combo of good food for adults and a nice kid's menu... always a sure bet with tots in tow... tasty Mexican food with a simple kids menu (especially the quesedillas)... the tortilla making machine is sure to grab your toddler's attention until the food arrives... an occasional balloon making man... party-like atmosphere with colorful decorations... huge Margaritas for mom and dad... service generally excellent and fast, but you may have to wait for a table at peak hours... long tables can accommodate the multifamily get-together... **"**

Children's menu	✓	$$	Prices
Changing station	✓	❹	Customer service
Highchairs/boosters	✓	❹	Stroller access

WWW.CHEVYS.COM

TACOMA—3702 S FIFE ST (AT S 38TH ST); 253.472.5800

Cucina Cucina Italian Cafe ★★★★☆

"...you wouldn't think of this as your typical 'kid-friendly' Italian restaurant, but the staff is wonderful with children... kids are given edible bread dough to eat, or play with, while they wait for dinner... tables are covered with paper and crayons for children (and adults) to color away... excellent food and terrific service... putting paper under the highchairs is a smart touch... **"**

Children's menu	✓	$$	Prices
Changing station	✗	❹	Customer service

participate in our survey at

Highchairs/boosters .... ✓   **❹** ....Stroller access

WWW.CUCINACUCINA.COM

TACOMA—4201 S STEELE ST (AT TACOMA MALL); 253.475.6000; SU-TH 11-
  10, F-SA 11-11; MALL PARKING

El Toro

❝...friendly... home-style ambiance... authentic food... dim lighting for
breastfeeding... **❞**

Children's menu .... ✗ $$ .... Prices
Changing station......................... ✗   **❺** ....Customer service
Highchairs/boosters .... ✓   **❹** ....Stroller access

TACOMA—12914 PACIFIC HWY SW (AT 66TH AVE CT SW); 253.588.5888; SU-
  TH 11-10, F-SA 11-11

Firehouse Coffee

❝...lovely for an afternoon coffee stop or lunch... they even have a
children's room so that you can relax while they play... babies can be
on the floor while you enjoy a great cup of coffee... the staff seems to
love having kids come in—a great refreshing break in an otherwise
hectic day... **❞**

Children's menu .... ✓ $ .... Prices
Changing station......................... ✓   **❺** ....Customer service
Highchairs/boosters .... ✓   **❹** ....Stroller access

WWW.FIREHOUSECOFFEE.COM

ADAMS—3602 6TH AVE (AT UNION AVE); 253.606.4134; DAILY 5:30-9:30;
  PARKING GARAGE

Old Spaghetti Factory, The

❝...good for a fast, cheap meal if the place isn't too packed... apple
sauce for kids... fun for the whole family and easy to eat for under $25
(family of four)... if you've got a hankering for spaghetti and meatballs,
look no further... relatively inexpensive and you get big portions for
your money... a place with a relaxed feel... it is usually so busy that no
one will notice if your toddler is crying... the staff makes it easy to hang
out and have a good time... **❞**

Children's menu .... ✓ $$ .... Prices
Changing station......................... ✓   **❹** ....Customer service
Highchairs/boosters .... ✓   **❹** ....Stroller access

WWW.OLDSPAGHETTIFACTORY.COM

TACOMA—1735 JEFFERSON AVE (AT 17TH ST); 253.383.2214; M-F 11:30-
  9:30, F 5-10, SA 11:30-10, SU 11:30-9:30; PARKING IN FRONT OF BLDG

Olive Garden

❝...finally a place that is both kid and adult friendly... tasty Italian
chain with lot's of convenient locations... the staff consistently attends
to the details of dining with babies and toddlers—minimizing wait time,
highchairs offered spontaneously, bread sticks brought immediately...
food is served as quickly as possible... happy to create special orders...
our waitress even acted as our family photographer... **❞**

Children's menu .... ✓ $$ .... Prices
Changing station......................... ✓   **❹** ....Customer service
Highchairs/boosters .... ✓   **❹** ....Stroller access

WWW.OLIVEGARDEN.COM

TACOMA—1921 S 72ND ST (AT S HOSMER ST); 253.475.1772

Outback Steakhouse

❝...Aussie style eatery with big steaks and shrimp on the barbie...
don't miss the bloomin' onion, but be prepared to share—it's huge...
very understanding of our screaming infant and gave us a booth a little
out of the way... gave us extra whipped cream for dessert and on

occasion free ice cream... the wait for a table can get long so go early to avoid the masses... nice wide aisles makes maneuvering around with strollers easy... tables toys in the waiting area... **"**

Children's menu	✓	$$$ .... Prices
Changing station	✓	❹ ....Customer service
Highchairs/boosters	✓	❸ .... Stroller access

WWW.OUTBACKSTEAKHOUSE.COM

PUYALLUP—12920 MERIDIAN E (OFF 128TH ST); 253.864.7725

TACOMA—3111 S 38TH ST (AT PINE ST); 253.473.3669

Primo Grill ★★★★☆

"...*good children's menu that includes an entree and dessert... always friendly when we bring our kids. They give the kids a sketch pad and lunchbox of crayons. It's noisy inside so the kids don't disturb anyone even if they get a little loud...* **"**

Children's menu	✓	$$$ .... Prices
Changing station	✗	❹ ....Customer service
Highchairs/boosters	✓	❸ .... Stroller access

WWW.PRIMOGRILLTACOMA.COM

TACOMA—601 S PINE ST (AT 6TH AVE); 253.383.7000; M-TH 11:30-9:30, F 11:30-10:30, SA 5-10:30, SU 4:30-9

Ram Restaurant & Big Horn Brewery ★★★★⯪

"...*kids eat free two days a week and the children's menu includes a free scoop of ice cream—can also get apples instead of fries... high booths are a little hard with baby seats...* **"**

Children's menu	✓	$$ .... Prices
Changing station	✗	❹ ....Customer service
Highchairs/boosters	✓	❸ .... Stroller access

LAKEWOOD—10019 59TH AVE SW (AT 100TH); 253.584.3191; SU-TH 11-10, F-SA 11-11

Red Lobster Restaurants ★★★☆☆

"...*better than I expected from the TV commercials... food was enjoyable, especially the garlic-cheese biscuits... sea-themed decor is popular with kids... friendly staff was terrific with our kids—they must all be parents... servers even offered to heat up the baby food we brought along from home... not the cheapest prices around... kids menu offers lots of appealing choices... a comfortable place to bring kids...* **"**

Children's menu	✓	$$$ .... Prices
Changing station	✓	❹ ....Customer service
Highchairs/boosters	✓	❹ .... Stroller access

WWW.REDLOBSTER.COM

TACOMA—1929 S 72ND ST (AT HOSMER ST); 253.474.1262

Red Robin ★★★★★

"...*very kid-oriented—loud, balloons, bright lights, colorful decor and a cheerful staff make Red Robin a favorite among parents and children... the food is mainly burgers (beef or chicken)... loud music covers even the most boisterous of screaming... lots of kids—all the time... sometimes the wait can be long, but the arcade games and balloons help pass the time...* **"**

Children's menu	✓	$$ .... Prices
Changing station	✓	❹ ....Customer service
Highchairs/boosters	✓	❹ .... Stroller access

WWW.REDROBIN.COM

PUYALLUP—3609 9TH ST SW (AT 112TH ST E); 253.840.9901

TACOMA—3901 S STEELE ST (AT TACOMA MALL BLVD); 253.473.7447; MALL
  PARKING

Ruby Tuesday

"...nice variety of healthy choices on the kids' menu—turkey,
spaghetti, chicken tenders... you can definitely find something healthy
here... prices are on the high side, but at least everyone can find
something they like... service is fast and efficient... my daughter makes
a mess and they never let me clean it up... your typical chain, but it
works—you'll be happy to see ample aisle space, storage for your
stroller, and attentive staff... **"**

Children's menu ....✓ $$... Prices
Changing station..........................✓   ❹........................ Customer service
Highchairs/boosters ....✓   ❸.............................Stroller access

WWW.RUBYTUESDAY.COM

LAKEWOOD—2202 84TH ST S (AT RT 5); 253.581.5690; M-TH 11-10, F-SU
  11-11AM

PUYALLUP—13215 MERIDIAN E (AT 132ND ST E); 253.864.0610; SU-TH 11-
  11, F-SA 11-12

UNIVERSITY PLACE—2014 MILDRED ST W (AT 19TH ST); 253.460.3425; SU-
  TH 11-11, F-SA 11-12

TGI Friday's

"...good old American bar food with a reasonable selection for the
healthier set as well... I love that the kids meal includes salad... my
daughter requests the potato skins on a regular basis (which is good
because they are also my favorite)... moderately priced... cheerful
servers are used to the mess my kids leave behind... relaxed scene... I'd
steer clear on a Friday night unless you don't mind waiting and
watching the singles scene... **"**

Children's menu ....✓ $$... Prices
Changing station..........................✓   ❹........................ Customer service
Highchairs/boosters ....✓   ❸.............................Stroller access

WWW.TGIFRIDAYS.COM

PUYALLUP—3703 9TH ST SW (AT 43RD AVE SW); 253.845.0767; PARKING
  LOT

TACOMA—4219 S STEELE ST (AT S 38TH ST); 253.472.2474; SU-F 11-12, SA
  11-1; PARKING LOT

restaurants

doulas & lactation consultants

Editor's Note: Doulas and lactation consultants provide a wide range of services and are very difficult to classify, let alone rate. In fact the terms 'doula' and 'lactation consultant' have very specific industry definitions that are far more complex than we are able to cover in this brief guide. For this reason we have decided to list only those businesses and individuals who received overwhelmingly positive reviews, without listing the reviewers' comments.

Greater Seattle Area

Association of Labor Assistants & Childbirth Educators (ALACE)

Labor doula .... ✓   ✗ .... Postpartum doula
Pre & post natal massage .... ✗   ✗ .... Lactation consultant

WWW.ALACE.ORG

SEATTLE—617.441.2500

Doulas of North America (DONA)

Labor doula .... ✓   ✓ .... Postpartum doula
Pre & post natal massage .... ✗   ✗ .... Lactation consultant

WWW.DONA.ORG

SEATTLE—888.788.3662

La Leche League

Labor doula .... ✗   ✗ .... Postpartum doula
Pre & post natal massage .... ✗   ✓ .... Lactation consultant

WWW.LALECHELEAGUE.ORG

SEATTLE—VARIOUS LOCATIONS; 847.519.7730; CHECK SCHEDULE ONLINE

participate in our survey at

exercise

Seattle

"lila picks"

- ★ Mind & Body
- ★ Santosha Yoga
- ★ Seattle Holistic Center
- ★ Stroller Strides

8 Limbs Yoga Center ★★★★★

"...excellent prenatal yoga... very knowledgeable instructor... relaxing and supportive environment... comfortable and welcoming... group discussion and sharing encouraged, which is especially great for a first time pregnancy..."

Prenatal	✓	$$$	Prices
Mommy & me	✓	❹	Decor
Child care available	✗	❹	Customer service

WWW.EIGHTLIMBSYOGA.COM

FIRST HILL—500 E PIKE ST (AT SUMMIT AVE); 206.325.1511; CHECK SCHEDULE ONLINE; STREET PARKING

WEDGEWOOD/RAVENNA—7345 35TH AVE NE (AT NE 75TH ST); 206.523.9722; CHECK SCHEDULE ONLINE; STREET PARKING

Allstar Fitness ★★★★☆

"...great gym, and tons of pregnant moms too—also adding more prenatal exercise classes—great pool..."

Prenatal	✓	$	Prices
Mommy & me	✗	❺	Decor
Child care available	✗	❸	Customer service

WWW.ALLSTARFITNESS.COM

EASTLAKE/LAKE UNION—509 OLIVE WAY (AT 5TH AVE); 206.292.0900; M-F 5-9 SA 9-5 SU 9-3; PARKING AT 5TH & VIRGINIA

Aquarobics ★★★☆☆

"...pre-natal is nice... focuses on total body conditioning for all ages..."

Prenatal	✓	$$$	Prices
Mommy & me	✗	❸	Decor
Child care available	✗	❸	Customer service

WWW.AQUAROBICS.NET/

REDMOND—17535 NE 104TH ST (AT 176 AVE NE); 425.883.0475; M W F 7:30, T TH 8

Baby Boot Camp ★★★★☆

"...a great, low-cost, outdoor mom and baby workout... I've met some really fun moms and babies at these classes... not only fun, but more

importantly I got results... the first class is free so there's no excuse not to give it a try... instructors are well-trained physical therapists that really know their stuff... class sizes are limited... it's like a personal trainer and motivational system all in one... I do their exercises even when I'm on my own with my baby... **"**

Prenatal	✗	$$$	Prices
Mommy & me	✓	❸	Decor
Child care available	✗	❸	Customer service

WWW.BABYBOOTCAMP.COM

SEATTLE—VARIOUS LOCATIONS; 206.856.8892; CHECK SCHEDULE ONLINE

Maya Whole Health Studio

"...*they have everything from prenatal classes to mommy and me classes... Tami is a wonderful instructor and I really benefitted from her pre- and post-natal class ...* **"**

Prenatal	✓	$$	Prices
Mommy & me	✓	❹	Decor
Child care available	✗	❹	Customer service

WWW.MAYAWHOLEHEALTH.COM

WALLINGFORD/FREMONT—701 N 36TH ST (AT FREMONT AVE N); 206.632.4900; CHECK SCHEDULE ONLINE

Mind & Body ★★★★★

"...*pre-natal pilates felt safe, but substantial... I always energized from class (feeling two inches taller)... great way to stay fit and get back into shape after the baby is born... babies are welcome at the postnatal class... be sure to bring a blanket or car seat for the little one...* **"**

Prenatal	✓	$$	Prices
Mommy & me	✗	❹	Decor
Child care available	✗	❺	Customer service

WWW.SEATTLEPILATES.COM

CENTRAL DISTRICT—2022 E UNION ST (AT 20TH AVE); 206.325.3328; CHECK SCHEDULE ONLINE; STREET PARKING

Moms on the Move ★★★☆☆

"...*prenatal and postpartum workout (W-F)... good hard workout with fun music to keep your energy up... instructor knows her stuff and makes sure no injuries occur... she really attends to the technique... childcare is free as part of the class... the moms who watch the children are very sensitive toward the kids...* **"**

Prenatal	✓	$$$	Prices
Mommy & me	✓	❸	Decor
Child care available	✓	❹	Customer service

WWW.MOMSONTHEMOVE.ORG

BALLARD—5449 BALLARD AVE NW (AT NW MARKET ST); 206.789.3857; CHECK SCHEDULE ONLINE

Olympic Athletic Club ★★★★★

"...*a great family gym!.. there is something for everyone here, and they have a great kids corner too... there are classes for pre/post natal yoga, and occasionally that offer parent/infant or toddler swim classes... if you enjoy having an nice place to workout out, this is it!...* **"**

Prenatal	✓	$$	Prices
Mommy & me	✗	❺	Decor
Child care available	✓	❸	Customer service

WWW.OLYMPICATHLETICCLUB.COM

BALLARD—5301 LEARY AVE NW (AT 20TH AVE); 206.789.5010; SU-F OPEN 24HRS SA 12-6:30PM ; 4 PARKING LOTS

exercise

Overlake Hospital Medical Center (Prenatal Yoga)

★★★★☆

"...a really great class... prenatal and mommy and me... wonderful instructors..."

Prenatal	✓	$$$	Prices
Mommy & me	✓	❷	Decor
Child care available	✗	❺	Customer service

WWW.OVERLAKEHOSPITAL.ORG

BELLEVUE—1035 116TH AVE NE (AT NE 8TH ST); 425.688.5259; CALL FOR SCHEDULE; GARAGE PARKING

Pro Sports Club

★★★★☆

"...very expensive, but beautiful and relaxing facilities, and an amazing massage staff..."

Prenatal	✗	$$$	Prices
Mommy & me	✗	❺	Decor
Child care available	✓	❺	Customer service

WWW.PROCLUB.COM

EASTLAKE/LAKE UNION—501 EASTLAKE AVE E (OFF RT 5); 206.332.1873; M-F 5-11, SA-SU 7-10; PARKING LOT

Santosha Yoga

★★★★★

"...postpartum class is a great way to stretch without leaving your newborn behind... kind and knowledgeable instructors... a real treat for a new mom... childcare available... superb prenatal class... I made great friends who I'm still in touch with... nurturing environment ..."

Prenatal	✓	$$$	Prices
Mommy & me	✓	❹	Decor
Child care available	✓	❹	Customer service

WWW.SANTOSHA-YOGA.COM

CAPITOL HILL—2812 E MADISON ST (AT 28TH AVE E); 206.264.5034; CHECK SCHEDULE ONLINE

Seattle Holistic Center

★★★★★

"...prenatal class was excellent preparation for my delivery... I love having time every week to bond with other moms-to-be... a perfect way to de-stress and take time for myself... the instructors are very knowledgeable and professional... they tailor each class and focus on any body areas that are causing you problems..."

Prenatal	✓	$$	Prices
Mommy & me	✓	❹	Decor
Child care available	✗	❹	Customer service

WWW.SEATTLEHOLISTICCENTER.COM

NORTH SEATTLE—7700 AURORA AVE N (AT N 77TH ST); 206.525.9035; VIEW SCHEDULE ONLINE

Skate King Stroller Fitness

★★★★★

"...great fun!.. get exercise 'stroller skating' with your little one!..."

Prenatal	✗	$	Prices
Mommy & me	✗	❹	Decor
Child care available	✗	❸	Customer service

WWW.BELLEVUESKATEKING.COM

BELLEVUE—2301 140TH AVE NE; 425.641.2046

Sound Yoga

★★★★★

"...the staff is wonderful... I had never even tried yoga before becoming pregnant... nonintimidating... prenatal classes were offered twice a week at convenient times... the studio is on the small side

participate in our survey at

which is actually better—more personal and allows you to tune into yourself and your baby... **"**

Prenatal.. ✓
Mommy & me .... ✗
Child care available...................... ✗

$ .... Prices
5 .... Decor
5 .... Customer service

WWW.SOUNDYOGA.COM

WEST SEATTLE—5639 CALIFORNIA AVE SW (AT SW FINDLAY ST); 206.938.8195

Stroller Strides ★★★★★

"...*fantastic fun and very effective for losing those post-baby pounds... this is the greatest way to stay in shape as a mom—you have your baby in the stroller with you the whole time... the instructors are very professional, knowledgeable and motivating... beautiful, outdoor locations... classes consist of power walking combined with body toning exercises using exercise tubing and strollers... a great way to bond with my baby and other moms...* **"**

Prenatal.. ✗
Mommy & me .... ✓
Child care available...................... ✗

$$ .... Prices
4 .... Decor
5 .... Customer service

WWW.STROLLERSTRIDES.NET

ISSAQUAH—VARIOUS LOCATIONS; 800.569.1624; CHECK SCHEDULE ONLINE

SEATTLE—VARIOUS LOCATIONS; 800.917.4592; CHECK SCHEDULE ONLINE

SNOHOMISH—VARIOUS LOCATIONS; 800.518.2357; CHECK SCHEDULE ONLINE

Whole Life Yoga ★★★★☆

"...*excellent instructors that really care about you... the mommy and me class is a great way to get back in shape after pregnancy...* **"**

Prenatal.. ✓
Mommy & me .... ✓
Child care available...................... ✗

$$ .... Prices
4 .... Decor
5 .... Customer service

WWW.WHOLELIFEYOGA.COM

NORTH SEATTLE—8551 GREENWOOD AVE N (AT N 87TH ST); 206.784.2882; CALL FOR SCHEDULE; PARKING LOT ACROSS ST; GARAGE IN BLDG

YMCA ★★★★☆

"...*the variety of fitness programs offered is astounding... class types and quality vary from facility to facility, but it's a must for new moms to check out... most facilities offer some kind of kids' activities or childcare so you can time your workouts around the classes... aerobics, yoga, pool—our Y even offers Pilates now... my favorite classes are the mom & baby yoga... the best bang for your buck... they have it all—great programs that meet the needs of a diverse range of families...* **"**

Prenatal.. ✓
Mommy & me .... ✓
Child care available...................... ✓

$$$ .... Prices
3 .... Decor
3 .... Customer service

WWW.SEATTLEYMCA.ORG

AUBURN—1620 PERIMETER RD SW (AT 15TH ST SW); 253.833.2770; M-F 5-9, SA 8-6, SU 11-6; FREE PARKING

BELLEVUE—14230 BEL-RED RD (AT 140TH ST); 425.746.9900; CALL FOR SCHEDULE; FREE PARKING

BELLEVUE—5225 119TH AVE SE (AT SE 52ND ST); 425.644.8417; M-F 6:30-8:30, F 6:30-6:30, SA 9-3; PARKING LOT

BELLEVUE—777 108TH AVE NE (AT NE 8TH ST); 425.451.2422; M-F 6-8; PARKING LOT

BOTHELL—11811 NE 195TH ST (AT 120TH AVE NE); 425.485.9797; CALL FOR SCHEDULE; PARKING LOT

exercise

CENTRAL DISTRICT—1700 23RD AVE (AT E MADISON ST); 206.322.6969; CHECK SCHEDULE ONLINE

DOWNTOWN—909 4TH AVE (AT MARION ST); 206.382.5000; CALL FOR SCHEDULE; STREET PARKING

ISSAQUAH—4221 228TH SE AVE (AT SE 40TH ST); 425.391.4840; M-F 6-9, SA 8-4, SU 12-4; PARKING LOT

REDMOND—10315 CEDAR PARK CRES NE (AT NE ALDER CREST DR); 425.868.4399; CHECK SCHEDULE ONLINE

SHORELINE—1220 NE 175TH ST (AT 15TH AVE NE); 206.364.1700; M-F 6-10, SA 8-5, SU 12-5; PARKING LOT

UNIVERSITY DISTRICT/UNIVERSITY VILLAGE—5003 12TH AVE NE (AT NE 50TH ST); 206.524.1400; M-F 6-10, SA 8-5, SU 12-5

WEST SEATTLE—4515 36TH AVE SW (AT SW OREGON ST); 206.382.5003; CALL FOR SCHEDULE

WEST SEATTLE—9260 CALIFORNIA AVE SW (AT SW ROXBURY ST); 206.937.1000; M-F 7:30-9:30, SA 8-5, SU 1-5; PARKING LOT

Yoga On Beacon ★★★★★

"...friendly and inviting yoga for beginners to advanced... I like the mommy and me and prenatal option as well..."

Prenatal	✓	$	Prices
Mommy & me	✓	❺	Decor
Child care available	✗	❸	Customer service

BEACON HILL—3013 BEACON AVE S (AT S STEVENS ST); 206.324.9642; CALL FOR SCHEDULE

Tacoma

Birthing Inn ★★★★☆

"...offer excellent relevant classes and they are tons of fun because you are surrounded by women who are going through the same things you are—you build good friendships... I took prenatal yoga with Diane Demars and highly recommend this class to anyone and everyone... my last few weeks of pregnancy would have been very hard had it not been for the classes I took....**"**

Prenatal	✓	$$$	Prices
Mommy & me	✗	❹	Decor
Child care available	✗	❹	Customer service

WWW.THEBIRTHINGINN.COM

TACOMA—6002 WESTGATE BLVD (AT N PEARL ST); 253.761.8939; CHECK SCHEDULE ONLINE

Fife Swimming Pool ★★★☆☆

"...exercise in the water is less stressful on a pregnant body... and you can go your own pace... mommy and me class is fun, too...**"**

Prenatal	✗	$$$	Prices
Mommy & me	✓	❷	Decor
Child care available	✗	❸	Customer service

FIFE—5410 20TH ST E (AT 54TH AVE E); 253.922.7665; CHECK SCHEDULE ONLINE; PARKING LOT

YMCA ★★★★☆

"...the variety of fitness programs offered is astounding... class types and quality vary from facility to facility, but it's a must for new moms to check out... most facilities offer some kind of kids' activities or childcare so you can time your workouts around the classes... aerobics, yoga, pool—our Y even offers Pilates now... my favorite classes are the mom & baby yoga... the best bang for your buck... they have it all—great programs that meet the needs of a diverse range of families...**"**

Prenatal	✓	$$$	Prices
Mommy & me	✓	❸	Decor
Child care available	✓	❹	Customer service

WWW.YMCATACOMA.ORG

TACOMA—1002 S PEARL ST (AT S 12TH ST); 253.564.9622; CALL FOR SCHEDULE

TACOMA—1144 MARKET ST (AT S 13TH ST); 253.597.6444; M-F 5-9:30, SA 7-8, SU 10-5; PARKING LOT

TACOMA—9715 LAKEWOOD DR SW (AT 100TH ST SW); 253.584.9622; CALL FOR SCHEDULE

parent education & support

Greater Seattle Area

★★★★★
"lila picks"

- ★ Community Birth & Family Center
- ★ Evergreen Hospital (Women's & Children's Services)
- ★ Program for Early Parent Support
- ★ Swedish Medical Center (Women & Infant Services)
- ★ Tacoma General Hospital (Childbirth & Family Education)

Birthing Inn

Childbirth classes.........................✗   ✓.................Breastfeeding support
Parent group/club ....✗   ✗.............................Child care info

WWW.THEBIRTHINGINN.COM

TACOMA—6002 WESTGATE BLVD (AT N PEARL ST); 253.761.8939; CHECK SCHEDULE ONLINE

Birthways Childbirth Resource

Childbirth classes.........................✗   ✗.................Breastfeeding support
Parent group/club ....✗   ✗.............................Child care info

VASHON—PO BOX 2069; 206.463.9572; M-F 9-5

Bradley Method, The   ★★★½☆

❝...12 week classes that cover all of the basics of giving birth... run by individual instructors nationwide... classes differ based on the quality and experience of the instructor... they cover everything from nutrition and physical conditioning to spousal support and medication... wonderful series that can be very educational... their web site has listings of instructors on a regional basis...**❞**

Childbirth classes.........................✓ $$$.......................................Prices
Parent group/club ....✗   ❸............................Class selection
Breastfeeding support..................✗   ❸.........................Staff knowledge
Child care info ....✗   ❸.........................Customer service

WWW.BRADLEYBIRTH.COM

SEATTLE—VARIOUS LOCATIONS; 800.422.4784; CHECK SCHEDULE & LOCATIONS ONLINE

TACOMA—VARIOUS LOCATIONS; 888.265.0923; CHECK SCHEDULE & LOCATIONS ONLINE

Community Birth Center Of Seattle

Childbirth classes.........................✗   ✓.................Breastfeeding support
Parent group/club ....✓   ✓.............................Child care info

WWW.COMMUNITYBIRTH.ORG

CAPITOL HILL—2200 24TH AVE E (AT ON LYNN ST); 206.328.0910

Community Birth & Family Center ★★★★★

"...the childbirth preparation class was incredible... I learned a lot, met some great people and was prepared for my delivery... the support group for new parents helps navigate those trying first weeks (babies through 12 wks are welcome)... weekly on Thursday from 12pm to 2pm in the Montlake Childbirth Center... they request a nominal $5 contribution per week... **"**

Childbirth classes	✓	$	Prices
Parent group/club	✓	❺	Class selection
Breastfeeding support	✓	❺	Staff knowledge
Child care info	✗	❹	Customer service

WWW.COMMUNITYBIRTH.ORG

MONTLAKE—2200 24TH AVE E (AT E LYNN ST); 206.720.0511; ALL AND ON-CALL; PARKING AT 2200 24TH AVE

Evergreen Hospital (Women's & Children's Services) ★★★★★

"...not only was my birthing experience wonderful, but the pre and postnatal education and support was outstanding... they offer a wide range of topics from pregnancy and child birth to parenting... the staff is knowledgeable and the class material is well presented... I can't say enough good things about the services they offer new parents... **"**

Childbirth classes	✓	$$	Prices
Parent group/club	✓	❹	Class selection
Breastfeeding support	✓	❺	Staff knowledge
Child care info	✓	❺	Customer service

WWW.EVERGREENHEALTHCARE.ORG

KIRKLAND—12040 NE 128TH ST (AT 120TH AVE NE); 425.899.3494; M-F 8:30-4:30, SA 9-4

Gracewinds Perinatal Services

Childbirth classes	✗	✓	Breastfeeding support
Parent group/club	✓	✓	Child care info

WWW.GRACEWINDSPERINATAL.COM

BALLARD—1421 NW 70TH ST (AT ALONZO AVE); 206.781.9871

Great Starts Birth and Family Education

Childbirth classes	✗	✓	Breastfeeding support
Parent group/club	✓	✗	Child care info

WWW.GREATSTARTS.ORG

GREENLAKE/GREENWOOD/PHINNEY RIDGE—2517 EASTLAKE AVE EAST (AT EASTLAKE & ROANOKE); 206.789.0883; CHECK SCHEDULE ONLINE; PARKING LOT

Great Starts Birth & Family Education ★★★⯨☆

"...excellent child birth education and comprehensive support services for after the baby arrives... they provide lots of classes including childbirth prep, breastfeeding, newborn care, infant safety and CPR... good support groups for breastfeeding—we made some great friends through these groups... instructors are very knowledgeable... **"**

Childbirth classes	✓	$$	Prices
Parent group/club	✓	❹	Class selection
Breastfeeding support	✓	❸	Staff knowledge

parent education & support

Child care info .... ✗   ❹ ....Customer service

WWW.GREATSTARTS.ORG

NORTH SEATTLE—2517 EASTLAKE AVE E (AT E ROANOKE ST); 206.789.0883;
  CHECK SCHEDULE ONLINE

Group Health

Childbirth classes	✗	✓	Breastfeeding support
Parent group/club	✗	✗	Child care info

WWW.GHC.ORG/CLASSESANDEVENTS

SEATTLE—VARIOUS LOCATIONS; 206.326.2800; CHECK SCHEDULE ONLINE

Healthy Mothers, Healthy Babies

Childbirth classes	✗	✗	Breastfeeding support
Parent group/club	✗	✗	Child care info

WWW.HMHBWA.ORG

NORTH SEATTLE—11000 LAKE CITY WAY NE (AT NE 110TH ST);
  206.284.2465

Lamaze International ★★★★☆

❝...thousands of women each year are educated about the birth
process by Lamaze educators... their web site offers a list of local
instructors... they follow a basic curriculum, but invariably class quality
will depend on the individual instructor... in many ways they've set the
standard for birth education classes... **❞**

Childbirth classes	✓	$$$	Prices
Parent group/club	✗	❸	Class selection
Breastfeeding support	✗	❸	Staff knowledge
Child care info	✗	❸	Customer service

WWW.LAMAZE.ORG

SEATTLE—VARIOUS LOCATIONS; 800.368.4404; CHECK SCHEDULE AND
  LOCATIONS ONLINE

Mocha Moms ★★★★⯪

❝...a wonderfully supportive group of women—the kind of place you'll
make lifelong friends for both mother and child... a comfortable forum
for bouncing ideas off of other moms with same-age children... easy to
get involved and not too demanding... the annual membership dues
seem a small price to pay for the many activities, play groups, field
trips, Moms Nights Out and book club meetings... local chapters in
cities nationwide... **❞**

Childbirth classes	✗	$$$	Prices
Parent group/club	✓	❸	Class selection
Breastfeeding support	✗	❸	Staff knowledge
Child care info	✗	❸	Customer service

WWW.MOCHAMOMS.ORG

SEATTLE—VARIOUS LOCATIONS

MOMS Club ★★★★☆

❝...an international nonprofit with lots of local chapters and literally
tens of thousands of members... designed to introduce you to new
mothers with same-age kids wherever you live... they organize all sorts
of activities and provide support for new mothers with babies... very
inexpensive for all the activities you get... book clubs, moms night out,
play group connections... generally a very diverse group of women... **❞**

Childbirth classes	✗	$$$	Prices
Parent group/club	✓	❸	Class selection
Breastfeeding support	✗	❸	Staff knowledge
Child care info	✗	❸	Customer service

WWW.MOMSCLUB.ORG

participate in our survey a

Mothers and More

"...a very neat support system for moms who are deciding to stay at home... a great way to get together with other moms in your area for organized activities... book clubs, play groups, even a 'mom's only' night out... local chapters offer more or less activities depending on the involvement of local moms..."

Childbirth classes	✗	$$$ .... Prices
Parent group/club	✓	❸ .... Class selection
Breastfeeding support	✗	❸ .... Staff knowledge
Child care info	✗	❸ .... Customer service

WWW.MOTHERSANDMORE.COM

SEATTLE—VARIOUS LOCATIONS; CHECK SCHEDULE & LOCATIONS ONLINE

Overlake Hospital Medical Center (Family & Community Education)

"...enjoyed our classes... friendly, helpful and knowledgeable... make sure to register early..."

Childbirth classes	✓	$$ .... Prices
Parent group/club	✓	❹ .... Class selection
Breastfeeding support	✓	❺ .... Staff knowledge
Child care info	✗	❹ .... Customer service

WWW.OVERLAKEHOSPITAL.ORG

BELLEVUE—1035 116TH AVE NE (AT NE 8TH ST); 425.688.5259; CALL FOR SCHEDULE; GARAGE PARKING

Program for Early Parent Support (PEPS)

"...PEPS is a great way to meet other families... extremely positive experience in my newborn group—amazing new friends and support... volunteer organization that gets mothers from the same neighborhoods together... minimal fee to join and financial assistance is offered... we now have a baby-sitting coop... every new mom should join a PEPS group..."

Childbirth classes	✗	$$ .... Prices
Parent group/club	✓	❹ .... Class selection
Breastfeeding support	✗	❹ .... Staff knowledge
Child care info	✗	❹ .... Customer service

WWW.PEPSGROUP.ORG

WALLINGFORD/FREMONT—4649 SUNNYSIDE AVE N (BTWN NE 50TH & SUNNYSIDE); 206.547.8570; CALL FOR SCHEDULE

Safety for Toddlers of Kirkland

"...Safety for Toddlers is a great resource... these folks know their stuff, and do a great job of assessing your home and identifying childproofing opportunities... they are very knowledgeable and offer thorough information for why each product is needed... they also help you assess what's necessary and how to prioritize... two women, will come to your home and do a terrific job baby-proofing it... a sweet service for busy parents..."

Childbirth classes	✗	$$$ .... Prices
Parent group/club	✗	❸ .... Class selection
Breastfeeding support	✗	❸ .... Staff knowledge
Child care info	✗	❸ .... Customer service

WWW.SAFETY4TODDLERS.COM

parent education & support

Seattle Holistic Center

Childbirth classes......................**✗**   **✓**..................Breastfeeding support
Parent group/club .... **✓**   **✓**...........................Child care info

WWW.SEATTLEHOLISTICCENTER.COM

GREENLAKE/GREENWOOD/PHINNEY RIDGE—4649 SUNNYSIDE AVE N (AT 50TH ST); 206.525.9035; CHECK SCHEDULE ONLINE

NORTH SEATTLE—7700 AURORA AVE N (AT N 77TH ST); 206.525.9035; VIEW SCHEDULE ONLINE

St Francis Hospital (Family Education)

Childbirth classes......................**✗**   **✓**..................Breastfeeding support
Parent group/club .... **✓**   **✗**...........................Child care info

WWW.FHSHEALTH.ORG

FEDERAL WAY—34515 9TH AVE S (OFF S 348TH ST); 253.944.7957; CALL FOR SCHEDULE; STREET PARKING

Stevens Hospital

Childbirth classes......................**✗**   **✓**..................Breastfeeding support
Parent group/club ....**✗**   **✗**...........................Child care info

WWW.STEVENSHEALTHCARE.ORG/PG_CLASSES.PHP?C=6

EDMONDS—21601 76TH AVE W (AT 216TH ST SW); 425.640.4066; CALL FOR SCHEDULE

Swedish Medical Center (Women & Infant Services) ★★★★★

"...it doesn't get much better than this if you're a new parent in need of information... lots of classes covering everything from before, during and after childbirth... the Baby Club is a good deal—both monetarily as well as in terms of the information you'll get... good instructors... very convenient especially if you're giving birth at Swedish too... **"**

Childbirth classes...................... **✓** $$..Prices
Parent group/club .... **✓**   **❹** ....Class selection
Breastfeeding support.................. **✓**   **❺** ....Staff knowledge
Child care info ....**✗**   **❺** ....Customer service

WWW.SWEDISH.ORG

UNIVERSITY DISTRICT/UNIVERSITY VILLAGE—747 BROADWAY (AT MADISON ST); 206.215.3338; CHECK SCHEDULE ONLINE; GARAGE AT MINOR AVE & JAMES STS

Tacoma General Hospital (Childbirth & Family Education) ★★★★★

"...a great selection of childbirth classes to fit a variety of needs... I was going back to work and had so many questions about breast feeding... the lactation department eased all of my concerns with just one session... the sibling and grandparent classes were well received in our family... supportive and fun environment... **"**

Childbirth classes...................... **✓** $$..Prices
Parent group/club .... **✓**   **❺** ....Class selection
Breastfeeding support.................. **✓**   **❹** ....Staff knowledge
Child care info ....**✗**   **❸** ....Customer service

WWW.MULTICARE.ORG

TACOMA—315 MARTIN LUTHER KING JR WY (AT 3RD ST); 253.403.1032; M-TH 9-5, SA 10-5, SU

UW Medical Center (Maternal & Infant Care Clinic Classes) ★★★☆☆

"...lactation course gets high marks in my book... classes are large with 15 plus couples on average... we found a wide range in the quality of the courses..."

Childbirth classes	✓	$$	Prices
Parent group/club	✗	❸	Class selection
Breastfeeding support	✓	❹	Staff knowledge
Child care info	✗	❹	Customer service

WWW.UWBABY.ORG

UNIVERSITY DISTRICT/UNIVERSITY VILLAGE—1959 NE PACIFIC ST (OFF MONTLAKE BLVD NE); 206.598.4070; CHECK SCHEDULE ONLINE; GARAGE ACROSS STREET FROM MAIN ENTRANCE

Valley Medical Center

Childbirth classes	✗	✓	Breastfeeding support
Parent group/club	✓	✗	Child care info

WWW.VALLEYMED.ORG/SERVICES/HEALTH_WELLNESS/BIRTHPREP.ASP

RENTON—400 S 43RD ST (AT VALLEY FWY); 206.575.2229

Women's Center At Overlake

Childbirth classes	✗	✓	Breastfeeding support
Parent group/club	✗	✗	Child care info

WWW.OVERLAKEHOSPITAL.ORG/SERVICES/WOMENSANDCHILDRENS/WOMENS CENTER/DEFAULT.ASPX

ISSAQUAH—6520 226TH PL SE (AT E LAKE SAMMAMISH PKY); 425.688.5787; CHECK SCHEDULE ONLINE

parent education & support

pediatricians

Editor's Note: Pediatricians provide a tremendous breadth of services and are very difficult to classify and rate in a brief guide. For this reason we list only those practices for which we received overwhelmingly positive reviews. We hope this list of pediatricians will help you in your search.

Seattle

Ballard Pediatric Clinic
WWW.BALLARDPEDIATRICS.COM

BALLARD—7554 15TH AVE NW (AT NW 75TH AVE); 206.783.9300; M-F 8-6, SA 9-12

Cascade Pediatrics
ISSAQUAH—22526 SE 64TH PL (AT E LAKE SAMMAMAISH PKY SE); 425.392.6500; M-F 8:30-5

Children's Clinic
EDMONDS—21600 HWY 99 (AT 215TH ST); 425.778.0191; M-F 8:15-5

Everett Clinic, The
WWW.EVERETTCLINIC.COM

EVERETT—1818 121ST ST SE (AT 19TH AVE); 425.357.3302; M-F 8-5, SA-SU 9-3

EVERETT—3901 HOYT AVE (AT 39TH ST); 425.339.5450; M-F 8-5, SA-SU 9-3

EVERETT—4410 106TH ST SW (AT AIRPORT RD); 425.493.6002; M-F 8-8 SA-SU 9-3

EVERETT—8910 VERNON RD (AT 87TH AVE NE); 425.335.0966; M-F 8-5, SA-SU 9-3

MARYSVILLE—4420 76TH ST NE (AT 44TH AVE NE); 360.651.7492; M-F 8-5, SA-SU 9-3

MUKILTEO—4410 106TH ST SW (AT MUKILTEO SPDWY); 425.493.6002; M-F 8-5, SA-SU 9-3

SNOHOMISH—401 SECOND ST (AT PINE AVE); 360.563.8600; M-F 8-5, SA-SU 9-3

Evergreen Medical Group
WWW.EVERGREENHEALTHCARE.ORG

KENMORE—18208 66TH AVE NE (AT 65TH AVE NE); 425.485.6561; M-SA 9-5

Federal Way Family Physicians
FEDERAL WAY—34616 11TH PL S (AT 11TH AVE S); 253.927.9460; M-F 8-5 SOMETIMES SA 8-12

Jinguji, Tom MD
KENT—23313 PACIFIC HWY S (AT S KENT DES MOINES RD); 206.870.8880; M-F 9-5; STREET PARKING

Kids Clinic
SEATTLE—12317 15TH AVE NE (AT NE 123RD ST); 206.957.1881; M-F 8-5; UNDERGROUND GARAGE

Medalia Medical Group
MONROE—14692 179TH AVE SE (AT VALLEY GENERAL HOSPITAL); 360.794.7996; M-TH 8-7, F 8-5, SA 9-3; PARKING IN FRONT OF BLDG

Medalia Silver Lake Clinic
EVERETT—12800 BOTHELL-EVERETT HWY (AT 132ND PL SE); 425.316.5160; M-F 8-6; PARKING LOT

participate in our survey at

Mercer Island Pediatrics Associates

WWW.MIPAKIDS.ORG

MERCER ISLAND—2553 76TH AVE SE (AT SE 27TH ST); 206.275.2122; M-F 8-5

Newcastle Pediatrics

NEWCASTLE—7203 129TH AVE SE (AT SE 69TH WAY); 425.656.5406; M-F 7-5

North Seattle Pediatrics

NORTH SEATTLE—10330 MERIDIAN AVE N (AT COLLEGE WAY N); 206.368.6080; M-F 9-5

North Sound Pediatrics

MILL CREEK—15808 MILL CREEK BLVD (AT 159 PL SE); 425.338.5668; M-F 9-5

Northgate Medical Center

WWW.GHC.ORG

MAPLE LEAF/ROOSEVELT—9800 4TH AVE NE (AT NE 100TH ST); 206.302.1400; M-F 8-5:30; PARKING AT 4TH AVE NE

Odessa Brown Children's Clinic

SEATTLE—2101 E YESLER WAY (AT 21ST AVE); 206.987.7200; M-F 8:30-5, SA 9-12

Pediatric Associates

WWW.MYPEDIATRICASSOCIATES.COM

BELLEVUE—4122 FACTORIA BLVD SE (AT FACTORIASQUARE MALL); 425.747.7202; M-F 8-5:30; MALL PARKING

ISSAQUAH—22717 SE 29TH ST (AT 226TH AVE SE); 425.391.7337; M-F 8-5:30

KIRKLAND—13030 121ST WY NE (AT NE 130 LN); 425.814.5170; M-F 8-5:30

REDMOND—8301 161ST AVE NE (AT NE 83RD ST); 425.885.9292; M-TH 8-5:30

RENTON—4033 TALBOT RD S (AT VALLEY MEDICAL CTR); 425.271.5437; M-F 9-6:30, SA 9-3, SU 10-2; GARAGE AT VALLEY MEDICAL CENTER

SAMMAMISH—22603 NE INGLEWOOD HILL RD (AT 228TH AVE NE); 425.836.5407; M-F 8-5:30

Pediatric Associates (Bellevue)

WWW.MYPEDIATRICASSOCIATES.COM

BELLEVUE—2700 NORTHUP WY (AT 116TH AVE NE); 425.827.4600; M-F 7:30-5:30 SA 8:30-4 SU 8:30-2

Pediatrics Northwest

FEDERAL WAY—34503 9TH AVE S (AT ST FRANCIS COMMUNITY HOSPITAL); 253.941.7229; M-F 8:30-5

Polyclinic Pediatrics

CENTRAL DISTRICT—1221 MADISON ST (AT MINOR AVE); 206.292.2249; M-F 8-12 & 1:15-5:30

Roxbury Family Health Care

WEST SEATTLE—9635 17TH AVE SW (NEAR ROXBURY); 206.763.5057; M-F 9-6; PARKING LOT

pediatricians

Seahurst Pediatrics

SEATTLE—16110 8TH AVE SW (AT HIGHLINE COMMUNITY HOSPITAL); 206.242.7822; M-F 9-5 SA 9-3

Snohomish Family Medical Center

WWW.FAMILYDOCTOR.ORG/SNOHOMISH

SNOHOMISH—629 AVE D (AT 7TH ST); 360.568.1554; M-TH 8-8, F 8-6, SA 9-4; PARKING AVAILABLE AT CLINIC

Swedish Physicians Children's Clinic

NORTH SEATTLE—1355 N 205TH ST (BTWN CALIFORNIA AVE & HINDS STS); 206.320.5780; M-F 8-8, SA 8-12; GARAGE OFF OF CALIFORNIA ST

UW Physicians

WWW.UWMEDICINE.ORG

SHORELINE—1355 N 205TH ST (BTWN HWY 99 AND 205TH ST); 206.542.5656; M 8-8, T 8-8, W 8-6, TH 8-7, F 8-5:30, SA 8-5; PARKING LOT

WOODINVILLE—17638 140TH AVE NE (AT NE178TH PL); 425.485.4100; M-TH 8-8, F 8-6, SA 8-5

Valley Childrens Clinic

RENTON—4011 TALBOT RD S (AT S 43RD ST); 425.656.5300; M-F 8:30-5

Virginia Mason

WWW.VMMC.ORG

FEDERAL WAY—33501 1ST WY S (AT S 336TH ST); 253.838.2400; M-F 8-5

ISSAQUAH—100 NE GILMAN BLVD (AT FRONT ST N); 425.557.8000; M-T 9-7, W-F 9-6, SA 9-1; PARKING LOT

LAURELHURST/SANDPOINT—4575 SAND POINT WY NE (AT 40TH AVE NE); 206.525.8000; M-F 9-5:30, SA 9-12; PARKING BEHIND BLDG

FIRST HILL—1201 TERRY AVE (AT SPRING ST); 206.223.6188; M-F 8:30-5:30

Wallingford Pediatrics

WALLINGFORD/FREMONT—4005 WALLINGFORD AVE N (AT N 40TH ST); 206.632.0542; M-F 8:30-5

Woodinville Pediatrics

WWW.WOODVILLEPEDIATRICS.COM

WOODINVILLE—17000 140TH AVE NE (AT NE 171ST ST); 425.483.5437; M-F 9-6; PARKING LOT

participate in our survey a

Tacoma

Allenmore Children & Young Adult Clinic

TACOMA—1924 S CEDAR ST (AT S 19TH ST); 253.627.9145; M-F 9-5:30

Commencement Bay Pediatrics

TACOMA—1901 S UNION AVE (AT ALLENMORE MEDICAL C ENTER);
253.572.5971; M-F 8:45-5; PARKING LOT

Lakewood Pediatric Associates

LAKEWOOD—7424 BRIDGEPORT WY W (AT 75TH ST W); 253.581.2111; M-F
7:30-6:30, SA 10-LAST APPT

Medalia Health Care

TACOMA—1708 S YAKIMA AVE (AT S 17TH ST); 253.627.9151; M-F 9-5

Pediatrics Northwest

GIG HARBOR—4700 POINT FOSDICK DR NW (AT 45TH ST CT NW);
253.851.5665; M-F 8:30-5

TACOMA—1628 S MILDRED ST (AT 19TH ST); 253.564.8005; M-F 9-5

Tacoma South Medical Center

WWW.GHC.ORG

TACOMA—9505 S STEELE ST (AT 96TH ST S); 253.597.6800; M-F 8-6

Union Avenue Pediatrics

WWW.UNIONAVEPEDS.COM

TACOMA—1530 S UNION AVE (OFF 19TH ST); 253.759.3333; M-F 8-5

Woodcreek Pediatrics

WWW.WOODCREEKPEDIATRICS.COM

PUYALLUP—1706 S MERIDIAN (AT 19TH AVE SE); 253.848.8797; M-F 8-6

pediatricians

breast pump sales & rentals

Greater Seattle Area

★★★★★

"lila picks"

- ★Birth and Beyond
- ★Pacific Mothers Support

Babies R Us

❝...*Medela pumps, Boppy pillows and lots of other breastfeeding supplies... staff knowledge varies from store to store, but everyone was friendly and helpful... clean and well-stocked... not a huge selection, but what they've got is great and very competitively priced...* **❞**

Customer Service .... ❸ $$$ .... Prices

WWW.BABIESRUS.COM

LYNNWOOD—19500 ALDERWOOD MALL PKWY (AT 196TH ST NW); 425.672.3220; M-SA 9:30-9:30, SU 11-7; PARKING IN FRONT OF BLDG

TACOMA—2502 S 48TH ST (AT TACOMA MALL); 253.472.4441; M-SA 9:30-9:30; FREE PARKING

TUKWILA—17500 SOUTHCENTER PKWY (AT SOUTHCENTER MALL); 206.575.1819; M-SA 9:30-9:30, SU 11-7; MALL PARKING

Birth & Beyond ★★★★★

❝...*carries just about everything you could possibly need and more... high quality brands... staff seemed to have a great knowledge base... no discounts here, but they have a lot of specialty items you wouldn't ordinarily see anywhere else...* **❞**

Customer Service .... ❹ $$$ .... Prices

WWW.BIRTHANDBEYOND.COM

ISSAQUAH—317 NW GILMAN BLVD (AT 224TH AVE SE); 425.392.6665; M-F 10-11:30AM; PARKING LOT BY BLDG

MADISON VALLEY/MADISON PARK—2610 E MADISON ST (AT 26TH AVE E); 206.324.4831; M-F 10-6, SA-SU 11-5; STREET PARKING

Breast Pump Rental Station

NORTH SEATTLE—1530 N 115TH ST (AT NORTHWEST HOSPITAL); 206.365.2277; M-F 9-5; PARKING IN FRONT OF BLDG

Evergreen Hospital (Women's & Children's Services)

WWW.EVERGREENHEALTHCARE.ORG

KIRKLAND—12040 NE 128TH ST (AT 120TH AVE NE); 425.899.3494; M-F 8:30-4:30, SA 9-4

Overlake Hospital Medical Center (Breast Pump Rental Station)

"...breast pumps for rental and sale... Medela Symphony, Hollister and Whittlestone... friendly and caring staff... carries replacement parts... very helpful, especially at answering questions from postpartum moms..."

Customer Service......................**5** $$$ .... Prices

WWW.OVERLAKEHOSPITAL.ORG

BELLEVUE—1051 116TH AVE NE (AT NE 8TH ST); 425.688.5389; M-SA 9-5; STREET LEVEL PARKING

Overlake Hospital Medical Center (Family & Community Education)

"...excellent supplies... offers nursing bra fittings... easy to rent deluxe pump and extend rental time if necessary... great customer service and care for new mothers..."

Customer Service......................**5** $$$ .... Prices

WWW.OVERLAKEHOSPITAL.ORG

BELLEVUE—1035 116TH AVE NE (AT NE 8TH ST); 425.688.5259; CALL FOR SCHEDULE; GARAGE PARKING

Pacific Mothers Support, Inc (PMSI)

"...the owner is a first-rate lactation consultant... special prices for people who aren't covered by insurance... a nice family-owned and operated breastfeeding support business... they really go the extra mile to make your breastfeeding experience successful... they delivered my pump to the hospital when my baby was born prematurely—thank you, thank you, thank you!... they give you what you need, and at a great price..."

Customer Service......................**5** $$ .... Prices

WWW.PACIFICMSI.COM

BELLEVUE—1407 132ND AVE NE (AT BEL RED RD); 425.462.0577; M-F 9-5, SA 12-3; PARKING IN FRONT OF BLDG

QFC View Ridge Pharmacy

"...Medela Lactina rentals available at $2.50/day or $145 for 3 months... good availability and customer service..."

Customer Service......................**4** $$$ .... Prices

WEDGEWOOD/RAVENNA—7501 35TH AVE NE (AT NE 75TH ST); 206.524.1800; M-F 9-7, SA 9-5, SU 12-5; PARKING LOT AND STREET PARKING

Right Start, The

"...a small selection of pumps for sale... their prices are on the higher side, and the pump selection is pretty limited... they carry the Medela Pump In Style... they only carry the best... good quality and customer service might make it totally worthwhile..."

Customer Service......................**4** $$ .... Prices

WWW.RIGHTSTART.COM

BELLEVUE—168 BELLEVUE SQ (AT NE 2ND ST); 425.451.2445; M-SA 9:30-9:30, SU 11-7

WEDGEWOOD/RAVENNA—4520 UNION BAY PL NE (ACROSS FROM UNIVERSITY VLG); 206.729.7458; M-SA 10-6:30, SU 11-6

breast pump sales & rentals

Swedish Medical Center
(Women & Infant Services)

WWW.SWEDISH.ORG

UNIVERSITY DISTRICT/UNIVERSITY VILLAGE—747 BROADWAY (AT MADISON
ST); 206.215.3338; CHECK SCHEDULE ONLINE; GARAGE AT MINOR AVE &
JAMES STS

Tacoma General Hospital
(Breast Pump Rental Depot)

"...*very caring and knowledgeable lactation consultant... they help
ensure you get the best breast pump for you, your body and your
baby... not the cheapest option, but very convenient for new moms...* **"**

Customer Service ....❺ $$$..Prices

WWW.MULTICARE.COM

TACOMA—315 MARTIN LUTHER KING JR WY (AT MARY BRIDGE CHILDRENS
HEALTH CTR); 253.403.3020; M-F 9-5, SA 10-5, SU 12-5; PARKING IN
FRONT OF BLDG

Tacoma General Hospital
(Mom & Baby Boutique)

WWW.MULTICARE.ORG

TACOMA—315 MARTIN LUTHER KING JR WY (AT 3RD ST); 253.403.6081; M
TH-F 9-5, T-W 9-8, SA 10-5, SU 12-5

takecare.com

WWW.TAKE-CARE.COM

CAPITOL HILL—125 16TH AVE E (AT E DENNY WY); 206.326.3496; ONLINE;
FREE PARKING

USA Baby

WWW.USABABY.COM

TUKWILA—720 ANDOVER PK E (AT MINKLER BLVD); 206.575.1476; M-SA 10-
8, SU 11-6

Village Maternity

"...*Medela pumps for rental or purchase... not too many pumps in
stock so best to call and reserve or order... they also carry the
replacement parts for the Medela pumps which comes in very
helpful...* **"**

Customer Service ....❺ $$$$$ ....Prices

WWW.VILLAGEMATERNITY.COM

UNIVERSITY DISTRICT/UNIVERSITY VILLAGE—2615 NE UNIVERSITY VILLAGE
ST (AT UNIVERSITY VILLAGE MALL); 206.523.5167; M-SA 9:30-9, SU 11-6;
MALL PARKING

Women's Center At Overlake

WWW.OVERLAKEHOSPITAL.ORG

ISSAQUAH—6520 226TH PL SE (AT SE 64TH PL); 425.688.5787; M-SA 9-5:30;
FREE PARKING

Online

amazon.com

"...I'm always amazed by the amount of stuff Amazon sells—including a pretty good selection of pumps... Medela, Avent, Isis, Ameda... prices range from great to average... pretty easy shopping experience... free shipping on bigger orders... **"**

babycenter.com

"...they carry all the major brands... prices are competitive, but keep in mind you'll need to pay for shipping too... the comments from parents are incredibly helpful... excellent customer service... easy shopping experience... **"**

birthexperience.com

"...Medela and Avent products... great deal with the Canadian currency conversion... get free shipping with big orders... easy site to navigate... **"**

breast-pumps.com

breastmilk.com

ebay.com

"...you can get Medela pumps brand new in packaging with the warranty for $100 less than retail... able to buy immediately instead of having to bid and wait... wide variety... be sure to check for shipping price... great place to find deals, but research the seller before you bid... **"**

express-yourself.net

healthchecksystems.com

lactationconnection.com

"...Ameda and Whisper Wear products... nice selection and competitive prices... quick delivery of any nursing or lactation product you can imagine... the selection of mom and baby related items is fantastic... **"**

medela.com

"...well worth the money... fast, courteous and responsive... great site for a full listing of Medela products and links to purchase online... quality of customer service by phone varies... licensed lactation specialist answers e-mail via email at no charge and with quick turnaround... **"**

mybreastpump.com

"...a great online one-stop-shop for all things breast feeding... you can purchase hospital grade pumps from them... fast service for all you breastfeeding needs... **"**

diaper delivery services

Greater Seattle Area

★★★★★

"lila picks"

★ Baby Diaper Service
★ Sunflower Diaper Service

Baby Diaper Service ★★★★★

"...they take the fear out of using cloth diapers... love this professional and eco-friendly diaper service service... always easy to change our orders... wide delivery area... drivers are excellent and will answer any of your questions... prompt... also provide extra products like pins and diaper covers, which are hard to find other places... great gift for new parents... diapers are all cotton, always clean and sanitary... **"**

Customer Service .... ❸ $$$ .... Prices
Service Area .... Seattle & Tacoma
WWW.SEATTLEDIAPER.COM
MADISON VALLEY/MADISON PARK—6559 5TH PL S (AT S RIVER ST);
 206.767.1807; M-F 9-5

Josie's Baby Diaper Service ★★★★☆

"...service includes a weekly exchange of clean diapers for soiled diapers at your doorstep... charges are based on the number of diapers you order per week... the only diaper service available right now in Whatcom County ... **"**

Customer Service .... ❸ $$$ .... Prices
Service Area .... call for delivery
WWW.JOSEPHINENET.COM
STANWOOD—9901 272ND PLACE NW (AT 99TH AVE NW); 360.629.2126

Sunflower Diaper Service ★★★★★

"...love this service... run by a mom... she picks up and delivers diapers 2x per week... provides everything you need and her diapers are the form fitting kind with snaps... I have been using Sunflower Diaper Service for a year now and I recommend it to everyone... especially friendly and community oriented... **"**

Customer Service .... ❸ $$$ .... Prices
Service Area .... Seattle area
WWW.GOCITYKIDS.COM/BROWSE/ATTRACTION.JSP?ID=50296
BALLARD—7519 28TH AVE NW (AT NW 75TH ST); 206.782.4199; M-F 9-5

haircuts

Greater Seattle Area

★★★★★

"lila picks"

★Hair Chair

Beach Combers Kids' Cuts

"*...making what could be a scary experience fun... the kids can watch DVD's to distract them while they get a cut... terrific haircuts... nice playroom for the kids... always calm and mellow, never the screaming zone of other shops... a bit spendy for a kids' cut, but a fun environment and overall experience... nice first-cut certificate and hair locket...* **"**

Customer Service ....❹ $$$.. Prices

BALLARD—6417 PHINNEY AVE N (AT NW 65TH ST); 206.783.1554; T-SA 10-7; FREE PARKING

Brat Pack

"*...this has been the only place that has been able to successfully cut our son's hair... we tried going to regular 'big people' places and they just couldn't handle it... he would leave with either half a haircut or no haircut and everyone would be upset... they've got it down pat at the Brat Pack—even if you end up with a child with a lollipop in both hands, bubbles being blown around him, a bucket of toys on their adorable non-threatening chairs and the child's favorite movie chosen from their huge selection on their own personal television, they get the job done and done well...* **"**

Customer Service ....❺ $$$.. Prices

REDMOND—7335 164TH AVE NE (REDMOND TOWN CENTER); 425.883.1006; CALL FOR APPT

Fantastic Sams

"*...good prices on kids' haircuts (includes a wash if needed, unlike other drop-in salons)... they take the time to talk with the kids, who are treated as the customer (the parent is included too)... haircuts have been excellent every time we've gone... they often run specials... nothing fancy, but they do the trick...* **"**

Customer Service ....❺ $$.. Prices

WWW.FANTASTICSAMS.COM

RENTON—12638 164TH AVE SE (AT SE 128TH ST); 425.226.5353; CALL FOR APPT

Fun Kuts

"*...great place to take your child for their first haircut... even wigglers will get a good cut... we don't go anywhere else... always on time... for the first haircut, you get a picture, a bag of your child's locks and a card for your baby book... you pay for the luxury of a kid-friendly environment...* **"**

Customer Service ....❹ $$$.. Prices

WWW.FUNKUTS.COM

LYNNWOOD—3333 184TH ST SW (AT ALDERWOOD MALL); 425.776.7777; M-F
9-8, SA 9-6, SU 10-6

TACOMA—3815 S STEELE ST (AT S 78TH ST); 253.474.9847; M-F 9-8, SA-SU
9-6

Great Clips ★★★★☆

"...cheap, decent cuts... not specifically tailored around children so
there aren't any horses or cars to sit in... stylists' experience with kids
vary, but we generally walk away satisfied... you can't beat the price
and you don't have to make an appointment... the balloon at the end
makes it all worthwhile... **"**

Customer Service......................... ❸ $$ .... Prices

WWW.GREATCLIPS.COM

NORTH SEATTLE—8551 GREENWOOD AVE N (AT N 85TH ST); 206.297.7733;
M-F 9-9, SA 9-6, SU 10-5

TACOMA—5738 N 26TH ST (AT N PEARL ST); 253.752.4305; M-F 9-9, SA 9-7,
SU 10-5

Hair Chair ★★★★★

"...a crying kid won't frazzle these pros... the adjacent toy store
comes in handy for bargaining with my tot... on the spendy side, but
you get what you pay for... best and most consistent haircuts... the kid-
friendly environment and special little touches make us keep coming
back... painless haircutting experience... **"**

Customer Service......................... ❹ $$$ .... Prices

BELLEVUE—15600 NE 8TH ST (AT CROSSROADS SHOPPING CTR);
425.562.0430; M-SA 10-8, SU 11-5; FREE PARKING

UNIVERSITY DISTRICT/UNIVERSITY VILLAGE—2676 NE UNIVERSITY VLG (AT
UNIVERSITY VILLAGE MALL); 206.525.0499; M-SA 10-8, SU 11-6; MALL
PARKING

Haircuts For Kids ★★★★⯪

"...great for kids and parents nervous about the first haircut... cool
car-shaped seats, boxes of fun toys and competent stylists... the
sweetest stylists... great people... great haircuts!.. **"**

Customer Service......................... ❺ $$ .... Prices

MAPLE LEAF/ROOSEVELT—6104 ROOSEVELT WY NE (AT NE 61ST ST);
206.522.4906; T-F 10-6, SA 9-5, SU 10-2

Hairmasters ★★★★☆

"...stylists are relaxed enough to let my girls play with the combs and
brushes... they even give out stickers... my girls love to go there, they
allow them to brush their own or baby dolls hair... very inexpensive...
only $10 for a cut... **"**

Customer Service......................... ❹ $$$ .... Prices

BOTHELL—18811 BOTHELL WY NE (AT NE 188TH ST); 425.486.7304; CALL
FOR APPT

Kids Cuts ★★★★☆

"...Kids cuts offers reliable, fast service with reasonable prices...
friendly staff and accomodating to children... great decor, toys, chairs,
you name it... this place has it all... great cuts, too... **"**

Customer Service......................... ❺ $$ .... Prices

WWW.KIDSCUTS.COM

LYNNWOOD—19410 36TH AVE W (AT 196TH ST SW); 425.774.3960; CALL
FOR APPT

haircuts

Kids Cuts-N-Play ★★★★⯪

"...wonderful kid friendly environment... finish the girls off with a cute pony tail and ribbon... fast and fabulous haircuts... they work hard to make kids feel welcome... they even have cute seats to get your haircut in and toys to play with... go for ice cream at the Town Center afterwards..."

Customer Service .... **❺** $$$.......................................Prices

REDMOND—7551 166TH AVE NE (AT REDMOND TOWN CTR); 425.869.2527; M-F 9:30-9, SA 10-10:30, SU 11-7

Kids Haircuts ★★★★☆

"...great service... really friendly stylists, and cute cars for the kids to sit in... makes the experience that much better..."

Customer Service .... **❹** $$$.......................................Prices

BURIEN—12845 1ST AVE S (AT S 128TH ST); 206.246.9483

Kids Kuts ★★★★☆

"...talented hairdresser who knows how to work with kids really well... tons of toys and videos... my boys loves the police car and motorcycle seats... we have had great experiences here... one of my daughters even asked if she could have a haircut for her birthday..."

Customer Service .... **❺** $$$.......................................Prices

WWW.KIDKUTS.COM

EVERETT—12811 8TH AVE W (AT 128TH ST SW); 425.710.9393; M-F 10-7, SA 9-4

Lil' Klippers ★★★★☆

"...they always do a good job... kids get to sit in beautiful wooden boats, horses, or cars... kids are offered boxes of toys to play with while they're getting their hair cut... great first haircut spot complete with certificate and lock booklet... make your appointment in advance and enjoy the professional and efficient cuts..."

Customer Service .... **❹** $$$.......................................Prices

WALLINGFORD/FREMONT—1815 N 45TH ST (AT WALLINGFORD AVE N); 206.633.2158; M-F 9-8, SA-SU 9-5

Picture Perfect Kids

EDMONDS—317 MAIN STR (AT 3RD AVE N); 425.744.1866; CALL FOR APPT

Rudy's Barber Shop ★★★★☆

"...this is a great place to go if you just need to get your child's hair cut on the spot... they also have kid prices and no appointments are needed... my daughter has always liked going there because she feels like a big girl... reasonable prices, and friendly, fun staff with a cool decor..."

Customer Service .... **❹** $ ....Prices

WWW.NEVERSTOP.COM/RUDYS

WALLINGFORD/FREMONT—475 N 36TH ST (AT FRANCIS AVE); 206.547.0818; M-SA 9-9, SU 11-7

Supercuts ★★★⯪☆

"...results definitely vary from location to location... they did their best to amuse my son and an okay job with his hair... cheap and easy, with decent results... some locations have toys for kids to play with... walk-ins welcome, but make an appointment if you are going on the weekend... ask for the cutter who's best with kids... great cut for the price... fast and easy..."

Customer Service .... **❸** $$...Prices

WWW.SUPERCUTS.COM

BELLEVUE—12660 SE 38TH ST (AT FACTORIA SQUARE MALL); 425.747.4686;
M-F 9-9, SA 8-7, SU 10-5; MALL PARKING

KIRKLAND—8421 122ND AVE NE (AT NE 85TH ST); 425.822.5020; M-F 9-9,
SA 8-7, SU 9-7

LAKEWOOD—6111 LAKEWOOD TWN CTR BLVD (AT LAKEWOOD TOWN CTR);
253.584.2121; M-F 8-9, SA 8-8, SU 9-7

RENTON—20 SW 7TH ST (AT RAINIER AVE S); 425.226.1115; M-F 8-9, SA 8-
8, SU 9-6

BALLARD—2232 NW MARKET ST (AT 22ND AVE NW); 206.789.8656; M-F 8-9,
SA 9-7, SU 10-5

RAINIER VALLEY—383 STRANDER BLVD (AT ANDOVER PARK E);
206.575.3609; M-F 9-9, SA 8-8, SU 9-7

UNIVERSITY DISTRICT/UNIVERSITY VILLAGE—4722 UNIVERSITY WY NE (AT
NE 47TH ST); 206.524.0126; M-F 9-9, SA 8-7, SU 9-7

WEST SEATTLE—4736 42ND AVE SW (S OF SW ALASKA ST); 206.932.0400; M-
F 8-9, SA 8-8, SU 9-7

TACOMA—141ST PACIFIC AVE S (AT 112TH ST E); 253.536.1130; M-F 9-9, SA
8-8, SU 9-7

TACOMA—2941 S 38TH ST (AT S PINE ST); 253.473.0444; M-SA 8-9, SU 9-7

West Seattle Kids ★★★★☆

❝...so great with kids and our son loves to go sit in the tractor for his
haircuts... it's hard to get an appointment so remember to book
early...**❞**

Customer Service......................... ❺ $$.. Prices

WEST SEATTLE—6969 CALIFORNIA AVE SW (AT SW FRONTENAC ST);
206.937.7017; CALL FOR APPT

Wild Child

TACOMA—2310 MILDRED ST W (AT 19TH ST); 253.564.0709; CALL FOR APPT

haircuts

nanny & babysitter referrals

Greater Seattle Area

★★★★★

"lila picks"

★ Childcare Referral Resources
★ Home Details

Annie's Nannies ★★★★☆

"...the oldest agency in Seattle... super-friendly owner... expensive, but well worth it for quality service... good selection of nannies and knowledgeable staff... they place live-in, live-out, full-time, part-time, temporary, on-call and emergency nannies... well-trained and well-screened... "on-call" service is great—have always been able to find someone on short notice... will not work with nannies who are mothers and want their own children with them during the day... "

Baby nurses	✗	$$$$	Prices
Nannies	✓	❹	Candidate selection
Au pairs	✗	❹	Staff knowledge
Babysitters	✓	❹	Customer service

WWW.ANNIESNANNIES-SEATTLE.COM

BALLARD—2236 NW 58TH ST (AT 22ND AVE NW); 206.784.8462; M-F 9-5

Best Sitters & Homemakers ★★★½☆

"...nice option for emergency or hotel babysitter... we found the babysitters to be variable... reasonable rates...pricey, but the nanny was very experienced... they charge more for extra children but we have had excellent results with their employees and will continue to happily use their service ... "

Baby nurses	✗	$$$	Prices
Nannies	✗	❸	Candidate selection
Au pairs	✗	❸	Staff knowledge
Babysitters	✓	❸	Customer service

Service AreaSeattle & the seaside from Federal way to Lynwood

WWW.BESTSITTERSINC.COM

ISSAQUAH—24514 SE 46TH ST; 206.682.2556; M-F 8-5, SA 9-1

Care Works ★★★★☆

"...nanny placement services for families... I was very impressed with the effort they put into ensuring that there were good personality and parenting-style matches between my family and the nannies they presented to us... they did get us a great nanny fairly quickly, and provided ongoing help and service... "

Baby nurses	✗	$$$$	Prices
Nannies	✓	❺	Candidate selection
Au pairs	✗	❺	Staff knowledge
Babysitters	✗	❺	Customer service

WWW.CAREWORKSSEATTLE.COM

SEATTLE—206.325.7510

Childcare Referral Resources ★★★★★

"...CRR is a nonprofit organization that provides referrals for free, though donations are appreciated... wonderful childcare resource... top-notch customer service... loaded with information... get info by phone or online... search for childcare by zip code, neighborhood, children's ages, pickup/drop-off times, family home/daycare center/preschool, etc... you need to call each provider to make sure their info is updated and accurate..."

Baby nurses	✗	$	Prices
Nannies	✓	❹	Candidate selection
Au pairs	✗	❹	Staff knowledge
Babysitters	✓	❹	Customer service

WWW.CHILDCARE.ORG

CAPITOL HILL—1225 S WELLER (AT 12TH ST); 206.329.5544; M-TH 9-3, F 9-1 (OFFICE HOURS)

Home Details ★★★★★

"...these folks are a great resource... they do an excellent job of helping you define your staff needs, and communicating that to potential candidates... all of the candidates they have sent to us have been amazing!.. Leann is very professional and passionate about her work... everyone I know who has worked with her has had a good experience... though her fees are not the cheapest, her work is worth it..."

Baby nurses	✗	$$$	Prices
Nannies	✓	❺	Candidate selection
Au pairs	✗	❺	Staff knowledge
Babysitters	✓	❺	Customer service

WWW.HOMEDETAILSINC.COM

SEATTLE—4616 25TH AVE NE (AT UNIVERSITY VLG MALL); 206.285.7656

Judi Julin RN Nannybroker, Inc.

Baby nurses	✗	✓	Nannies
Au pairs	✗	✓	Babysitters

Service AreaSeattle—east side, King County, Pierce County

WWW.NANNYBROKER.COM

ISSAQUAH—25620 SE 157TH ST (AT 256TH AVE SE); 206.624.1213; DAILY 24 HOURS

McDonald Nanny Services

Baby nurses	✗	✓	Nannies
Au pairs	✗	✗	Babysitters

WWW.MCDONALDEMPLOYMENT.COM

LOWER QUEEN ANNE/SEATTLE CENTER—2 NICKERSON ST (AT QUEEN ANNE AVE N); 206.284.5244

Nannies and More ★★★★☆

"...Margie is great at matching families with the right nanny..."

Baby nurses	✓	$$$	Prices
Nannies	✓	❺	Candidate selection
Au pairs	✗	❺	Staff knowledge
Babysitters	✗	❺	Customer service

Service Area....... Greater Seattle Area

MUKILTEO—206.240.0907; CALL FOR APPT

Nanny & Company ★★★★☆

"...they are very dedicated to understanding each family's needs and referring a nanny that will compliment a particular family's dynamics...

nanny & babysitter referrals

very confidential and professional and they have a low turnover rate ... "

Baby nurses	✗	
Nannies	✓	
Au pairs	✗	
Babysitters	✗	

$$$	Prices
❹	Candidate selection
❹	Staff knowledge
❹	Customer service

WWW.NANNYANDCOMPANY.NET

BELLEVUE—40 LAKE BELLEVUE DR (AT 120TH AVE NE); 425.454.1183

Seattle Nanny Network

"...they really know their business... help with all stages of finding the right nanny, from identifying the candidates to interview, to finally how to incorporate them into your home... low replacement rate... both permanent and temporary placements... "

Baby nurses	✗	
Nannies	✓	
Au pairs	✗	
Babysitters	✗	

$$$$	Prices
❸	Candidate selection
❹	Staff knowledge
❹	Customer service

Service Area ...... Greater Seattle Area

WWW.SEATTLENANNY.COM

SEATTLE—206.374.8688; M-F 9-5

participate in our survey at

Online

★ ★ ★ ★ ★
"lila picks"

★craigslist.org

4nannies.com

| Baby nurses | ✗ | ✓ | Nannies |
| Au pairs | ✗ | ✗ | Babysitters |

Service Area..................... nationwide
WWW.4NANNIES.COM

aupaircare.com

| Baby nurses | ✗ | ✗ | Nannies |
| Au pairs | ✓ | ✗ | Babysitters |

Service Area................ International
WWW.AUPAIRCARE.COM

aupairinamerica.com

| Baby nurses | ✗ | ✗ | Nannies |
| Au pairs | ✓ | ✗ | Babysitters |

Service Area................ International
WWW.AUPAIRINAMERICA.COM

babysitters.com

| Baby nurses | ✗ | ✗ | Nannies |
| Au pairs | ✗ | ✓ | Babysitters |

Service Area..................... nationwide
WWW.BABYSITTERS.COM

craigslist.org

★ ★ ★ ★ ★

❝...you can find just about anything on craigslist... good starting point, especially if you don't want to spend a lot of money and are willing to do your own screening... we received at least 50 responses to our 'nanny wanted' ad... helped me find very qualified baby-sitters... includes all major cities in the US... ❞

| Baby nurses | ✓ | ✓ | Nannies |
| Au pairs | ✗ | ✓ | Babysitters |

WWW.CRAIGSLIST.ORG

enannysource.com

| Baby nurses | ✗ | ✓ | Nannies |
| Au pairs | ✗ | ✗ | Babysitters |

Service Area..................... nationwide
WWW.ENANNYSOURCE.COM

findcarenow.com

| Baby nurses | ✗ | ✗ | Nannies |
| Au pairs | ✗ | ✓ | Babysitters |

Service Area..................... nationwide
WWW.FINDCARENOW.COM

nanny & babysitter referrals

get-a-sitter.com

Baby nurses .... ✗   ✗ .... Nannies
Au pairs .... ✗   ✓ .... Babysitters
Service Area .... nationwide
WWW.GET-A-SITTER.COM

householdstaffing.com

Baby nurses .... ✓   ✓ .... Nannies
Au pairs .... ✗   ✗ .... Babysitters
WWW.HOUSEHOLDSTAFFING.COM

interexchange.org

Baby nurses .... ✗   ✗ .... Nannies
Au pairs .... ✓   ✗ .... Babysitters
Service Area .... International
WWW.INTEREXCHANGE.ORG

nannies4hire.com

Baby nurses .... ✗   ✓ .... Nannies
Au pairs .... ✗   ✗ .... Babysitters
WWW.NANNIES4HIRE.COM

nannylocators.com

★★★⯨☆

"...many listings of local nannies available... I have found that the listings are not always up to date... $100 subscriber fee to respond and contact nannies that have posted... different regions have varying amounts of listings available... "

Baby nurses .... ✗   ✓ .... Nannies
Au pairs .... ✗   ✗ .... Babysitters
Service Area .... Nationwide
WWW.NANNYLOCATORS.COM

sittercity.com

★★★★☆

"...wSonderful online resource... an online baby-sitter database filled with mostly college and graduate students looking for baby-sitting and nanny jobs... candidates are not prescreened so you must check references... Fee to access the database is $35 plus $5 per month... tends to be be more useful for baby-sitters than regular daytime nannies... "

Baby nurses .... ✗   ✗ .... Nannies
Au pairs .... ✗   ✓ .... Babysitters
Service Area .... nationwide
WWW.SITTERCITY.COM

student-sitters.com

Baby nurses .... ✗   ✗ .... Nannies
Au pairs .... ✗   ✓ .... Babysitters
WWW.STUDENT-SITTERS.COM

photographers

Greater Seattle Area

"lila picks"

- ★ Bellen Drake Photography
- ★ EK Photography
- ★ Kiddie Kandids
- ★ Yuen Lui Studios

Bella Photography ★★★★☆

"...her work is beautiful... the children always look natural and comfortable—no stiff poses or awkward props!... **"**

Customer service.........................❺ $$$...Prices

WWW.BELLAPHOTOGRAPHYNW.COM

REDMOND—425.836.4080

Bellen Drake Photography ★★★★★

"...unique, unposed and natural... black and white or color photography... art with your child as the subject... babies, children and families presented in stunning handmade albums... **"**

Customer service.........................❺ $$$...Prices

WWW.BELLENDRAKE.COM

COLUMBIA CITY—4524 35TH SOUTH (AT S ALASKA ST); 206.941.2714; CALL FOR APPT

Chapters Photography ★★★☆☆

"...great location in Country Village in Bothell... the first year panel (3, 6 and 12 months) is an excellent value!.. my baby's 3 month picture from Chapters is fabulous, I am looking forward to the next one at 6 months... **"**

Customer service.........................❹ $$$...Prices

WWW.CHAPTERSPHOTO.COM

BOTHELL—23176 8TH AVE SE (AT COUNTRY VILLAGE); 425.415.1267

EK Photography ★★★★★

"...photographers are polite, friendly, and obviously love children... photos are much more artistic than most and reasonably priced... gives you the option of buying a CD of all the images... wonderful, natural photos that I will treasure forever...main studio is on Whidbey Island, but also does a lot of sessions at Gracewinds Perinatal Services in Ballard... **"**

Customer service.........................❺ $$...Prices

WWW.EKPHOTOGRAPHY.COM

BALLARD—709 NW 60TH ST (AT 7TH AVE NW); 206.849.9398

Hanson Photography ★★★★★

"...Brad managed to catch our son's personality in the pics he took... we set up a custom package to have pregnancy pics taken, then

     participate in our survey at

followed up with pics of our son several months later... took his time getting the candids we were looking for... expensive, but worth the price for the quality and service... fresh, original, artistic... **"**

Customer service .... **❺** $$$ .... Prices

Service Areaavailable for worldwide travel

WWW.HANSONPHOTOGRAPHY.COM

WEST SEATTLE—310 1ST AVE S (AT S MAIN ST); 206.652.5071; CALL FOR APPT

Heather Quintans

WWW.HEATHERPHOTO.COM

GREENLAKE/GREENWOOD/PHINNEY RIDGE—7017 GREENWOOD AVE N (AT N 70TH ST); 206.297.2064

Janet Klinger Photography

"*...we had some wonderful photos taken here (by the photographer's assistant as Janet Klinger was out on maternity leave at the time)... the photos and sitting fee seemed fairly expensive, and I'm not sure we could afford it multiple years, but the photos are truly wonderful and really capture our children's personalities...* **"**

Customer service .... **❹** $$$$ .... Prices

WWW.JANETKLINGER.COM

GREENLAKE/GREENWOOD/PHINNEY RIDGE—6120 PHINNEY AVE N (AT N 61ST ST); 206.622.7478

JCPenney Portrait Studio

"*...don't expect works of art, but they are great for a quick wallet photo... photographers and staff range from great to not so good... a quick portrait with standard props and backdrops... definitely join the portrait club and use coupons... waits are especially long around the holidays, so consider taking your Christmas pictures early... the e-picture option is a time saver... wait time for prints can be up to a month... look for coupons and you'll never have to pay full price...* **"**

Customer service .... **❹** $$ .... Prices

WWW.JCPENNEYPORTRAITS.COM

BELLEVUE—300 BELLEVUE SQ (AT NE 4TH ST); 425.451.8213; M-F 10-6:20, SA 10-5:20, SU 11-5:20; MALL PARKING

LYNNWOOD—18601 33RD AVE W (AT ALDERWOOD MALL); 425.771.2107; CALL FOR APPT; MALL PARKING

MAPLE LEAF/ROOSEVELT—401 NE NORTHGATE WY (AT NORTHGATE SHOPPING CTR); 206.364.2232; M-SA 10-7, SU 11-6

TACOMA—4502 S STEELE (AT TACOMA MALL); 253.474.5035; CALL FOR APPT; MALL PARKING

Joy Fischer Photography

"*...beautiful photos from her in-home studio... color and black and white... personal attention... easy to work with...* **"**

Customer service .... **❺** $$$$ .... Prices

Service AreaSeattle-Bellevue area (Eastside)

WWW.JOYFISCHERPHOTOGRAPHY.COM

KIRKLAND—13002 NE 102ND PL (AT 132ND AVE); 425.822.1731; CALL FOR APPT

Kiddie Kandids

"*...good quality photos for all occasions... they made a big effort to get a smile out of my grumpy son... you don't need to make a reservation, just pop in and have the pictures taken... no sitting fee... photographers take the extra time necessary to get a great shot and they have the cutest props... lots of items to buy with your pictures on*

photographers

them—cups, bags, mouse pads... buy the CD of pictures rather than buying the prints... pictures are available right after the sitting... **"**

Customer service.........................**❹** $$$...Prices

WWW.KIDDIEKANDIDS.COM

LYNNWOOD—19500 ALDERWOOD MALL PKWY (AT 196TH ST SW); 425.967.0060; M-SA 9:30-8:30, SU 11-6; MALL PARKING

TUKWILA—17500 S CTR PKWY (AT MINKLER BLVD); 253.479.0035; M-SA 9:30-8:30, SU 11-6

Lily Waner Photography ★★★★☆

"*...Lily has a knack for taking some very artistic and alternative pictures of children and their families... she is very good about expressing personality in her photos...* **"**

Customer service.........................**❺** $$...Prices

DOWNTOWN—115 PREFONTAINE PL (AT YESTER WAY); 206.915.4055

Peggy Washburn Photography ★★★★☆

"*...stunning works of art with my baby as the subject... creative poses that capture the wonderful expressions of children and parents... special... takes absolutely beautiful black and white photographs of your children that will be a cherished for a lifetime... gentle and patient working with my very active toddler...* **"**

Customer service.........................**❺** $$$...Prices
Service Area ....Greater Seattle area

WWW.PEGGYWASHBURN.COM

MONTLAKE—414 31ST AVE E (AT E HARRISON ST); 206.323.6705; CALL FOR APPT

Photographic Essays ★★★★☆

"*...Corinne and Steven, the photographers, created an album of our daughter that was phenomenal... their use of color and composition is original and breathtaking... they took enough time with our baby to get a wide variety of poses, but were efficient with their time... the shoot was friendly and fun for everyone... it's clear that photography is their passion and my pictures were beyond my expectations...* **"**

Customer service.........................**❺** $$$...Prices
Service Area ....Greater Seattle area

WWW.PHOTOGRAPHICESSAYS.COM

WOODINVILLE—14700 148TH AVE NE (AT 147TH PL); 425.424.9500; CALL FOR APPT

Photography By Trina ★★★★★

"*...Trina has a private studio which makes for a very comfortable setting and fun time for baby and parents!.. she is incredible with babies... she has two kids herself and she is a lot of fun!.. I was hardly clothed for pregnancy pictures (which would have made me nervous anywhere else) and she made my husband and I feel totally at home...* **"**

Customer service.........................**❺** $$$...Prices

WWW.PHOTOGRAPHYBYTRINA.COM

PUYALLUP—10812 149TH ST E (AT 109TH AVE E); 253.840.5709

Phottazz ★★★★☆

"*...I had my pregnancy and 'belly' shots taken here... they turned out wonderfully... we were not rushed during our photo shoot and I felt the poses were creative... a little pricey, but worth it...* **"**

Customer service.........................**❺** $$$$...Prices

WWW.PHOTTAZZ.COM

BELLEVUE—1014 BELLEVUE SQUARE (AT BELLEVUE SQUARE); 425.635.0200

Picture People ★★★½☆

" *...this well-known photography chain offers good package deals that get even better with coupons... generally friendly staff despite the often 'uncooperative' little customers... they don't produce super fancy, artistic shots, but you get your pictures in under an hour... reasonable quality for a fast portrait... kind of hit-or-miss quality and customer service...* **"**

Customer service .... **❹** $$$ .... Prices

WWW.PICTUREPEOPLE.COM

LYNNWOOD—3000 184TH ST SW (AT ALDERWOOD MALL); 425.744.0752; MALL PARKING

MAPLE LEAF/ROOSEVELT—401 NE NORTHGATE WY (AT NORTHGATE SHOPPING CTR); 206.362.9520; MALL PARKING

TACOMA—4502 S STEELE ST (AT TACOMA MALL); 253.474.2484; MALL PARKING

TUKWILA—804 SOUTHCENTER MALL (AT TUKWILA PKY); 206.431.5545; MALL PARKING

Purely Kids Photography ★★★★½

" *...by far, the most beautiful photos of children I have seen... I selected Marissa after seeing a co-workers photos... light and bright, Marissa and her exceptional helpers captured the essence of our child and family... she visits Seattle once a month at the Right Start...* **"**

Customer service .... **❺** $$$$ .... Prices

WWW.PURELYKIDS.COM

SEATTLE—866.787.3543

Render's Photography ★★★★★

" *...Michelle render captures great pictures of baby, pregnancy and the whole family...* **"**

Customer service .... **❺** $$$ .... Prices

WWW.RENDERSPHOTOGRAPHY.COM

TACOMA—253.922.4242

Sears Portrait Studio ★★★☆☆

" *...the price is right, but the service and quality are variable... make an appointment to cut down on the wait time... bring your coupons for even better prices... perfect for getting a nice wallet size portrait without spending a fortune... I wish the wait time for prints wasn't so long (2 weeks)... the quality and service-orientation of the photographers really vary a lot—some are great, some aren't...* **"**

Customer service .... **❸** $$ .... Prices

WWW.SEARSPORTRAIT.COM

EVERETT—1302 EVERETT MALL WY (AT EVERETT MALL); 425.356.6767; M-F 10-8, SA 9-8, SU 10-6; MALL PARKING

FEDERAL WAY—1701 S SEATAC MALL (AT 320TH ST); 253.529.8312; M-SA 10-8, SA 9-8, SU 10-5; MALL PARKING

LYNNWOOD—18600 ALDERWOOD MALL PKWY (AT ALDERWOOD MALL); 425.670.6229; MALL PARKING

PUYALLUP—3500 S MERIDIAN (AT SOUTH HILL MALL); 253.770.5700; MALL PARKING

REDMOND—2200 148TH AVE NE (AT NE 22ND ST); 425.644.6581

NORTH SEATTLE—15711 AURORA AVE N (AT N 155TH ST); 206.364.9000

SODO—76 S LANDER ST (AT UTAH AVE S); 206.344.4959

TACOMA—4502 S STEELE ST (AT TACOMA MALL); 253.471.7187; MALL PARKING

photographers

Tanya Davis Photography

WWW.TANYADAVISPHOTOGRAPHY.COM

BALLARD—913 NW 64TH ST (AT 9TH AVE NW); 206.619.5221

Teddi Yaeger Photography

66*...wonderful... Teddi has a great way with infants and a great eye... she takes the time to work with you and makes your home a terrific backdrop for the photos... the album she supplies is beautiful and we couldn't be happier... she is not insanely expensive as some photographers are, so you can have her take pictures more than once!.. we think she is great, but hope she doesn't get so busy we can't get an appointment!!...* **99**

Customer service.........................❺ $$$...Prices

WWW.TEDDIYAEGER.COM

SEATTLE—206.856.7960

Vakker Portraits

WWW.VAKKER.COM

BELLEVUE—1940 124TH AVE NE (AT NORTHRUP WY); 425.455.2827; T-F 10-6, SA 10-5

Yuen Lui Studios

66*...kudos for going digital... professional, quality studio portraits with extensive choice of backdrops... everyone knows 'the chair' at Yuen Lui's... find your favorite photographer and stick with him or her for consistently great pictures everytime... lots of locations to choose from...* **99**

Customer service.........................❹ $$$$.....................................Prices

WWW.YUENLUISTUDIO.COM

BELLEVUE—10855 NE 8TH ST (AT 108TH AVE NE); 425.453.1606; CALL FOR APPT

BELLTOWN—900 VIRGINIA ST (AT 9TH AVE); 206.622.0338; CALL FOR APPT

EVERETT—1205A EVERETT MALL WAY (AT EVERETT MALL PLAZA); 425.353.5151; CALL FOR APPT; MALL PARKING

FEDERAL WAY—2120 S 320TH ST (AT SEATAC MALL); 253.839.4633; CALL FOR APPT; MALL PARKING

KENT—25607 101ST AVE S (AT SE 256TH ST); 253.854.8600; CALL FOR APPT

LYNNWOOD—18411 ALDERWOOD MALL PKWY (AT ALDERWOOD MALL); 425.771.3423; CALL FOR APPT; MALL PARKING

REDMOND—16640 CLEVELAND ST (AT REDMOND TOWN CTR); 425.882.1168; CALL FOR APPT

TACOMA—4020 S STEELE ST (AT TACOMA MALL); 253.475.1303; CALL FOR APPT; MALL PARKING

UNIVERSITY DISTRICT/UNIVERSITY VILLAGE—924 NE 63RD ST (AT ROOSEVELT WAY NE); 206.523.5707; CALL FOR APPT

Online

clubphoto.com
WWW.CLUBPHOTO.COM

dotphoto.com
WWW.DOTPHOTO.COM

flickr.com
WWW.FLICKR.COM

kodakgallery.com

"...the popular ofoto.com is now under it's wings... very easy to use desktop software to upload your pictures on their site... prints, books, mugs and other photo gifts are reasonably priced and are always shipped promptly... I like that there is no limit to how many pictures and albums you can have their site..."

WWW.KODAKGALLERY.COM

photoworks.com
WWW.PHOTOWORKS.COM

shutterfly.com

"...I've spent hundreds of dollars with them—it's so easy and the quality of the pictures is great... they use really nice quality photo paper... what a lifesaver—since I store all of my pictures with them I didn't lose any when my computer crashed... most special occasions are take care of with a personal photo calendar, book or other item with the cutest pictures of our kids... reasonable prices..."

WWW.SHUTTERFLY.COM

snapfish.com

"...great photo quality and never a problem with storage limits... we love their photo books and flip books—easy to make and fun to give... good service and a good price... we have family that lives all over the country and yet everyone still gets to see and order pictures of our new baby..."

WWW.SNAPFISH.COM

indexes

alphabetical

by city/neighborhood

alphabetical

5 Spot 120
8 Limbs Yoga Center 150
A Pea In The Pod 64
Again & A Gain 14
Alderwood Mall 78
Alki Bakery 120
Alki Beach Park 102
Alki Community Center 78
All For Kids Books & Music 14
Allenmore Children & Young Adult
   Clinic 169
Allstar Fitness 150
Alphabet Soup Books 15
American Legion Memorial Park 102
Angelina's Trattoria 120
Annie's Nannies 186
Anthony's Beach Cafe 121
Anthropologie 15
April Cornell..15
Aquarobics..150
Arnies Restaurant 121
Ashleigh's Attic 16
Association of Labor Assistants &
   Childbirth Educators (ALACE)..........148
Atlas Foods 121
Auburn Gymnastics Center 78
Azteca Mexican Restaurant 121, 142
Babies R Us 16, 46, 172
Baby Boot Camp 151
Baby Depot At Burlington Coat
   Factory 16, 46, 64, 70
Baby Diaper Service 178
BabyGap/GapKids 17
Bagel Oasis..121
Ballard Community Center 79
Ballard Pediatric Clinic 166
Ballard Playfield 102
Ballard Pool 79
Barnes & Noble 79, 98
Barneys New York 17
Beach Combers Kids' Cuts 180
Bella Photography 192
Bella Rose..17
Bellen Drake Photography 192
Bellevue Downtown Park......................103
Bellevue Square 80
Bellini 18
Benihana 122
Best Sitters & Homemakers 186
BF Day Playground 103
Big Time Uncommon Pizzeria 122
Bing's Bodacious Burgers 122
Birth & Beyond 18, 172
Birthing Inn 155, 158
Birthways Childbirth Resource 158
Bitter Lake Community Center 80
Bitter Lake Playground.........................103
Blyth Park 103

Bootyland 18
Borders Books...................................80, 98
Boston Street Baby Store 18
Bradley Method, The 158
Brasa 122
Brat Pack 180
Breast Pump Rental Station................. 172
Bryant Playground 103
Buca di Beppo 122
Build-A-Bear Workshop 80, 99
Burke-Gilman Playground Park........... 103
Burrito Loco 123
Café Besalu 123
Cafe Flora 123
California Pizza Kitchen 123
Capers 19
Care Works 186
Carkeek Park 104
Carter's 19
Casa Mia 142
Cascade Pediatrics 166
Cedar Park 104
Celebration Park 104
Chapters Photography 192
Charlestown Street Cafe...................... 123
Cheesecake Factory, The..................... 124
Chevys Fresh Mex 124, 142
Childcare Referral Resources 187
Children's Clinic.................................. 166
Children's Closet 19
Children's Place, The............................ 20
Children's Shop, The............................ 20
Childrens Warehouse, A 20
Childs Closet, A 20
Chili's Grill & Bar 124
Chinook's At Salmon Bay..................... 124
Chuck E Cheese's 81, 99
City Kids 21
City Peoples Mercantile........................ 21
Claim Jumper Restaurant 125
Clover.. 21
Coastal Kitchen 125
Colman Pool 81
Commencement Bay Pediatrics 169
Community Birth Center Of Seattle.... 159
Community Birth & Family Center 159
Costco...22, 47
Cottage Lake Park 104
Cotton Caboodle.................................. 22
Country Village Playground................. 104
Cowen Park 104
Creative Dance Center.......................... 81
Crossroads Shopping Center Food
   Court 125
Cucina Cucina Italian Cafe......... 125, 143
Curious Kidstuff................................... 22
Dad Watson's 125
DeLong Park 116

participate in our survey a

Delridge Community Center...............81
Discovery Park 104
Dish D'Lish 126
Doulas of North America (DONA).......148
Edmonds City Park 105
EK Photography 192
El Toro 143
Elliott Bay Brewery & Pub 126
Elysian TangleTown 126
Endolyne Joe's.....................................126
Essenza 23
Etta's Seafood.....................................126
Evans Pool...81
Everett Clinic, The 166
Evergreen Hospital (Women's &
    Children's Services) 159, 172
Evergreen Medical Group....................166
Fantastic Sams....................................180
Farrel-Mc Whirter Park 105
Federal Way Family Physicians 166
Fife Swimming Pool............................155
Finders 23
Firehouse Coffee 143
Fireworks Galleries 23
Flora and Henri................................23, 24
Forest Park 105
Fred Meyer..24
Froula Playground 105
Fun Kuts...181
Funtasia 82
Gap Maternity.......................................65
Garfield Community Center 82
Garfield Playfield 105
Gas Works Park Play Barn...................105
Gene Coulon Memorial Beach Park 106
Gilman Playground..............................106
Go To Your Room 24
Golden Gardens Park 106
Gordon Biersch 127
Gracewinds Perinatal Services............159
Grady's Montlake Pub & Eatery 127
Grass Lawn Community Park..............106
Great Clips 181
Great Harvest Bread Company 127
Great Starts Birth and Family
    Education 159
Great Starts Birth & Family
    Education 160
Green Lake Community Center 82
Green Lake Park 106
Group Health 160
Gymagine Gymnastics 82
Gymboree............................... 24, 25, 47
Gymboree Play & Music.................82, 99
Gymnastics East.....................................83

air Chair...181
aircuts For Kids 181
airmasters..181
anna Andersson....................................25
anson Photography.............................193
ealthy Mothers, Healthy Babies 160

Heather Quintans 193
Heaven Sent 25
Helene Madison Pool 83
Hi-Life, The 127
Hiawatha Community Center 83
Hiawatha Playfield 107
High Point Community Center 83
Highland Community Center 83
Hiram M Chittenden Locks 83
Home Details 187
IKEA 26, 128
Il Fornaio 128
Imagine Children's Museum 84
Imperial Garden Seafood Restaurant.. 128
Inside Out Home & Garden.................. 26
Ivar's Acres of Clams............................ 128
Ivar's Salmon House............................. 128
Ixtapa Restaurant................................. 129
Izilla Toys 26
Janet Klinger Photography 193
Janie And Jack 26
JCPenney 27, 47, 65, 70
JCPenney Portrait Studio..................... 193
Jefferson Community Center 84
Jefferson Park 107, 116
Jennings Memorial Park 107
Jewish Community Center 84
Jinguji, Tom MD 166
Johnny Rockets 129
Jojo Kids 27
Jose O'Reilly's Cantina 129
Josie's Baby Diaper Service................. 178
Joy Fischer Photography...................... 193
Judi Julin RN Nannybroker, Inc. 187
Judy's Intimate Apparel......................... 70
Just Babies Baby Shop........................... 27
Just For Kids 28, 65
Kanishka... 129
KB Toys 28
Kelsey Creek Farm 84
Kelsey Creek Park 107
Kid's Club 28
Kid's On 45th 29
Kiddie Kandids..................................... 194
Kids Clinic 166
Kids Cuts 181
Kids Cuts-N-Play 182
Kids Gig, The 116
Kids Haircuts... 182
Kids Kuts 182
Kinder Britches 29
Kindermusik.. 84
Kubota Garden 107
Kym's Kiddy Corner 29
La Leche League 148
Lake Boren Park 107
Lake Route Cafe 129
Lakeshore Learning Store..................... 29
Lakewood Pediatric Associates............ 169
Lakewood Playfield 107
Lamaze International 160
Lamb's Ears 30

Land of Nod 30
Laurelhurst Community Center 85
Laurelhurst Playfield 108
Leschi Park 108
Licton Springs Park 108
Lil' Klippers...182
Lily Waner Photography 194
Lincoln Park...108
Little Artist, The......................................85
Little Gym, The............................85, 99
Lollipops..30
Lowery C Mounger Pool........................85
Lowman Beach Park 108
Loyal Heights Community Center 86
Luisa's Mexican Grill 129
Luna Park Café.......................................130
Macy's 30, 31, 48, 65, 71
Madison Park 108
Madrona Eatery & Ale House 130
Madrona Moose.....................................31
Madrona Park 109
Maggie Bluff's Grill...............................130
Magnolia Community Center 86
Magnolia Park 109
Magnuson Community Center 86
Maneki Restaurant 130
Maple Leaf Playground........................109
Market Street Music 86
Marymoor Regional Park 109
Maternity Factory 66
Math 'n' Stuff 31
Matthews Beach Park...........................109
Maya Whole Health Studio.................151
Mayas 130
Mayuri Indian Cuisine.........................130
McCormick & Schmicks......................131
McDonald Nanny Services 187
Me 'n Mom's Consignment
  Boutique...31, 66
Meadowbrook Community Center 86
Meadowbrook Playfield......................109
Meadowbrook Pool..............................86
Medalia Health Care............................169
Medalia Medical Group 166
Medalia Silver Lake Clinic 166
Medgar Evers Pool.................................87
Mercer Island Pediatrics Associates 167
Meridian Playground 110
Merry Go Round 32
Mervyn's 32, 48, 71
Miller Community Center.....................87
Miller Playfield.....................................110
Mimi Maternity 66
Mind & Body...151
Mocha Moms.......................................160
MOMS Club 161
Moms on the Move...............................151
Montlake Community Center 87
Motherhood Maternity..................67, 71
Mothers and More 161
Mountlake Terrace Community
  Center 87

Mr. Villa.. 131
Mt Baker Park 110
Museum of Flight 87
Museum Of History & Industry 87
Music Center of the Northwest............ 88
Music Together....................................... 88
Musik Nest, The 88
Musik Place, The.................................... 88
My Coffee House.................................... 131
Nana's Children's World 48
Nannies and More 187
Nanny & Company 188
New Eden Music Academy.................... 89
Newcastle Pediatrics 167
Noah's Bagels 131
Nordstrom 33, 49
North Seattle Pediatrics........................ 167
North Sound Pediatrics 167
Northacres Park & Playfield 110
Northgate Medical Center 167
Northwest Aerials School 89
Northwest Puppet Center 89
Northwest Trek Wildlife Park................. 99
Odessa Brown Children's Clinic........... 167
Odyssey Maritime Discovery Center 89
Oilily 33
Old Country Buffet 131
Old Navy....................................... 33, 49, 67
Old Spaghetti Factory, The......... 132, 143
Olive Garden 132, 143
Olympic Athletic Club 151
Once Upon A Child.......................... 34, 49
Ooba's Mexican Grill............................ 132
Orca Swim School.................................. 89
Original Pancake House 132, 133
OshKosh B'Gosh 34
OshKosh B'Gosh Outlet 34
Other Mothers.................. 34, 50, 67, 72
Outback Steakhouse.................... 133, 144
Overlake Hospital Medical Center
  (Breast Pump Rental Station) 173
Overlake Hospital Medical Center
  (Family & Community Education)... 161,
  173
Overlake Hospital Medical Center
  (Prenatal Yoga)............................... 152
Pacific Mothers Support, Inc (PMSI).... 173
Pacific Science Center 90
Pagliacci Pizzeria 133
Pallino Pastaria........................... 133, 134
Pasta & Co.. 134
Pasta Nova... 134
Payless Shoe Source 35, 50
Pediatric Associates.............................. 167
Pediatric Associates (Bellevue)............ 167
Pediatrics Northwest 167, 169
Peggy Washburn Photography........... 194
Peter Kirk Park 110
Phinney Ridge Playground................... 110
Photographic Essays............................. 194
Photography By Trina........................... 194
Phottazz 194

Picture People 195
Picture Perfect Kids...........................182
Pike Place Market 90
Pine Lake Park 110
Pinocchio's Toys 35
Plum 35
Point Defiance Zoo & Aquarium 100
Polyclinic Pediatrics...........................167
Pop Tots 36
Portage Bay Cafe 134
Portage Bay Goods 36
Pottery Barn Kids 36
Pratt Park Water Spray 90
Pregnant Pause 37
Primo Grill 144
Pro Sports Club 152
Program for Early Parent Support
    (PEPS) 161
Puerto Vallarta Restaurant 134
Pump It Up 90
Purely Kids Photography 195
QFC View Ridge Pharmacy 173
Queen Anne Cafe 134
Queen Anne Community Center 90
Queen Anne Dispatch/Undies &
    Outies 37
Queen Anne Pool 91
Rainforest Cafe 135
Rainier Beach Community Center........91
Rainier Beach Pool 91
Rainier Community Center 91
Ram Restaurant & Big Horn
    Brewery 144
Ram Restaurant & Brewery 135
Ravenna Eckstein Community
    Center 91
Ravenna Park 111
Red Lobster Restaurants 144
Red Mill Burgers 135
Red Robin 135, 136, 144, 145
Redmond Town Center 91
Reel Moms (Loews Theatres) 92
Regrade Park 111
REI 37, 50
Render's Photography 195
Right Start, The 38, 173
Rising Stars..38
Roanoke Park 111
Robins Nest Childrens Resale 38
Robinswood Community Park 111
Romano's Macaroni Grill 136
Ross Dress For Less 38, 68
Ross Playfield......................................111
Roxbury Family Health Care...............167
Roxhill Park 111
Ruby Tuesday 145
Ruby's Diner 136, 137
Rudy's Barber Shop 182
Safe N Sound Swimming 92
Safety for Toddlers of Kirkland 162
Sahib..137
Salmon Bay Park 112

Sam Smith Park 112
Sand Point Magnuson Park
    Playground 112
Sandel Playground 112
Santosha Yoga 152
Saturday's Child Consignment 39
Seahurst Pediatrics 168
Sears 39, 68
Sears Portrait Studio 195
Seattle Aquarium 92
Seattle Center House 92
Seattle Central Community College
    (Parent Child Center)...................... 93
Seattle Gymnastics Academy 93
Seattle Holistic Center 152, 162
Seattle Nanny Network 188
Seattle Symphony / Benaroya Hall 93
Seward Park 112
Shiki Japanese Restaurant 137
Shoe Zoo 40
Shoefly 40
Sip & Ship 137
Skate King Stroller Fitness 152
Snohomish Family Medical Center 168
Sole Food Shoes 40
Sound Yoga 153
Soundbridge 93
Soundview Playfield 112
South 47 Farm 93
South Hill Community Park 116
South Park Community Center 93
Southwest Community Center 94
Southwest Pool 94
Space Needle Restaurant 137
Spectrum Dance Studio 94
Spoiled by Nana 40
Spruce Street Mini Park....................... 112
St Clouds Restaurant 137
St Edward State Park 113
St Francis Hospital (Family Education). 162
Steel Lake Park 113
Stellar Pizza & Ale 138
Stevens Hospital 162
Strasburg Children 41
Stride Rite Shoes 41
Stroller Strides 153
Stuhlberg's 41
Sunflower Diaper Service 178
Sunset Park.. 113
Supercuts 183
Susan's 5100 Bistro 138
Swedish Medical Center (Women &
    Infant Services)...................... 162, 174
Swedish Physicians Children's Clinic... 168
Sweet Baby Jess.................................. 41
Sweet Cheeks....................................... 42
Sweet Pea's 42
Taco Del Mar 138
Tacoma General Hospital (Breast
    Pump Rental Depot) 174
Tacoma General Hospital (Childbirth
    & Family Education)........................ 162

Tacoma General Hospital (Mom & Baby Boutique) 51, 174
Tacoma South Medical Center 169
takecare.com 174
Talbots Kids...42
Tall Grass Bakery 139
Tanya Davis Photography 196
Target 42, 43, 51, 69, 72
Teddi Yaeger Photography 196
Teri's Toybox 43
TGI Friday's 139, 145
Thai Ginger 139
The Children's Museum Of Seattle 94
Thornton A Sullivan Park 113
Tin Horse...43
Titlow Park 116
Top Ten Toys..44
Toys R Us 44, 51
Tree House 44
Tutta Bella Neapolitan Pizzera 139
Union Avenue Pediatrics.....................169
University Playfield.............................113
University Village 94
USA Baby 45, 174
UW Medical Center (Maternal & Infant Care Clinic Classes)...............163
UW Physicians Shoreline Clinic 168
Uw Physicians Woodinville Clinic 168
Vakker Portraits..................................196
Valley Childrens Clinic 168
Valley Medical Center.........................163
Value Village 45, 69
Victory Heights Playground 113
View Ridge Playfield 114
Village Maternity 45, 69, 174
Vios Cafe and Marketplace 139
Virginia Mason (Federal Way).............168
Virginia Mason (Issaquah)...................168
Virginia Mason (Sand Point Pediatrics) 168
Virginia Mason (Seattle Pediatrics) 168
Volunteer Park 114
W Magnolia Park.................................114
W Queen Anne Playfield......................114
W Woodland Park Playground.............114
Wading Pool (at Hiawatha Community Center) 95
Wading Pool (at Lincoln Park)...............96
Wading Pool (Beacon Hill) 95
Wading Pool (Bitter Lake Playfield) 95
Wading Pool (Cal Anderson Park).........95
Wading Pool (Dahl Playfield)................95
Wading Pool (Delridge Playfield)...........96
Wading Pool (E Queen Anne Playfield).......................................95
Wading Pool (EC Hughes Playground) 95
Wading Pool (Georgetown Playfield).......................................95
Wading Pool (Gilman Playground) 95
Wading Pool (Green Lake Park) 95
Wading Pool (Highland Park Playfield) 95
Wading Pool (Judkins Park)..................95
Wading Pool (Miller Playfield)...............95
Wading Pool (Northacres Park)..............95
Wading Pool (Peppi's Playground)........95
Wading Pool (Powell Barnett Park) 95
Wading Pool (Ravenna Park) 95
Wading Pool (Sand Point Magnuson Park) 95
Wading Pool (Sandel Playground) 95
Wading Pool (Soundview Playfield) 95
Wading Pool (South Park Playground) ..95
Wading Pool (Van Asselt Playground)...95
Wading Pool (View Ridge Playfield) 95
Wading Pool (Volunteer Park) 95
Wading Pool (Wallingford Playfield) 95
Wallingford Pediatrics 168
Wallingford Playfield 114
Wapato Lake Park...............................117
Wasabi Bistro.....................................139
Washington Park Arboretum 115
Washington Park Playfield...................115
Waterbabies 96
Webster Playground 115
West Seattle Kids 183
White Horse Toys..................................45
Whole Life Yoga 153
Wilburton Hill Park & Bellevue Botanical Garden............................115
Wild Child 183
Wild Mountain Café 140
Wild Waves & Enchanted Village..........96
Women's Center At Overlake 163, 174
Woodcreek Pediatrics 169
Woodinville Pediatrics 168
Woodland Park Zoo 96
World Wrapps 140
Yesler Community Center......................96
YMCA 97, 100, 153, 154, 155
Yoga On Beacon..................................154
Yuen Lui Studios.................................196
Zao Noodle Bar 140
Zeek's Pizza 141

by city/neighborhood

Adams

Firehouse Coffee 143

Algona

Children's Place, The........................20
Red Robin.......................................135

Auburn

Auburn Gymnastics Center 78
Baby Depot At Burlington Coat
Factory 16, 64
Carter's 19
Johnny Rockets..............................129
Motherhood Maternity 67
Old Navy..................................33, 67
Red Robin.......................................136
Robins Nest Childrens Resale 38
Sunset Park....................................113
YMCA 97, 153

Ballard

Annie's Nannies..............................186
Ballard Community Center...............79
Ballard Pediatric Clinic...................166
Ballard Playfield 102
Ballard Pool 79
Beach Combers Kids' Cuts 180
Café Besalu 123
Clover..21
EK Photography..............................192
Fred Meyer.......................................24
Gilman Playground 106
Golden Gardens Park.......................106
Gracewinds Perinatal Services 159
Great Harvest Bread Company........127
Gymboree Play & Music 82
Hi-Life, The 127
Hiram M Chittenden Locks 83
Lake Route Cafe 129
Loyal Heights Community Center......86
Luisa's Mexican Grill 129
Me 'n Mom's Consignment
Boutique....................................31, 66
Moms on the Move 151
Olympic Athletic Club 151
Salmon Bay Park 112
Sip & Ship......................................137
Sunflower Diaper Service 178
Supercuts 183
Taco Del Mar 138
Tall Grass Bakery............................139
Tanya Davis Photography................196
Webster Playground 115
Wild Mountain Café 140

Beacon Hill

Jefferson Community Center 84
Wading Pool (Beacon Hill)................95
Wading Pool (Van Asselt
Playground).....................................95
Yoga On Beacon 154

Bellevue

April Cornell.....................................15
BabyGap/GapKids 17
Barnes & Noble 79
Bellevue Downtown Park................103
Bellini 18
California Pizza Kitchen....................123
Cheesecake Factory, The 124
Children's Place, The 20
Chili's Grill & Bar 124
Chuck E Cheese's..............................81
Crossroads Shopping Center Food
Court 125
Fireworks Galleries 23
Fred Meyer..24
Go To Your Room 24
Gymboree 24
Gymnastics East 83
Hair Chair..181
Highland Community Center............83
Janie And Jack..................................26
JCPenney 27, 65
JCPenney Portrait Studio 193
Jojo Kids...27
Kelsey Creek Farm 84
Kelsey Creek Park............................107
Kid's Club 28
Kindermusik 84
Lakeshore Learning Store 29
Lamb's Ears 30
Little Gym, The..................................85
Macy's 30
Maternity Factory 66
Mayuri Indian Cuisine......................130
Merry Go Round 32
Mervyn's 32
Mimi Maternity 66
Motherhood Maternity.......................67
Nanny & Company 188
Nordstrom...33
Oilily...33
Old Navy 33, 67
Orca Swim School 89
OshKosh B'Gosh Outlet.....................34
Outback Steakhouse 133
Overlake Hospital Medical Center
(Breast Pump Rental Station) 173
Overlake Hospital Medical Center
(Family & Community Education)... 161,
173
Overlake Hospital Medical Center
(Prenatal Yoga)...............................152
Pacific Mothers Support, Inc (PMSI) 173
Pagliacci Pizzeria.............................133
Pallino Pastaria 133
Pasta & Co 134

Payless Shoe Source 35
Pediatric Associates.........................167
Pediatric Associates (Bellevue).........167
Phottazz 194
Pottery Barn Kids 36
Red Robin 136
Right Start, The.........................38, 173
Robinswood Community Park........111
Skate King Stroller Fitness 152
Stride Rite Shoes..............................41
Supercuts 183
Taco Del Mar 138
Talbots Kids 42
Target.......................................42, 69
Toys R Us...44
Vakker Portraits 196
Waterbabies......................................96
Wilburton Hill Park & Bellevue
Botanical Garden 115
World Wrapps 140
YMCA 97, 153
Yuen Lui Studios.............................196

Belltown

Etta's Seafood 126
Old Spaghetti Factory, The.............132
Regrade Park 111
Wasabi Bistro...................................139
Yuen Lui Studios.............................196

Bothell

Blyth Park 103
Chapters Photography.....................192
Country Village Playground.............104
Hairmasters 181
Outback Steakhouse........................133
Saturday's Child Consignment 39
YMCA 97, 153

Burien

Fred Meyer 24
Kids Haircuts...................................182
Lollipops 30
Sweet Cheeks....................................42

Capitol Hill

Bella Rose 17
Bing's Bodacious Burgers 122
Bootyland 18
Cafe Flora 123
Childcare Referral Resources...........187
Children's Shop, The.........................20
Coastal Kitchen 125
Community Birth Center Of
Seattle 159
Flora and Henri 23
Miller Community Center 87
Miller Playfield 110
Noah's Bagels 131
Pagliacci Pizzeria 133
Santosha Yoga 152
Seattle Central Community

College (Parent Child Center) 93
takecare.com 174
Value Village 45, 69
Vios Cafe and Marketplace 139
Volunteer Park 114
Wading Pool (Miller Playfield) 95
Wading Pool (Volunteer Park)...........95
Washington Park Arboretum 115
Washington Park Playfield 115
World Wrapps...................................140

Central District

Garfield Community Center 82
Garfield Playfield 105
Medgar Evers Pool............................87
Mind & Body 151
Payless Shoe Source 35
Polyclinic Pediatrics.........................167
Pratt Park Water Spray 90
Sam Smith Park 112
Spruce Street Mini Park 112
Wading Pool (Judkins Park) 95
Yesler Community Center 96
YMCA......................................97, 154

Columbia City

Bellen Drake Photography 192
Rainier Community Center 91
Sweet Pea's......................................42
Tutta Bella Neapolitan Pizzera 139

Des Moines

Red Robin 136

Downtown

A Pea In The Pod...............................64
Anthropologie...................................15
April Cornell......................................15
BabyGap/GapKids 17
Barnes & Noble 79
Borders Books 80
Brasa 122
Cheesecake Factory, The 124
Children's Place, The 20
Fireworks Galleries 23
Flora and Henri................................24
Gap Maternity..................................65
Gordon Biersch 127
Gymboree 25
Il Fornaio 128
Ivar's Acres of Clams 128
Johnny Rockets 129
Land of Nod.....................................30
Lily Waner Photography 194
Macy's 31, 65
Maneki Restaurant 130
Mimi Maternity 66
Motherhood Maternity.....................67
Nordstrom..33
Old Navy 33, 67
Pallino Pastaria 133
Payless Shoe Source 35

Red Robin 136
Reel Moms (Loews Theatres)............92
REI 37
Ross Dress For Less 38, 68
Seattle Symphony / Benaroya Hall 93
Soundbridge.....................................93
Strasburg Children............................41
Taco Del Mar 138
Thai Ginger.....................................139
World Wrapps 140
YMCA 97, 154

Downtown Bellevue

Bellevue Square 80
Build-A-Bear Workshop 80

Eastlake/Lake Union

Allstar Fitness...............................150
Buca di Beppo 122
McCormick & Schmicks 131
Outback Steakhouse.......................133
Pro Sports Club.............................152

Eatonville

Northwest Trek Wildlife Park.............99

Edmonds

Anthony's Beach Cafe 121
Baby Depot At Burlington Coat
Factory 16, 64
Children's Clinic.............................166
City Kids 21
Edmonds City Park...........................105
Funtasia..82
Kinder Britches 29
Picture Perfect Kids 182
Sahib 137
Stevens Hospital 162
Teri's Toybox 43

Everett

American Legion Memorial Park 102
Azteca Mexican Restaurant............121
Borders Books...................................80
Costco...22
Everett Clinic, The...........................166
Forest Park.......................................105
Imagine Children's Museum 84
Just For Kids 28, 65
Kids Kuts 182
Kindermusik......................................84
Little Gym, The 85
Medalia Silver Lake Clinic................166
Mervyn's..32
Olive Garden 132
Other Mothers............................34, 67
Outback Steakhouse........................133
Red Robin 136
Sears...39, 68
Sears Portrait Studio 195
Thornton A Sullivan Park...................113
Waterbabies......................................96

Yuen Lui Studios 196

Federal Way

Borders Books................................ 80
Celebration Park............................ 104
Costco 22
Federal Way Family Physicians 166
Heaven Sent.................................... 25
Old Navy 33, 67
Olive Garden 132
OshKosh B'Gosh 34
Outback Steakhouse 133
Pediatrics Northwest........................ 167
Red Robin 136
Sears.. 39, 68
Sears Portrait Studio 195
St Francis Hospital (Family
Education)...................................... 162
Steel Lake Park 113
Target 42, 69
Toys R Us 44
Virginia Mason (Federal Way) 168
Wild Waves & Enchanted Village 96
Yuen Lui Studios 196

Fife

Costco 47
Fife Swimming Pool........................ 155

First Hill

8 Limbs Yoga Center...................... 150
Pallino Pastaria 133
Virginia Mason (Seattle Pediatrics) .. 168
Wading Pool (Cal Anderson Park)..... 95
World Wrapps................................ 140

Georgetown

Jefferson Park.................................. 107
Stellar Pizza & Ale.......................... 138
Taco Del Mar.................................. 138
Wading Pool (Georgetown
Playfield) 95

Gig Harbor

Kids Gig, The.................................. 116
Pediatrics Northwest........................ 169
Target 51, 72

Greenlake/Greenwood/
Phinney Ridge

Dad Watson's.................................. 125
Evans Pool...................................... 81
Great Starts Birth and Family
Education.. 159
Green Lake Community Center 82
Green Lake Park 106
Heather Quintans............................ 193
Ivar's Salmon House 128
Janet Klinger Photography 193
Music Center of the Northwest 88
Music Together 88
Red Mill Burgers.............................. 135

Rising Stars 38
Ross Playfield 111
Seattle Holistic Center.................162
Shoefly 40
Taco Del Mar 138
W Woodland Park Playground 114
Wading Pool (Gilman
Playground) 95
Wading Pool (Green Lake Park).........95
Woodland Park Zoo 96
World Wrapps 140
Zeek's Pizza 141

Issaquah

Barnes & Noble 79
Best Sitters & Homemakers 186
Birth & Beyond 18, 172
Cascade Pediatrics 166
Chili's Grill & Bar.......................124
Costco 22
Cucina Cucina Italian Cafe.............125
Gymboree Play & Music 82
Judi Julin RN Nannybroker, Inc. 187
Me 'n Mom's Consignment
Boutique..............................31
Motherhood Maternity 67
Musik Nest, The........................88
Pallino Pastaria.........................134
Pediatric Associates....................167
Red Robin 136
Spoiled by Nana........................40
Stroller Strides 153
Taco Del Mar 138
Target.............................42, 69
Virginia Mason (Issaquah) 168
Waterbabies 96
White Horse Toys.......................45
Women's Center At Overlake 163, 174
YMCA 97, 154

Kenmore

Evergreen Medical Group 166
Little Gym, The 85
St Edward State Park 113

Kent

Children's Closet 19
Chuck E Cheese's 81
Imperial Garden Seafood
Restaurant............................128
Jinguji, Tom MD 166
Little Gym, The 85
Music Together..........................88
Old Country Buffet 131
Once Upon A Child......................34
Red Robin 136
Target.............................42, 69
Yuen Lui Studios........................196

Kirkland

Costco 22
Cucina Cucina Italian Cafe.............125

Evergreen Hospital (Women's &
Children's Services)................ 159, 172
Fred Meyer.............................. 24
Joy Fischer Photography 193
Market Street Music 86
Northwest Aerials School 89
Olive Garden 132
Original Pancake House................. 132
Outback Steakhouse 133
Pediatric Associates 167
Peter Kirk Park 110
Pump It Up.............................. 90
Safety for Toddlers of Kirkland 162
Supercuts 183
Taco Del Mar............................ 138
TGI Friday's 139
Waterbabies............................. 96
World Wrapps 140

Lakewood

Barnes & Noble 98
Lakewood Pediatric Associates 169
Motherhood Maternity................... 71
Old Navy 49
Ram Restaurant & Big Horn
Brewery................................ 144
Ruby Tuesday 145
Supercuts 183

Laurelhurst/Sandpoint

Burke-Gilman Playground Park 103
City Peoples Mercantile 21
Great Harvest Bread Company 127
Gymboree Play & Music................. 82
Laurelhurst Community Center 85
Laurelhurst Playfield 108
Magnuson Community Center 86
Sand Point Magnuson Park
Playground............................ 112
Virginia Mason (Sand Point
Pediatrics)............................ 168
Wading Pool (Sand Point
Magnuson Park).................... 95

Leschi

Leschi Park 108
Wading Pool (Peppi's Playground) 95
Wading Pool (Powell Barnett Park) ...95

Lower Queen Anne/Seattle Center

McDonald Nanny Services 187
Pagliacci Pizzeria......................... 133
Queen Anne Cafe 134
Space Needle Restaurant................ 137
The Children's Museum Of Seattle ... 94

Lynnwood

Alderwood Mall 78
Babies R Us 16, 172
BabyGap/GapKids 17
Barnes & Noble 79

Borders Books......................................80
Build-A-Bear Workshop 80
Chevys Fresh Mex.............................124
Chuck E Cheese's 81
Fun Kuts 181
Gymboree 24
JCPenney 27, 65
JCPenney Portrait Studio.................193
KB Toys 28
Kiddie Kandids..................................194
Kids Cuts 181
Mervyn's..32
Motherhood Maternity 67
Nordstrom 33
Old Navy..33
Old Spaghetti Factory, The..............132
Payless Shoe Source...........................35
Picture People...................................195
Red Robin 136
REI...37
Romano's Macaroni Grill..................136
Ruby's Diner 136
Sears 39, 68
Sears Portrait Studio 195
Stride Rite Shoes.................................41
Target...43, 69
Toys R Us...44
Yuen Lui Studios...............................196

Madison Valley/Madison Park

Baby Diaper Service 178
Birth & Beyond 18, 172
Izilla Toys 26
Madison Park.....................................108
My Coffee House................................131
Plum..35
Pregnant Pause 37

Madrona

Madrona Eatery & Ale House 130
Madrona Moose 31
Madrona Park.....................................109
Spectrum Dance Studio 94
St Clouds Restaurant 137

Magnolia

Chinook's At Salmon Bay..................124
Discovery Park 104
Maggie Bluff's Grill 130
Magnolia Community Center.............86
Magnolia Park 109
New Eden Music Academy..................89
Red Mill Burgers 135
W Magnolia Park 114

Maple Leaf/Roosevelt

Azteca Mexican Restaurant..............121
California Pizza Kitchen 123
Froula Playground..............................105
Gymboree 25
Haircuts For Kids...............................181

JCPenney 27, 65
JCPenney Portrait Studio 193
Little Gym, The...................................85
Macy's...31
Maple Leaf Playground....................109
Math 'n' Stuff 31
Motherhood Maternity......................67
Mr. Villa 131
Nordstrom...33
Northgate Medical Center..............167
Northwest Puppet Center..................89
Picture People 195
Pop Tots 36
Red Robin 136
Sandel Playground............................112
Target 43, 69
Toys R Us 44

Marysville

Everett Clinic, The 166
Jennings Memorial Park...................107

Mercer Island

Finders 23
Jewish Community Center 84
Mercer Island Pediatrics Associates . 167
Music Together 88

Mill Creek

North Sound Pediatrics...................167

Monroe

Medalia Medical Group....................166

Montlake

Community Birth & Family Center .. 159
Costco 22
Grady's Montlake Pub & Eatery 127
Montlake Community Center...........87
Museum Of History & Industry 87
Peggy Washburn Photography 194

Mount Baker

Mt Baker Park 110

Mountlake Terrace

Mountlake Terrace Community
Center..87

Mukilteo

Arnies Restaurant 121
Childrens Warehouse, A....................20
Everett Clinic, The 166
Gymagine Gymnastics.......................82
Just Babies Baby Shop 27
Nannies and More............................187

Newcastle

Lake Boren Park 107
Newcastle Pediatrics........................167

North Bend

BabyGap/GapKids 17
Carter's 19
OshKosh B'Gosh Outlet 34
Stride Rite Shoes 41

North Seattle

Bitter Lake Community Center 80
Bitter Lake Playground 103
Breast Pump Rental Station 172
Carkeek Park 104
Cedar Park 104
Creative Dance Center 81
Fred Meyer 24
Great Clips 181
Great Harvest Bread Company 127
Great Starts Birth & Family
Education 160
Healthy Mothers, Healthy Babies 160
Helene Madison Pool 83
Kym's Kiddy Corner 29
Licton Springs Park 108
Matthews Beach Park 109
Meadowbrook Playfield 109
Music Together 88
North Seattle Pediatrics 167
Northacres Park & Playfield 110
Outback Steakhouse 133
Ross Dress For Less 38, 68
Sears 39, 68
Sears Portrait Studio 195
Seattle Gymnastics Academy 93
Seattle Holistic Center 152, 162
Soundview Playfield 112
Swedish Physicians Children's
Clinic 168
Taco Del Mar 138
Top Ten Toys 44
Victory Heights Playground 113
Wading Pool (Bitter Lake
Playfield) 95
Wading Pool (Northacres Park) 95
Wading Pool (Sandel Playground) 95
Wading Pool (Soundview
Playfield) 95
Whole Life Yoga 153

Pike Market

Boston Street Baby Store 18
Dish D'Lish 126
Sweet Baby Jess 41

Pike Place Market

Pike Place Market 90

Pioneer Square

Fireworks Galleries 23

Portage Bay

Red Robin 136
Roanoke Park 111

Puyallup

Borders Books 98
Casa Mia 142
Costco 47
Gymboree 47
Little Gym, The 99
Macy's 48, 71
Mervyn's 48, 71
Old Navy 49
Outback Steakhouse 144
Payless Shoe Source 50
Photography By Trina 194
Red Robin 144
Ruby Tuesday 145
Sears Portrait Studio 195
South Hill Community Park 116
Target 51, 72
TGI Friday's 145
Woodcreek Pediatrics 169
YMCA 100

Queen Anne

5 Spot 120
Cotton Caboodle 22
Lowery C Mounger Pool 85
Orca Swim School 89
Pasta & Co 134
Queen Anne Community Center 90
Queen Anne Dispatch/Undies &
Outies 37
Queen Anne Pool 91
Safe N Sound Swimming 92
Shiki Japanese Restaurant 137
Stuhlberg's 41
Taco Del Mar 138
W Queen Anne Playfield 114
Wading Pool (E Queen Anne
Playfield) 95
World Wrapps 140

Rainier Beach

Kubota Garden 107
Rainier Beach Community Center 91
Rainier Beach Pool 91

Rainier Valley

KB Toys 28
Mayas 130
Payless Shoe Source 35
Supercuts 183

Redmond

Aquarobics 150
Ashleigh's Attic 16
BabyGap/GapKids 17
Bella Photography 192
Big Time Uncommon Pizzeria 122
Borders Books 80
Brat Pack 180
Claim Jumper Restaurant 125
Farrel-Mc Whirter Park 105
Grass Lawn Community Park 106

Gymboree 25
Gymboree Play & Music 82
Ixtapa Restaurant 129
Kanishka 129
Kids Cuts-N-Play 182
Marymoor Regional Park...............109
Mervyn's...............................32
Musik Place, The.........................88
Ooba's Mexican Grill.....................132
Orca Swim School.........................89
Pasta & Co.............................134
Pediatric Associates....................167
Red Robin...............................136
Redmond Town Center...................91
REI...............................37
Ruby's Diner 136
Sears...............................39, 68
Sears Portrait Studio 195
Shoe Zoo...............................40
South 47 Farm 93
Taco Del Mar...............................138
Target...............................43, 69
Tree House 44
YMCA 97, 154
Yuen Lui Studios............................196

Renton

Fantastic Sams 180
Fred Meyer 24
Gene Coulon Memorial Beach
Park...............................106
IKEA 26, 128
Pediatric Associates.....................167
Supercuts 183
Valley Childrens Clinic....................168
Valley Medical Center 163

Sammamish

Pediatric Associates........................167
Pine Lake Park 110

Seattle

Association of Labor Assistants &
Childbirth Educators (ALACE)..........148
Baby Boot Camp............................151
Barneys New York 17
Benihana 122
Bradley Method, The 158
Care Works 186
Doulas of North America (DONA)....148
Group Health...............................160
Home Details 187
Kids Clinic...............................166
La Leche League 148
Lamaze International 160
Mocha Moms 160
Mothers and More..........................161
Odessa Brown Children's Clinic.......167
Original Pancake House 133
Pallino Pastaria...............................134
Payless Shoe Source.........................35
Purely Kids Photography 195

Seahurst Pediatrics 168
Seattle Nanny Network...................188
Stroller Strides...............................153
Taco Del Mar...............................138
Teddi Yaeger Photography 196

Seattle Center

Pacific Science Center.......................90
Seattle Center House........................92

Seward Park

Lakewood Playfield...........................107
Seward Park 112
Susan's 5100 Bistro 138

Shoreline

UW Physicians Shoreline Clinic 168
YMCA.......................................97, 154

Silverdale

JCPenney 65
Sears...............................68
Target 69

Snohomish

Everett Clinic, The 166
Inside Out Home & Garden 26
Ixtapa Restaurant 129
Snohomish Family Medical Center.. 168
Stroller Strides...............................153

SODO

Costco 22
Sears...............................39, 68
Sears Portrait Studio 195

South Park

South Park Community Center..........93
Wading Pool (South Park
Playground).......................................95

Spanaway

Nana's Children's World...................48

Stanwood

Josie's Baby Diaper Service 178

Tacoma

Allenmore Children & Young Adult
Clinic...............................169
Azteca Mexican Restaurant 142
Babies R Us 46, 172
Baby Depot At Burlington Coat
Factory...............................46, 70
Birthing Inn 155, 158
Borders Books 98
Bradley Method, The.......................158
Build-A-Bear Workshop....................99
Chevys Fresh Mex............................142
Chuck E Cheese's.............................99
Commencement Bay Pediatrics 169
Costco 47

Cucina Cucina Italian Cafe.............143
DeLong Park 116
El Toro 143
Fun Kuts 181
Great Clips 181
JCPenney 47, 70
JCPenney Portrait Studio................193
Jefferson Park 116
Judy's Intimate Apparel....................70
Macy's.......................................48, 71
Medalia Health Care 169
Mervyn's....................................48, 71
Motherhood Maternity 71
Nordstrom 49
Old Navy..49
Old Spaghetti Factory, The.............143
Olive Garden 143
Once Upon A Child............................49
Other Mothers..........................50, 72
Outback Steakhouse........................144
Payless Shoe Source..........................50
Pediatrics Northwest.......................169
Picture People 195
Point Defiance Zoo & Aquarium......100
Primo Grill 144
Red Lobster Restaurants..................144
Red Robin 145
REI..50
Render's Photography.....................195
Sears Portrait Studio 195
Supercuts 183
Tacoma General Hospital (Breast
Pump Rental Depot).........................174
Tacoma General Hospital
(Childbirth & Family Education).......162
Tacoma General Hospital (Mom
& Baby Boutique)......................51, 174
Tacoma South Medical Center 169
Target.......................................51, 72
TGI Friday's.....................................145
Titlow Park 116
Toys R Us..51
Union Avenue Pediatrics 169
Wapato Lake Park............................117
Wild Child 183
YMCA 100, 155
Yuen Lui Studios..............................196

Tukwila

Azteca Mexican Restaurant.............121
Babies R Us................................16, 172
BabyGap/GapKids.............................17
Barnes & Noble 79
Borders Books...................................80
Children's Place, The.........................20
Costco..22
Cucina Cucina Italian Cafe.............125
Gymboree 25
JCPenney....................................27, 65
Kiddie Kandids................................194
Macy's..31
Mervyn's...32

Motherhood Maternity......................67
Museum of Flight..............................87
Nordstrom...33
Old Navy....................................33, 67
Outback Steakhouse 133
Picture People 195
Rainforest Cafe 135
Red Robin 136
Ross Dress For Less 38, 68
Sears 39, 68
Taco Del Mar...................................138
Target..43, 69
Toys R Us 44
USA Baby 45, 174

University District/University Village

All For Kids Books & Music 14
Anthropologie...................................15
Atlas Foods 121
BabyGap/GapKids.............................17
Barnes & Noble 79
Burrito Loco 123
Childs Closet, A.................................20
Fireworks Galleries 23
Hair Chair..181
Hanna Andersson.............................25
Kid's Club 28
Pagliacci Pizzeria............................133
Pasta & Co 134
Portage Bay Cafe............................134
Pottery Barn Kids..............................36
Sole Food Shoes 40
Supercuts 183
Swedish Medical Center (Women &
Infant Services)......................162, 174
University Playfield..........................113
University Village...............................94
UW Medical Center (Maternal &
Infant Care Clinic Classes) 163
Village Maternity 45, 69, 174
World Wrapps..................................140
YMCA......................................97, 154
Yuen Lui Studios 196

University Place

Gymboree Play & Music....................99
Ruby Tuesday 145

Vashon

Birthways Childbirth Resource 158

Wallingford/Fremont

Alphabet Soup Books 15
BF Day Playground 103
Capers 19
Elysian TangleTown 126
Essenza 23
Gas Works Park Play Barn 105
Jose O'Reilly's Cantina....................129
Kid's On 45th...................................29

Lil' Klippers 182
Maya Whole Health Studio 151
Meridian Playground........................110
Portage Bay Goods 36
Program for Early Parent Support
(PEPS) 161
Rudy's Barber Shop..........................182
Tin Horse 43
Wading Pool (Wallingford
Playfield)..95
Wallingford Pediatrics 168
Wallingford Playfield........................114

Waterfront

Odyssey Maritime Discovery
Center 89
Seattle Aquarium 92

Wedgewood/Ravenna

8 Limbs Yoga Center 150
Bagel Oasis 121
Bryant Playground 103
Cowen Park 104
Jewish Community Center 84
Meadowbrook Community
Center 86
Meadowbrook Pool 86
Phinney Ridge Playground...............110
Pinocchio's Toys..................................35
QFC View Ridge Pharmacy 173
Ram Restaurant & Brewery 135
Ravenna Eckstein Community
Center 91
Ravenna Park 111
Right Start, The.........................38, 173
Taco Del Mar 138
View Ridge Playfield.........................114
Wading Pool (Dahl Playfield)............95
Wading Pool (Ravenna Park) 95
Wading Pool (View Ridge
Playfield)..95
Zao Noodle Bar 140

West Seattle

Again & A Gain 14
Alki Bakery 120
Alki Beach Park 102
Alki Community Center 78
Angelina's Trattoria 120
Capers...19
Charlestown Street Cafe.................123
Colman Pool 81

Curious Kidstuff 22
Delridge Community Center.............81
Elliott Bay Brewery & Pub 126
Endolyne Joe's...................................126
Great Harvest Bread Company 127
Hanson Photography.......................193
Hiawatha Community Center 83
Hiawatha Playfield...........................107
High Point Community Center 83
Lincoln Park.......................................108
Little Artist, The..................................85
Lowman Beach Park 108
Luna Park Café 130
Puerto Vallarta Restaurant 134
Roxbury Family Health Care............167
Roxhill Park 111
Sound Yoga 153
Southwest Community Center 94
Southwest Pool 94
Supercuts 183
Target 43, 69
Wading Pool (at Hiawatha
Community Center)..............................95
Wading Pool (at Lincoln Park)...........96
Wading Pool (Delridge Playfield).......96
Wading Pool (EC Hughes
Playground)...95
Wading Pool (Highland Park
Playfield) 95
West Seattle Kids 183
YMCA 97, 154

Woodinville

Barnes & Noble 79
Cottage Lake Park 104
Gymnastics East 83
Hanna Andersson 25
Ooba's Mexican Grill 132
OshKosh B'Gosh Outlet.....................34
Pallino Pastaria 134
Pasta Nova 134
Photographic Essays 194
Red Robin 136
Reel Moms (Loews Theatres) 92
Ruby's Diner.......................................137
Target 43, 69
Uw Physicians Woodinville Clinic 168
Woodinville Pediatrics.....................168

Notes

Notes

Notes

Notes

Notes

Notes

....

....

....

....

....

....

....

....

....

....

....

....

....

....

....

Notes

Notes

Notes

Notes